What Readers Are Saying about
AMERICAN SHOES

"*American Shoes* is one of the most poignant books on the market. It's a page-turner that should be read by every age."

—Brit Elders, writer, editor, and CEO at ShirleyMacLaine.com

"Stories of terror and profound sadness about World War II are not new, but to follow Rosel as she navigates the horror, endures the challenges, and boards the Marine Flasher very much alone . . . it is a journey we all need to take. *American Shoes* has a power I will not forget."

—Mary Ellen Wood, Schuler Books, Okemos, Michigan

"*American Shoes* will encourage and ever so gently challenge you to enlarge your vision and create a healthier future for you and for those around you. Powerful, intense, hopeful!"

—Gerard Mauzé, educator and juvenile justice trainer

"This gripping real life story is about unpleasant experiences, perseverance, hope, and love of family. A book you will always remember."

—James M. Wahl, retired family court specialist

"This is not a passe, young adult story of historical and autobiographical significance. *American Shoes* is an exemplar of the psychological, sociological, historical, and political influences of pain, suffering, perseverance, and ultimately, love."

—Jordan Horan, psychotherapist

"The book *American Shoes* was wonderful and well-written. Its scenery pulled me in, and I just could not put it down. I think this story would make reading historical books in the classroom fun again!"

—Caleb Hart, 15-years-old

"My parents asked me to read this book about Nazi Germany, and I am glad they did! I found my questions about what is happening in today's world answered inside the pages of *American Shoes*. My mind kept switching between 1930s Germany and what is happening today. A must read and a warning for us all."

—Yusuf Abbas, 19-years-old

"A powerful book for understanding life and justice . . . with important lessons for our times. *American Shoes* is a powerful, emotional, sensual, intimately woven story teaching us how wounds morph into wisdom."

—Carla Guggenheim

"*American Shoes* will quickly draw you into the life of a teenage girl and her family during World War II. A memoir of courage and determination."

—Stefanie Kyte

"*American Shoes* is a beautifully written, powerful story. I was drawn into the account from the first page . . . and inspired throughout."

—Ruth Seagull

"Rosemarie Turke, with Garrett's help, has given us a tremendous gift. I hope that we can accept and fully appreciate it. We must guard against the kind of horrors she experienced and relates. To paraphrase Rosel: *Maybe America is still out there, alive and well, ready to help us.*"

—David Hopkinson

"A sobering look at the far-reaching effects of war, *American Shoes* is an enlightening and painful reminder that wars forever damage those who are forced to live through them."

—S. Russick

"Rosemarie's stories are treasures, and I am so glad she has shared them with the world in *American Shoes*."

—Carla Starrett-Bigg

"*American Shoes* shows how destructive political division can be, but also how people can pull together to provide help and support between one another regardless of nationality or origin. This is how the world should operate, and the blueprint for that is found within these pages."

—Mody Diagne Diop

"*American Shoes* is the reflection of all immigrants from all over the world. As an immigrant from West Africa, I found myself inside the mind of young Rosemarie chapter after chapter. Captivating, exciting, educational, and ultimately uplifting—a life changing read!"

—Amadou Nikhor Mbenge

"A lesson on life from a most horrific and terrible time, this is the story of a small child, now a grown woman, who opened her scars and wounds to the world. May we move forward from her journey inspired to make this world peaceful!! *American Shoes* is a must read for all ages."

—Norma M. C. Myers

AMERICAN SHOES

A Refugee's Story

Rosemarie Lengsfeld Turke
and Garrett L. Turke

BEYOND WORDS

Portland, Oregon

BEYOND WORDS

1750 S.W. Skyline Blvd., Suite 20
Portland, OR 97221-2543
503-531-8700 / 503-531-8773 fax
www.beyondword.com

First Beyond Words hardcover edition February 2022

BEYOND WORDS PUBLISHING and colophon are registered trademarks of Beyond
Words Publishing. Beyond Words is an imprint of Simon & Schuster, Inc.
For more information about special discounts for bulk purchases, please contact
Beyond Words Special Sales at 503-531-8700 or specialsales@beyondword.com.

Managing editor: Lindsay S. Easterbrooks-Brown
Editor: Lindsay Marie Scott, Chelsea Lobey, Brennah Hale, Linda M. Meyer
Proofreader: Kristin Thiel
Cover design: Marie Kar (Redframe Creative), Sara E. Blum
Interior design: Sara E. Blum
Composition: William H. Brunson Typography Services

Manufactured in the United States of America

10 9 8 7 6 5 4 3 2 1

Library of Congress Cataloging-in-Publication Data:

Names: Turke, Rosemarie Lengsfeld, 1930– author. | Turke, Garrett L.
   author.
Title: American shoes : a refugee's story / Rosemarie Lengsfeld Turke, and
   Garrett L. Turke.
Description: First Beyond Words hardcover edition | Portland, Oregon:
   Beyond Words, 2022. | Audience: Ages 12+
Identifiers: LCCN 2021040490 (print) | LCCN 2021040491 (ebook) |
ISBN 9781582708522 (hardcover) | ISBN 9781582708539 (ebook)
Subjects: LCSH: Turke, Rosemarie Lengsfeld, 1930—Childhood and
   youth—Juvenile literature. | Turke, Rosemarie Lengsfeld,
   1930—Family—Juvenile literature. | World War, 1939–1945—Germany
   —Personal narratives, American—Juvenile literature.
   | National socialism—Social aspects—Juvenile literature. | World War,
   1939–1945—Children—Poland—Wrocław—Biography—Juvenile literature. |
   World War, 1939–1945—Refugees—Germany—Juvenile literature. | Marine
   Flasher (Ship)—Juvenile literature. | Refugees—United
   States—History—20th century—Juvenile literature. | Wrocław
   (Poland)—Biography—Juvenile literature.
Classification: LCC D811.5 .T86 2022 (print) | LCC D811.5 (ebook) | DDC
   940.53/43092 [B]—dc23
LC record available at https://lccn.loc.gov/2021040490
LC ebook record available at https://lccn.loc.gov/2021040491

The corporate mission of Beyond Words Publishing, Inc.: *Inspire to Integrity*

For Papa and Ezra
As one beautiful soul departs,
another beautiful soul enters

For Eli
The great-grandfather of my children,
who found safe harbor in America,
the lone survivor of an entire family
lost to the Nazi evil

and

For Eleonore
Our reunion waits in another time
and realm, a peaceful place where we
can walk hand in hand and collect
wildflowers once again

*The past is all that makes the present coherent,
and further, that the past will remain horrible for
exactly as long as we refuse to assess it honestly.*

JAMES BALDWIN, from *Notes of a Native Son*, 1955

AUTHOR'S INTRODUCTION

For seven decades, my mother's story lay dormant, suppressed but festering, periodically reminding her that she had yet to heal. As she was unable to speak of the war years and unable to cry, the story of *American Shoes* waited nearly her entire lifetime to be told. In 2013, spurred on by photographs I had taken during a recent trip to Europe, my mother began talking about a period of her life she had never spoken of to me. Not yet realizing the magnitude of the journey I was about to embark on, I scrambled to find a pen and a pad of paper to get it all down. It would be eight years and hundreds of interview hours before I put my pen and paper to rest.

American Shoes recalls twelve years in the childhood of Rosemarie Lengsfeld Turke, an American-born U.S. citizen caught inside Nazi Germany during the rise of Adolf Hitler, waves of endemic ethnic and political purging, and the entirety of World War II. Trapped with her German-born parents after a visit to meet her relatives, she would find herself ensnared in a country that quickly became more sinister and macabre than any child's nightmare could ever be.

Elucidating the rapid breakdown of a fragile democratic society from a child's point of view, *American Shoes* gives an inside view of a nation that turned against itself, where millions of law-abiding citizens were targeted as "threats" and then systematically identified, removed, and eliminated. This is the story of a young girl nicknamed Rosel, perceived to be one of those threats. With her guided by her belief in guardian angels and a sense of self-determination instilled by her father, *American Shoes* tells the story of life within Hitler's Germany through the ever-widening eyes of a brave girl who dared to question Nazi lies and propaganda. Through it all, she fervently clung to her American identity and an undying hope that she would one day return home to New York.

Alternately a testament to humankind's compassionate spirit and history's unforgiving and destructive pattern of repeating itself, *American Shoes* illuminates a family's struggle against impossible odds to survive amid societal collapse, as a cataclysmic world war crept closer and closer until it was upon them. More than a story of survival, *American Shoes* portrays a child's internal battle to make sense of a world gone mad, to face and ultimately take a stand against evil, and to fight through overwhelming obstacles to reclaim her freedom.

Rosemarie's recollections of the war and Nazi oppression are conveyed in vivid flashbacks of her ten-day, cross-Atlantic voyage aboard the SS *Marine Flasher*, a troop transport ship mandated by President Truman to rescue "surviving Jews and other displaced persons" from war-ravaged Europe and bring them to a new life in America. Rosemarie is sharp and lucid in her accounts; her memories have been validated with painstaking historical research, including passenger and immigration lists, war reports, family photographs and letters, as well as archived newspaper articles, naval records, and weather charts. Weekly phone conversations with her little sister, Eleonore, who passed away in 2020, served to further corroborate and enhance her recollections of their shared history.

The evocative war and refugee scenes, social and religious persecution, and Nazi brutality depicted in *American Shoes* reflect actual events experienced by Rosemarie and her family, taken from scores of interviews over a five-year period. Captured in great detail, her largely intact and vividly imprinted memories of these events in Germany were painful reminders that these wounds could not be forgotten—no matter how badly she wanted to erase them.

By contrast, my mother's memories aboard the *Marine Flasher* were often little more than fleeting imagery. Although the main characters aboard ship were drawn from actual people who made passage with Rosemarie, their identities and day-to-day thematic ties are for the most part works of historical fiction created as a vehicle to tell the overarching story of one of the most tumultuous and violent periods in world history.

With a deep sense of conviction and purpose, I am honored to present my mother's story, *American Shoes*.

Garrett L. Turke
January 2022

REFLECTIONS FROM A HEALING SOUL

I was raised with the belief that life gives us a blank canvas on which to paint our lives. As a little girl born in America, I remember feeling so very happy exploring a world that seemed rich with uplifting colors and light. There was so much beauty around, in the wind and the trees, in the chirping of birds, in a patch of wildflowers, and in the kind faces of the people around me. I was eager to start filling my canvas.

Then the evil came, sweeping over the land like a pandemic. My childhood world soon became frightening and filled with shadows. Being trapped in Europe during the world's most horrific war soon placed so many dark and oppressive hues upon my palette. Feeling the hopelessness all around me, I feared I would lose my life-affirming colors forever, leaving me awash in tones unspeakably sad and cruel.

When I was fifteen, after a decade of darkness and so many dreams deferred, the SS *Marine Flasher*, a converted American troop transport ship, arrived to take me home to the United States. In America, I hoped I would find vibrant colors returned to my palette, bringing illumination and faith once again to my world. I could choose the shades with which to repaint my life, leaving behind the forlorn hues that had come with war.

At ninety-one years of age, I reflect upon that most wicked and sinister time. With the war now seventy-five years behind me, I wonder what history will think of what I have done with my life's canvas. Did I bring some good for others, and for the world? Were my colors and brushstrokes enough to inspire hope and compassion? Did I manifest my dreams and aspirations for peace, freedom, and equality? And perhaps most of all, did I leave enough of my canvas blank, trusting that there was still room for the future, for positive and necessary events yet to come?

God gave me a shining beacon called America. To her I was born, and to her colors and light I did return. I pray we never forget about who she is, the strong people she has forged, and the marvelous contribution she has made to the world's canvas.

Rosemarie

Rosemarie Lengsfeld Turke
January 2022

PRECAUTIONS FOR PARENTS AND TEACHERS

In accordance with my mother's wishes, *American Shoes* is presented as a first-person narrative and memoir, in order to capture the intensity and raw emotional power of her childhood experiences. The author and publisher have not taken any steps to diminish or whitewash the realities of World War II, which left over seventy-five million dead in a global swath from Europe and the Soviet Union and across North Africa to China, Japan, and the Pacific. Passages throughout the book describe ethnic and religious bigotry, violence, torture, and genocide. **Parental and teacher discretion is advised for younger readers.**

PROLOGUE

I was born Rosemarie Katarina Ingeborg Lengsfeld on October 13, 1930, at Fordham Hospital in New York City. My mother told me, many years later, that I was a captivating baby with a strong will and ever-curious eyes.

When I was almost four years old, my parents, Herman and Hilde, known to me as Papa and Mutti, took me on my first trip, an exciting voyage across the Atlantic Ocean aboard an ocean liner. We were going to meet my relatives in Germany, the country where my parents were born. Although Papa and Mutti were dedicated to their new life in America and had been living in the United States for years, they did not yet have their final citizenship papers. I did, however, the proud birthright of having been born in America, a nation that welcomed immigrants, new beginnings, and lofty aspirations.

We had traveled to Germany for what Papa said would be only a short stay, maybe a few weeks, a month at most. Papa needed to say goodbye to his father, whose heart was failing. He wanted to introduce me as his American girl, to tell his father that he was loved one last time, and that his family had "made it" in America.

When we arrived at my grandparents' home in the eastern German city of Breslau, there was a big family party. My German relatives were in great anticipation of meeting me, the headstrong little American girl Papa had written about. I had never seen so many people gathered inside such a small apartment! Playing music I hadn't heard before and enjoying a tableful of food unfamiliar to me, they all seemed happy to be celebrating our arrival. Although my grandfather was ailing and in a wheelchair, he smiled and stood when he met me, patting me on the back and lifting me high into the air. That made me so happy, but I remember that it also made him so tired he had to immediately sit back down.

With my grandfather elated to be with us, my parents decided to stay a little longer in Germany to be with him during his final days. But he lingered longer than expected. Soon our short stay became months, and then seasons. It didn't matter to me, however. My days were still bright and cheerful back then, surrounded by my loving relatives who took every opportunity to shower me with activities and attention.

My grandfather passed away peacefully the following year—the first death in my young life. I remember being confused and full of questions at the funeral. I didn't really understand what death meant or the finality of it all.

At last the day came for us to return home to America. I was so happy to see Papa join Mutti and me in the boarding line, with our return ocean liner tickets in his hand. But the German authorities at the Port of Bremerhaven said we couldn't board the ship. They told my parents that Germany's supreme leader, Chancellor Adolf Hitler, had closed the borders to German citizens leaving the country.

My parents reassured me that it would be just weeks before the borders would be reopened and we could return to New York. They were wrong. Months passed, a year, and then two. When the war broke out, all talk of going home ended.

Despite being unable to return home, I remember my first few years in Germany as being happy, even nurturing. After a while I started speaking German instead of English. Papa found work as a buyer in a textile factory. We soon moved out of his parents' home and into our own little apartment on the east side of Breslau. It was very small, just two rooms, but it had a charming little balcony overlooking a courtyard and garden. I loved going down there to pick flowers when spring came.

I began school in Breslau when I was six, a nearby elementary school I could walk to. Eager to learn and to make friends, I would tell them I was an American, back then, a novelty and topic of curiosity among my teachers and peers. I would race home after school each day to tell my parents of my new friends and what I had learned. I couldn't wait to go back the next day.

Although life seemed good to me during those first few years, there was chaos all around us in Germany. I was too young to understand it then, but people were becoming increasingly tense and saying angry, shameful things about their neighbors. At first, my parents said nothing to me about what was happening. Maybe they wanted to shelter me from the ugliness taking hold of the country. Still naïve and trusting, I felt safe and protected for a while yet—until the purges began.

I had a friend about my age who lived next door to us. His name was Adam. I didn't understand why the other children said I shouldn't play with him. One evening some neighbors came over to talk with my parents, and though I wasn't supposed to, I listened in to the conversation going on by the front door. The neighbors warned that Adam was Jewish and that I needed to stay away from him.

My parents did not agree. Papa told them I could play with whomever I wanted. Although we were not Jewish, Papa said that Lutherans and Catholics and Jews—and many other faiths he had studied—all believed in the same God. They even shared the same angels. I didn't know it yet, but my parents were risking everything by telling them that.

Papa's encouragement to remain friends with Adam wouldn't really matter, however. I never got another chance to play with him again. Within a few days, Adam and his parents were gone. My parents told me that he and his family had been whisked away to safety before it was too late. They had to be rescued, Papa said.

Rescued? I had to ask my father what that word meant. *Rescued from what?*

That seems so long ago now, and so innocent. Like an infection, the hateful lies were spreading. People were disappearing—and, I would learn, not all were being rescued. The Nazi tentacles were everywhere. Caught in their web, I feared it was only a matter of time before they found us.

FRIDAY MORNING, JULY 5, 1946

Mission Berlin

Lost in her own world, my little sister paused to play what looked like a game of hopscotch amid the rubble. I watched her jump, unencumbered by her light knapsack; the craters, piles of bricks, and broken pieces of concrete—the ruins of war—had become her momentary playground. A few steps behind, I prodded her to keep moving, my battered and over-stuffed cardboard suitcase bumping along at my side. Trailing us was our mother, our *Mutti*, struggling with the rest of our family's belongings, and the ghost of a man I once knew. The last decade had exacted its toll on Papa. His steps were now tentative and unsteady, his sunken face drained of his once formidable spirit.

As the headquarters of the Nazi party, Berlin had always been in harm's way. Stepping over the broken remains of a German war-eagle motif blown off some government building, we crossed what I remembered was once a wide and bustling avenue. Our destination beckoned some two hundred yards ahead. It was easy to find, as it was the first structure still standing on the Clayallee thoroughfare. The building, now utilized by the Americans, was not unscathed. Along the base of the west wing was a pile of shattered bricks, the ruins of a four-story wall torn open by the bombings.

For a moment I was reminded just how long it had been. Over a decade had passed since we had traveled to Germany. Papa's plan for a short family visit had become my entire childhood. I wondered if New York would still feel like home.

I remembered how upset my father got when the German officer said he would not approve our return to New York, way back when I was five. His face red with anger, Papa had told the officer it wasn't fair; we were just visiting and had our return ocean liner tickets in hand. I recalled Papa's words as if they had been spoken to me just yesterday, "Rosel, no one has the right to choose our destiny for us."

My father had done his best to keep New York City alive within me when I was younger, telling me of the majestic buildings and bustling city streets before he put me to bed each night in Breslau. Returning to New York was like a happy fairy tale, totally unlike the grim fairy tales many Germans told. When I was younger, America would sometimes return to me in my dreams, reminding me that I still belonged to her. Now, a decade later, I could barely remember our old home in New York.

Hurrying along the decimated street, I felt for the letter from the United States Consulate in my dress pocket. It had arrived by courier at my aunt Johanna's apartment, our temporary home, just a few days ago. The letter said I was to report to the American Embassy at 10:30 AM today, suitcase packed, ready to receive my passport and to board a transport truck for the Port of Bremerhaven.

Three months ago, in April, Mutti had coached me to write a request on behalf of our family, which Papa and I then hand-delivered to the embassy. We felt that our plea to return home was reasonable, and we were hopeful of the outcome. But one particular fact nagged at me: in dictating our letter, Mutti had reminded me that I was the only one in our family with a U.S. birth certificate.

I thought it strange that the consulate's return letter had been addressed only to me. Reading it aloud to my family, it seemed clear to me that there had been some sort of mistake. The vice-consul said that I was authorized to return home, but there was no mention of my parents or my nine-year-old sister, Eleonore.

I remembered the look on Mutti's face after I finished reading, as if all of her remaining spirit had evaporated.

We had endured so much. The agony of the last decade had been unimaginable. Why would they separate us, after all we had been through? Determined to keep my head up and sustain hope, I had asked Mutti to pack the rest of the family's bags before we left my aunt's apartment this morning.

I reassured myself that things would be different this time around. Much had changed since our ill-fated attempt to leave Bremerhaven the decade before. The United States was in charge now and would understand our plight. The Americans were the champions, our liberators, sent here to rescue us. Compassionate, fair-minded, and generous, they could be trusted. At least that was what Papa had taught me when I was growing up. He said that you could feel the American spirit by their handshakes—strong, firm, and confident.

America had been good to us. We had prospered when we lived in New York. My parents saw themselves as loyal Americans, even if they did not have their citizenship papers. It was reasonable that we wanted to make our home there once again. Of course we would all be allowed to return home as a family. Why would we think otherwise?

On the cusp of a momentous day, I bolstered my confidence that it was all going to work out. We didn't survive a six-year war to be thwarted again. Today would prove to be cause for celebration, a joyous return home for all of us, with me proudly leading the way.

"Come along, *meine Familie*. We are almost there, and we shouldn't be late. Let's keep together as a group now." I took my sister's hand and looked back over my shoulder. Mutti put one of the burdensome suitcases down and helped Papa step over a pile of rubble, as they tried their best to keep up.

As we drew closer to the American Embassy, I could see where more construction had occurred since I had been here last with Papa. The work crews had started to repair part of the building's support structure along the west wall, as best as could be done without any clear roads leading in. With the help of an enormous pulley, new beams were being placed to shore up the open space where the bombs had torn through.

The two red, white, and blue flags hanging outside identified the once stately building as now belonging to the Americans; its entrance was marked by two soldiers at attention, holding their guns in a familiar formal stance. As we approached the front steps, I could see the presence of the Red Army just a few paces beyond, their red hammer-and-sickle flag draped from a parked Bolshevik tank down the street. I reminded myself that we were not supposed to call them Bolsheviks or even Russians anymore. During the occupation, we were told to call them Soviet comrades.

The American Embassy straddled the line between Berlin's American- and Soviet-controlled zones. A makeshift headquarters that was set up more like a triage center for refugees, the embassy's temporary home was dubbed Mission Berlin by nearly everyone. I had spent a lot of time thinking about why it was called that. Did it mean *mission*, as in a military operation? Or was it *mission*, like some sort of physical sanctuary that welcomed people with safety, provisions, and protection? Oddly, both meanings seemed to fit.

The two soldiers watched us closely as we stepped onto the entrance stairs. One of them nodded as I held out my birth certificate and letter of authorization for him to inspect.

Wanting to appear sure of myself, I spoke first. "Hello, sir. We have an appointment with the vice-consul at 10:30 this morning."

"Good morning." The soldier took the papers from my hand, examined them for a moment. He smiled politely as he handed them back. "This is your family with you?"

"Yes, sir."

"Certainly, then. Please go on in."

The other soldier held the door for us. *A good omen*, I thought. The Americans seemed friendly, even welcoming, and so very different from their German and Soviet counterparts that I had come across during the war.

I took over holding the door and ushered in my family. "Come on now—let's hurry a little. We don't want to be late for our appointment." Again, I worried about my English, now that we were entering American property. Despite our family efforts to practice, other than my visits to the embassy, I hadn't had to rely on English since I was four.

Inside, we collected ourselves in what still looked like the hastily thrown together reception area where I had waited with Papa a few months before. The chairs, old and mismatched, had been paired with banged-up tables. The floor appeared to be a new addition, however, smelling clean and freshly waxed. Looking up at the wall clock across the room, I was relieved to see that we had arrived right at 10:30.

With no time to seat ourselves, I put my suitcase down beside me and collected my papers. As I did, Eleonore latched on to my free hand.

"*Meine hübsche* Rosel." Eleonore looked up at me with adoring eyes. I nudged her with my elbow to remind her where we were. Smiling, she repeated her words, this time in English. "My beautiful Rosel."

I squeezed Eleonore's hand before letting go, not wanting to be further distracted. I double-checked my documents, making sure I had everything organized: my birth certificate, letter of authorization, sponsor's name and address, and the recent black-and-white photograph of myself that the consul had asked for, sized for a passport. *Good. I've got it all.*

Raising my eyebrows, trying to remain confident, I glanced behind me. "Are we ready?"

The response was not the spirited show of determination I had hoped for. Mutti looked uneasy and pensive. Beside her, the specter of my father stood silent and stoop-shouldered, his essence lost somewhere in the remnants of the war. Oh, how I missed the Papa of old. I surely could have used his steadying hand right now.

"*Ja-ja*, Rosel, ready." My mother gave the only answer, and her voice quivered as the words came out.

Across the room I watched the consulate officer finish up with his prior appointment. Their meeting had concluded successfully, gauging by the family's smiles.

That family had their bags packed too, just as I had asked Mutti to do. With two school-aged children, the four of them did not look all that different from us. They too had dressed the best they could for the occasion. Perhaps finely tailored a long time ago, their clothes were badly worn and wrinkled, pressed with grime and soot that had come with the war. *But they still manage to wear their outfits with dignity*, I thought, as if their attire were brand-new. While watching them, I relaxed a bit, assuring myself that we were all in the same boat.

I took a deep breath and motioned for my family to come with me to the officer's well-polished desk; we stopped at the red line a couple paces back. I saw his nameplate: Officer Parker Wyatt, Vice-Consul. Although he looked kind enough, he was not the same officer Papa and I had met with back in April. I thought it might be a good sign—a chance to make our case all over again.

I felt a surge of apprehension work its way up from my stomach. As I tried to push it back down and stay composed, my inner voice sounded almost like Papa's. *Stay calm and pace yourself. Everything is going to work out fine. Remember, the Americans see things from our side.*

Drawing measured breaths, I again thought, *It's not that complicated, really. We just want to go home.* The officer would unquestionably see us as a close, loving family. I would explain that my father and mother had started our family in America before the war. Germany was not our home. We had not chosen to stay all these years; the war had trapped us here. It was the Nazis who closed the door on us. We were the victims. *Of course the officer will understand our predicament. We have suffered and lost enough.* For all of us to go home was certainly not too much to ask.

The family in front of us were handed their passports. The father smiled, giving the officer a firm and lingering handshake. "Thank you, Vice-Consul Wyatt." Unlike me, his English contained not even a trace of a German accent. *They must be American*, I thought.

His face welcoming and approachable, Officer Wyatt motioned for us to step forward. As I stepped toward his desk, Eleonore tried to come with me, but Mutti gently pulled her back to the red line. We had decided that I would speak first, empowered by the American birth certificate I held in my hand. It was up to me. I prayed that my English was good enough to be convincing. There was nothing I could do about my accent.

"Good morning, Officer. We are seeking authorization to go home to the United States of America."

"Good morning." Officer Wyatt's eyes met mine and then glanced over my shoulder at my family behind me. "What is your name and date of birth, miss?"

I swallowed hard, trying to suppress all the anxiety of the past decade, but reassured myself that Officer Wyatt didn't notice.

"Rosemarie Katarina Ingeborg Lengsfeld. My date of birth is October 13, 1930." I handed him my birth certificate and the letter of authorization.

"Oh yes, Rose Mary. Officer Turner was telling me you were here before, back in the spring, and you were authorized to leave today. I have your passport right here." He picked up my fraying birth certificate and examined it. Looking up at me, he offered an understated smile. "I see you were born in New York City. Me too."

"Yes, sir. I was born at Fordham Hospital." I didn't correct him on his mispronunciation of my name.

"Did you bring an identifying photo with you?"

"Yes, sir. It's right here." I handed him the black-and-white photograph taken a few weeks before.

Holding up the small photo, Officer Wyatt did a lingering double take of me. I was sure I knew what he was thinking. I was used to it. The war had left me skinny and underdeveloped. Although fifteen, I must have looked eleven or twelve to him.

"And this is your family with you? I see that there is no mention of them in your authorization letter. What are your nationalities?"

I answered, not fully realizing he was speaking to my mother behind me. "Yes, sir. They are my mother and . . ."

He shook his head a little, interrupting me mid-sentence. "I'm sorry, miss. I must hear it from a parent."

I needed my father, my old father, to answer. He had always known what to say in important circumstances. Although I could sometimes conjure up the healthy, vibrant Papa I remembered, this shell of a man could barely speak. He might as well have been an apparition.

My mother replied anxiously in her heavy, eastern German accent. "My husband and I had been living in New York City for many years; our daughter was born there."

"What is your country of birth, ma'am?"

An awkward pause followed. Finally, Mutti said in an anemic tone, "Germany."

I forced a painful lump in my throat back down as I swallowed, this time certain that Officer Wyatt had noticed.

Officer Wyatt looked at each one of us, and the tension grew uncomfortable. My mother's next words left her mouth in a burst. "Please, Officer, we have been through . . ."

Mutti's plea was cut short, as the vice-consul's manner became more formal. "And your little girl beside you, was she was born in New York too?"

My mother put both arms across my little sister's shoulders, pulling her in against her chest. "No, sir," she said quietly. "She was born in Breslau, Germany, in 1936." This questioning felt like the war all over again. For the past decade, we had lived in constant fear of interrogation, at first by the Nazis and then by the Soviets.

Officer Wyatt looked down at his papers before fixing his gaze on me once again. "Is your family of the Jewish faith?"

I paused; I had still been entertaining hope, but that felt shakier now. I knew that all surviving Jews had been authorized to go to America. But Papa had taught me never to lie. I couldn't do it.

"No, sir. We are Lutheran."

"I'm sorry, miss. They will not be able to return with you."

My heart sank before Officer Wyatt finished his sentence. Inside my head, I was screaming, devastated. I wanted to fall to my knees. I was unprepared for anything that would come next.

He went on, politely but methodically. "My apologies, miss, but only you, as a displaced American citizen, may return to the United States at this time." I bit down hard on my lip to try to maintain my outward composure.

Officer Wyatt then reaffirmed what my authorization letter had already told us. "President Truman has mandated that only Jews and displaced American citizens can enter the United States right now. You are the only one who is an American citizen. Maybe in time, the rest of your family will be able to . . ."

I didn't hear the rest of his words. I would have cried if I were able. Mutti had told me this would happen, but I had not believed her.

Officer Wyatt then offered me a choice. "Miss, do you still want to go . . . by yourself?"

I couldn't find the answer. I wanted my family, and I wanted to go home to New York. Now I knew I couldn't have both.

"Miss?"

I tried to maintain self-control. But it felt as if Officer Wyatt was looking right through me, able to see my inner turmoil.

"We have your passport and travel ticket all prepared from when you were here last. As is indicated in your letter of authorization, the next transport truck leaves for the Port of Bremerhaven early this afternoon. The SS *Marine Flasher* is already in port and filling up with passengers."

I needed to remain outwardly calm, but the pressure threatened to suffocate me. *This is so unfair!* I had longed for the chance to go back to America for years! I couldn't wait to get out of this godforsaken place. And despite everything the war and the Nazis had thrown at me, I had never given up hope. The thought of returning to New York with my family was all that had kept me going. Now what remained of my dream was this cruel choice.

"Miss, do you still want to go?"

Although I had waited nearly my entire life for this moment, I was suddenly unsure, and I couldn't let it show. *Oh dear God, how can I leave my family? But how can I stay?* Could I handle this? Was I still a child, fifteen but looking twelve? What would life bring me in America, by myself? I thought about what Papa would have said right now, if he only could. That answer was obvious. On his steadier days before the war, he had told me many times, "Sometimes we only get a moment to make a life-changing choice. We must be ready to take it. There can be no growth, no reward, without taking that risk."

I didn't need to seek approval from the beloved faces behind me. I could already feel the weight of their eyes, the heaviness of their hearts. My opportunity had arrived. *This is my only chance! It is* our *only chance.* To stay back would seal our fates, trapping us anew in this desolate place, forever infected by its terrible past.

"Yes!" I paused for an instant, to see how my decision felt. "Yes, Officer, I will travel alone." As Mutti took a deep, exhaustive breath, I heard the beginnings of muffled crying. I knew those sobs were Eleonore's, the only one of us who could still cry.

Officer Wyatt's expression now looked pained but sympathetic. He seemed to understand my agony. He had undoubtedly encountered similar pain in listening to the countless stories of other refugees trying to leave this miserable country. Then he said something that had never crossed my mind.

"Your little sister. Would you like to take her with you?"

I was stunned.

"I have the power to authorize you as an American citizen to assume guardianship of your sister, of course, with your parents' approval."

My sister's soft crying stopped as I turned around. Mutti looked terrified, her bottom lip trembling. Eleonore's eyes widened under crinkled brows. Papa seemed somewhere else, lost and vacant.

The answer came instantly. I watched my mother tighten her grip across my sister's shoulders. I didn't need to hear the words. In my mother's world, it was just too dangerous to let a nine-year-old venture out into the unknown.

"No, sir. Thank you, but I will travel alone." A pain in my throat prevented me from swallowing. The crying behind me resumed.

I felt the first pangs of guilt that I was already certain would haunt me forever. I had told my sister countless times that we would always stick together, no matter what. *Oh, my dear little sister . . .*

"Very well, Rose Mary. Let's review your sponsorship."

My hand now shaking, I gave him the sheet of paper my mother had drafted, with my aunt's and uncle's names on it, along with a post office box address. We did not know their street address.

"Verna and Klaus Wagner, of Queens, New York?"

"Yes, sir. They are my aunt and uncle-in-law from my mother's side. They live on Long Island." I tried to act as if I were familiar with them. Mutti had written months ago, asking them to sponsor us. We had not received a reply. I had met my aunt only a couple of times when I was a baby. I had never seen Mr. Wagner in my life.

"Good, then, everything seems to be in order. I am hereby authorizing you to return to the United States of America." The officer glued my photograph in place, pressed a hand seal over it, and stamped my passport. "This is a temporary passport, good until the last of this month. Once in America, you will want to apply for a more durable one, which will be valid for five years. Now I must ask your family to kindly step back to the waiting area."

Eleonore's whimpering became more plaintive. The razor-sharp hurt in my throat threatened to cut me.

"Please, Rosel, please. Take me with you! *Bitte*, Rosel, *bitte*!" Eleonore's pleas ripped a hole through my heart. My legs wobbled.

"I am sorry, Miss Lengsfeld. I can imagine how difficult this must be. Perhaps someday in the future you will be able to petition for your family to join you." Although Officer Wyatt sounded empathetic, what did it matter? He had made his decision, and I had made mine.

"Please, I want to go with you!" Eleonore pleaded desperately, unable to catch her breath in between sobs. I couldn't bear to turn my head toward her.

Officer Wyatt handed me my passport, along with what looked like a boarding ticket. The ticket said I was Passenger No. 155, my first name misspelled as Rose Mary Lengsfeld.

"Please follow the signs behind me to the loading area for the transport truck. The trip from Berlin to the Port of Bremerhaven will take a little over five hours. You will then board the SS *Marine Flasher*, which departs early this evening."

"Yes, sir." I stood stoically, voicing no more protests, making no more pleas, not even silent ones. It was all painfully obvious now. I had been fooling myself all along.

"The passage across the Atlantic will take ten days. You will arrive at New York Harbor on or about July 15. Meals and a bed will be provided for you aboard the ship, compliments of President Truman. Good luck to you, Miss Lengsfeld."

Eleonore's sobbing behind me escalated. I could hear Mutti quietly trying to calm her, to no avail.

"Thank you, Officer Wyatt." He offered me his hand, as if to seal the arrangement. I squeezed his hand firmly and looked him in the eyes, the way Papa had taught me.

Taking a deep breath, I pushed down the jagged edges of my hurt. I had come to the consulate ready to be my family's American-born hero and lead us all home. Though I tried to stay strong, I felt an all-encompassing sense of defeat, and a knot in my stomach reminded me of what I was losing. I had failed, miserably.

I thought of looking back at my family one last time to say goodbye, but I couldn't do it. I had said enough goodbyes already over the past ten years. Farewells never made anyone feel any better, and they never had happy endings. Drawing and holding a deep breath, trying hard to keep my panic in check, I headed toward the transport line, churning with all the feelings I could no longer express.

"Please, *meine hübsche* Rosel, come back to me!"

I looked down at the ticket I was holding, along with my passport. I could only think the words that I could not say aloud. *My poor, poor sister! Dearest Eleonore, I am sorry. Hopefully someday you will understand. The future is right here, in my hands. I cannot pass it by.*

I could see the point of no return a few steps in front of me, the juncture of all that was my past and all that my future could be. Hanging over the entrance to a roped-off area, the sign read, Restricted Area, Authorized Passengers and Personnel Only. Beyond that, an open sliding door revealed a paved, fenced-in outside yard, where I could see some American soldiers loading supplies into an open-backed military truck.

An American Red Cross relief worker stood smiling in front of the sign, a crate of Coca-Colas by his feet. His happy face completely incongruent with my strained, overwrought face, the one-man welcoming committee took out a single bottle, opening it as I approached. It would have been a nice gesture had my family been able to join me in celebration. But the scene only taunted me, telling me I was now alone.

"Safe voyage to America, miss." The young man's hazel eyes shone with an exuberance and light I hadn't seen in over a decade.

"Rosel, come back! I am so sad." Eleonore's heart-wrenching words stopped me in my tracks as I accepted the relief worker's gift. I turned and ran back to her.

"I'm scared, Rosel. What if we never—"

I cut her off, unable to bear the end of her question. "Be brave, my little sister. It will be all right; you will see. Here, this is for you." I handed her my Coca-Cola.

She sniffled and then took a sip. She had never tasted the prized drink before; she produced a weepy little smile. Papa had bought me one once, on a warm spring day in Central Park, when we were feeding the ducks.

"Little Eleonore, *mein Liebchen*, listen now, please." I bent down so my eyes could meet hers. "I am going to make you a promise. I will make a home for us in America, and then I will call for all of you to come join me."

She looked up at me, wiping her eyes, still clutching the bottle of soda.

"It's going to be all right, my little Eleonore."

"*Ja-ja*, my brave sister, we will see you in America." Eleonore's tear-stained face brightened; she trusted every word that came from my mouth.

I pressed her gently back into my mother's arms, blowing her a kiss after we separated. My mother forced a smile. The specter of my father only nodded.

I had to be strong now and couldn't be burdened with any more doubt. As I turned and stepped away, I put as many thoughts and feelings inside mental boxes as I could. Only Eleonore's voice remained, hanging in the air, already haunting me. "*What if we never . . .*"

My conscience finished her question. *What if we never see each other again?*

As I made my way beneath the RESTRICED AREA sign, choking with anxiety, I heard a familiar voice from my childhood, strong and with presence.

"Be brave, my Rosel*chen*. We will be together again someday."

The words came from my father. Papa's shell shock had lifted, if just for a moment. His essence was still within him, buried somewhere underneath the war's rubble. I should have looked back at my father to acknowledge him, but didn't. I wanted to remember his unexpectedly strong words, not this shadow of a man I once knew.

Allowing a smile meant only for myself, I stepped into the restricted area, ready to reclaim my freedom.

FRIDAY AFTERNOON, JULY 5, 1946

Bremerhaven, American-Occupied Germany

"Port of Bremerhaven. Please wait so we can help you step off the vehicle." The truck lurched to a stop, rattling all of us on board. I felt my weight shift as the driver put the transmission in neutral and forcefully applied the hand brake. Another American soldier who had ridden with us in the back jumped off to assist, lowering the truck's gate to access the stepping bar.

It had been a long and bumpy ride in the open bed of the military transport truck, zigzagging our way through broken towns on roadways scarred by bomb craters and littered with abandoned military machinery. I was still nauseated from the abrupt twists, turns, and stops.

"Safe voyage to America, folks."

The soldier's kind but exhausted brown eyes met mine as he took my hand to help me down from the truck. "You too, miss, good luck in America."

I suppose I should have thanked him, but wanting to get my feet back on solid ground, all I could muster was a feeble smile as I let go of the soldier's hand.

Stepping away from the transport truck, I stopped short when I caught sight of the boarding line. I had expected the thirty or so of us who had been crammed together in the truck bed to walk directly aboard the ship to our cabins. Daunting and somehow foreboding, the line before me seemed to stretch out for eternity. Hundreds of people were waiting to board, and the line wasn't moving.

Off in the distance, a massive, utilitarian-looking ship loomed stark and gray against the overcast sky. Neither the harbinger of freedom I had anticipated nor the luxurious ocean liner I felt I deserved, the SS *Marine Flasher* was a troop transport ship, and to me another depressing reminder of war.

A cloud of sea mist rolled in off the harbor, moistening my face like the tears that would neither form nor fall. The bitterness was hard to keep in check. *Papa should have known it would be unsafe to return to Germany. Hitler was already in power. Couldn't he see the war coming?* Nearly my entire childhood had been stolen from me. And now, my family had been taken from me too.

We should never have come to such a horrid place. None of this had to happen. We could have stayed safe in New York. Hitler was a madman; anyone could see that! Lost in a maze of resentful thoughts, I tried to push dark memories away as I stepped forward on shaky legs. I had built so many dams inside my mind. Now it felt as if they could burst at any moment, flooding me with feelings I didn't want to give in to and imagery I had tried so hard to forget.

As I made my way closer to the boarding entrance, I was uncomfortably aware of the silent, unemotional faces of the people ahead of me. Even the little ones maintained an eerie quiet as they clung to their mothers' and fathers' sides. Altogether missing was the celebratory send-off I had longed for. There was no jubilation, no boisterous conversation, no talk of better days ahead. Scanning the multitudes before me, I saw only tired, worn-down travelers with vacant eyes.

Self-conscious in my old blue dress, the only one I had, I tried not to look conspicuous. With no family by my side, wartime survival mechanisms still governed my behavior: keep a low profile, remain quiet with my head down, and never look directly at anyone unfamiliar. Everyone knew those rules. To stand out might have gotten me killed during Hitler's reign. I straightened my clothes, tucked my suitcase more closely against my side, and looked around, distracting myself from my swirling emotions. Hours before, I'd been thrust into adulthood, but right now I felt more like a little girl lost without her mother. I missed my family terribly and yet remained dry-eyed—my sadness and anxiety revealed only as a familiar knot festering in my stomach.

Ca-caw, ca-caw!

The sound of the seabirds broke through my sudden despair. I imagined they might be bidding me farewell, as I searched for them out over the water. In contrast to the ghostly reticence of the ship's passengers, the frothy sea looked angry and agitated, its surface whipped into a frenzy by strong winds blowing in from the open sea. The gulls swooped and dove, seemingly unbothered by the turbulence and unaware of my inner turmoil. It was all so terribly unfair. The war had not changed their world at all.

Beckoning remnants of my self-confidence, I whispered a handful of words meant solely for me. "I have made it through the worst; this will be all right too." Exhaling hard, I picked up my suitcase and quietly joined the other boarders.

The line swallowed me up almost immediately. Within seconds, I felt the press of bodies upon my back, pushing me forward as the passengers began to move.

The smell of wartime fear and hygiene neglect threatened to choke me, forcing me to breathe shallowly through my mouth. I should have been prepared. We had been unable to wash during the war, but for some reason, people continued to neglect their hygiene after the war ended and running water had been restored. Palpable and inescapable, the unpleasant odor rekindled another set of recollections I had tried hard to suppress. My family's homelessness. Hobbling along, my mother and little sister and me, through one decimated city after another, we had to survive with very little food, no working sewers, or clean water that could be spared for washing.

As I fought off the wretched memories, my heart pounded as the line inched closer and closer to the long ramp connecting the shore and the ship's sweeping lower deck.

As far as I could tell, my fellow travelers had come from all over eastern and northern Europe. Their languages may have differed, but their smells, threadbare clothes, and vacant looks were much the same.

I could see up ahead where the line narrowed as it neared a single-file boarding ramp that formed a bridge over the water. My breath quickened. Soon it would be too late to turn back. Without warning, a blast from the ship's horn sent me tumbling to my knees. Instinctively covering my head, I was instantly back inside the bunker, protecting myself from yet another bombing. Scanning every direction for impending threat and danger, I had once again left the current moment for the worst of the past.

"Oh-oh! *Entschuldigung*, excuse me ... *bitte*." Ruffled and embarrassed by my reaction, I looked up at my fellow passengers for some kind of response. But no one said a word or lifted a finger to help me. They seemed to be staring right through me, as if I was invisible.

"Here, let me help you, miss." A teenaged boy, perhaps my age, emerged from behind me, his English welcome within the crowd of silent strangers. He extended his hand to help me up, but I had already taken hold of the railing.

"I'm sorry. I am so embarrassed. I don't know why this is still happening." Brushing myself off, I felt my face flush with shame.

Shielded by his faded-blue newsboy's cap, the young man's deepbrown, nearly black eyes were sympathetic. "They call it shell shock, miss ... You know, when your body reacts on its own, like it is in danger." He lowered his voice. "We all have it from the war, but no one around here seems willing or able to acknowledge it."

All that came out of my mouth was a murmured thank you.

"You're welcome. Please. There is no need to be embarrassed." The young man smiled kindly. I wanted to talk with him a little, but no more words would come, so I just nodded.

"Well, you seem to be all right now. I should get back to my position in line." He pointed to a spot about ten steps behind, his place held by a narrow, peculiar-looking rectangular case, the only piece of luggage he was carrying. Gauging by the indifferent faces as he took his place back in line, I wondered if he was traveling alone, like me. I felt some comfort in that thought. Perhaps I was not the only young teenager aboard, traveling without family.

But I had no time to linger with such thoughts. I felt suitcases and bodies callously and insistently pushing me along as we climbed the boarding ramp toward the gigantic ship. Awash in a sea of nameless and emotionless faces, I felt small and insignificant. The stark and gray *Marine Flasher* dwarfed everything and everyone around us. It was hard to imagine we were being rescued.

The mass of bodies further compressed as we began to climb the narrow ramp. Although there were handrails and ropes along each side, I imagined myself falling into the dark water below, pushed by the unyielding people behind me. I had no choice other than to be herded along. *Just like sheep*, I thought, *blindly following the flock*. Unable to see over the heads in front of me and nearly gagging from wafts of body odor, I fought off the impulse to vomit.

As we climbed to the level of the lower deck, I peeked around and between other passengers to catch sight of the dark waters stretching out over the harbor. The waves and their foamy, tumbling surf scared me. Looking through the gaps in the ramp's flooring, I could see the seawater churning below. Momentarily transfixed, I felt dizzy and reached for the handrail.

With the ship's lower deck and my future just a few feet ahead, my thoughts reeled. *Do I have what it takes to do this?* After years of waiting, I suddenly wasn't sure.

"Next." An officer standing on the ship's lower deck waved me on, and a push from behind sent me stumbling forward before I was ready. Three shaky steps later, I found myself aboard the SS *Marine Flasher*.

"Please have your passports and tickets out for inspection," a male voice boomed out over the passengers in line.

The relief that came with secure footing on board the lower deck lasted mere seconds. Just ahead, an officer was examining passports and authorization tickets. I felt along the side seam of my dress, where I found my passport and boarding ticket inside a buttoned pouch I had sewn within one of the side pockets of my dress. I resisted the urge to feel for the small fold of American money Mutti had given me yesterday evening, which I had cleverly stitched into the hemline of my dress.

"Passport, please." The ship's officer towered over me. Handing him my only identification, for a moment, I felt threatened, an unnerving chill running down my spine. Everything had gone wrong for years. I worried that something unforeseen was about to happen here.

"Thank you, miss."

Concerned about my accent, I didn't say a word as the officer checked my face against the passport photograph.

"All seems in order, miss. Safe travels to New York. Next . . ."

I took my passport from the officer and fumbled anxiously as I buttoned it back inside my pocket. Glancing back up at the officer's gentle eyes, I realized that once again my fearful reaction had been more automatic than necessary.

Drawing a deep breath, I was immediately squeezed into yet another suffocating line. Soon we were bumping and pushing our way through a propped metal door to the interior of the ship. Lit only by yellowish strands of light, a dim corridor lay ahead. I felt like I was moving through some sort of dark and foreboding dreamworld.

The ever-present stench of the unwashed intensified and mixed with the smell of damp metal as we entered the confined passageway. It reminded me of so many underground and claustrophobic spaces during the war. I once again told myself that this was not a time or place in which I could afford to panic.

"Attention! Passengers of the SS *Marine Flasher* . . ." The words reverberated so forcefully through the constricted corridor that I jumped. The man's voice coming through the loudspeaker sounded eerily familiar as it echoed down the passageway. It seemed as if I had heard that voice before, although I couldn't put my finger on it.

The voice continued. "Your attention and compliance are required. Please listen carefully. Check-in to the sleeping quarters is now ongoing. This will be followed by dinner from 7:00 to 8:00 PM. A bell will sound when you are expected to make your way to the mess hall, which can be found just beyond the women's community bathrooms and before the stairs leading to the observation deck." A minute later the stark announcement was repeated in French and then in German.

Now I remember. The assertive yet intimidating voice was reminiscent of the countless government directives shouted from loudspeakers mounted on trucks or along the city streets in Breslau. The Nazis were good at scaring people, barking out orders to keep their sheep in line.

The passengers pressed slowly forward. We arrived at an interior hallway, now far from the last of the daylight-catching portholes behind us. Framed by a cast of haunting shadows along the walls, we had arrived at an intersection of sorts.

The line was splitting up ahead. Men and teenaged boys veered left, while women and younger children turned right. The piercing, discordant sound of crying children, followed by the shushing of their mothers, resonated through the narrow space, calling to mind more unwanted memories. Broken families were one of the war's cruel casualties. I thought about the day Papa was sent off to war, and of the sadness I needed to wall off after saying goodbye. He had never fully returned to us, and I felt a familiar lump lodge itself in my throat.

Following the other female passengers, I could see several large doors just ahead, each propped open by makeshift wooden doorstops. Signs marked WOMEN'S SLEEPING QUARTERS identified each entrance. As our line progressed, I peeked inside ROOM A, glimpsing scores of women unpacking their meager belongings, many with young children clutching their skirts. My heart sank at the sight. Our accommodations were not the private cabins I had envisioned. My home for the next week and a half would be an austere bunk in a crowded, dank, unwelcoming room. There would be no place to retreat, nowhere to be alone.

ROOM B also quickly filled, but the line thinned as we came to ROOM C, where there would presumably be space for me. Like the all-too-quiet women and children around me, I avoided direct eye contact as I discreetly scanned the room, surveying the sleeping arrangements.

The crude wooden beds were stacked in pairs, filling the room from one end to the other. While the design probably allowed for maximum use of space, I couldn't help but think of us as sardines packed into a tin. Built-in ladders gave access to the upper beds, placed at the rear of each bunk such that one couldn't really see the bunkmate below. Yellowing flaxen mattresses were sunk deep into walled bed frames.

How strange, I thought, pondering possible explanations. *It's almost like a crib. Do they think we are all toddlers who might fall out?* But before I could lapse into more internal complaints, I recalled the choppy waters I had seen in the distance. Perhaps the bunks were built this way to keep us from being tossed off.

A wave of fear washed over me. *It's going to get that rough out at sea?* Swallowing hard, I noticed the lump in my throat was still there.

Nothing aboard this ship had so far come anywhere close to what I had hoped for. Shaking my head a little, I searched for names, or at least passenger numbers, alongside the bunks to find the space reserved for me. But there were no identifiers on the beds or anywhere else, nothing to say where I or anyone else belonged.

The room was filling, and I needed to act decisively or risk not getting a space. I claimed one of the upper beds near a corner wall, hoping that particular spot might allow for a modicum of privacy. At least I could turn away and face the wall if I needed time to myself.

Aside from its corner placement, my bed was the same as all the rest. A clean but slightly musty sheet accompanied the mattress, along with a small pillow. At the foot of the bed was a folded woolen blanket, ready to make my eczema-afflicted skin itch.

Scaling the few rungs of the bunk's ladder, with my suitcase still in hand, I paused when I reached the top, contemplating how I was going to climb in. The open ceiling with its exposed pipes and beams was too low for me to step into the bed while standing up. Entering the bed on my hands and knees, I found an uneasy balance by propping my pillow against the modest headboard so I could sit back. It was uncomfortable, but how long had it been since comfort mattered? Already used to sleeping in numerous refugee camps and makeshift living arrangements, I found this was just more of the same.

Leaning forward from my awkward seat, I opened the flimsy, banged-up suitcase my mother had packed for me. Inside was all I had with which to start a new life: a single change of underclothes, my old homemade cotton pajamas, a drawstring canvas bag containing my brush and toiletries, and a couple of kerchiefs for my hair. Also included was what I had insisted on bringing, despite Mutti's protests that there was not enough room: a small, unlined notebook with a pouch that included a mechanical writing pencil, a handful of worn-down colored drawing pencils, a small sharpener, and a heavily used artist's gummy eraser. Beneath my sketchpad I found something unexpected—my extra pair of shoes, along with a note attached from my mother.

I cringed at the sight of those old shoes, my "marching shoes," as I called them. I hated them. They branded me as a person without a home, a discarded refugee, a victim. I had told Mutti I didn't want anything to do with those dilapidated shoes anymore. And yet, here they were, still traveling along with me, laden with bad memories. Why hadn't Mutti just thrown them out? The war was over, and these worthless shoes served no use other than to disturb me. Couldn't she have given me an extra set of underwear, a sweater, or a comforting shawl instead?

Perhaps the answer would be found in her note.

Meine liebe *Rosel,*

You of course remember these shoes. When the time is right, I want you to dispose of them. I couldn't bring myself to get rid of them for you. I think you need to do this on your own. Please be brave, Rosel. God willing, we will someday be together again.

Herzlich, *your loving mother,*
Mutti

For a moment I was reminded of my mother's bravery, found during the last years of the war. Despite my naïve insistence that we would all be allowed to return to New York as a family, she must have known that I was going to be traveling alone. Was her including my old shoes her way of telling me that I had to be the one to put the war years behind me?

I spoke softly to answer Mutti, as if she was standing next to me. "*Ja-ja*, Mutti, I understand."

As I took the wretched shoes out of my suitcase and placed them atop the bed, their long and painful story returned to me in flashes. They had been given to me as a gift by my parents three years ago, for school. Instead, they became my marching shoes as we fled the siege of Breslau for Dresden, some two hundred miles away. Months later, those shoes were again put to use when we, as war refugees, walked for weeks to get to Berlin and then northward to Mecklenburg Province. When my feet swelled from the relentless marching, my mother had loosened the stitching enough to let my toes peek out the front, to allow for some relief from the pain.

Staring down at them, ashamed to have those pathetic reminders out in the open, I thought about how to get rid of them. I already knew those old shoes, with their sorrowful history, couldn't possibly carry me to a new future. I spoke to them as if they were alive, like some familiar character in a children's book.

"So, my tired marching shoes, I will not need your service anymore. I'm afraid your time is coming to an end."

Snickering to myself, it dawned on me what I could do to get rid of them. *That's it, of course! When the time is right, I'll know just what to do.*

Satisfied with my plan, I stuffed the shoes back inside the lower shell of my suitcase and took out my sketchbook before latching the top shut.

As the minutes slowly passed, I was unsure of what to do next. Although the room had indeed filled with passengers, the strange silence of my roommates continued, broken only by occasional terse instructions given by mothers to their young children.

Just then I caught the scent of a light perfume, a relief to my beleaguered sense of smell. *What is that? It smells like lavender! What a relief to take in something so fresh and inviting.* Feeling my mood lift a bit, I looked around for the source of the perfume.

Across the room, an attractive, well-dressed young woman was carefully unpacking what looked like an abundance of expensive belongings. *The scent must be hers.*

Obviously well-off, she appeared calm and collected, as if she had been through all this before. Ever curious, my anonymity protected by my perch atop my bunk, I watched her place the smaller of two matching travel cases on her lower-bunk mattress and push her larger suitcase underneath her bed with her foot. Unlatching the case in front of her, she took out a mirror and what looked like a makeup kit, followed by a beautiful outfit already put together on a wooden coat hanger. After attaching the hanger to the lip of the upper bed frame, she took a couple steps back to inspect her apparel, as if wondering whether she had made the right choice.

Oh my word, that dress, it is so elegant! I fought off unexpected jealousy as I watched her pat down a lacey white-and-blue-trimmed *Dirndl* and its matching white shawl. I had seen such clothes many times before, in the shops of downtown Breslau, and I envied those who had the money to buy them.

She looked completely out of place in this group of women, and I wondered what she was doing aboard the SS *Marine Flasher*. She certainly didn't appear to be in need of rescue. Chuckling to myself, I mused, *Maybe she, too, was expecting an ocean liner.*

I felt a fleeting impulse to walk over and introduce myself, but it would be much too forward of me, wouldn't it? Even if her bed were closer, I was pretty sure I wouldn't have had the nerve to speak to her anyway. She was sophisticated, while I was plain and disheveled, an impoverished waif. She looked so much older than me too—at least in her middle twenties, I guessed. Why would she even want to talk to someone like me?

A resounding bell broke up my thoughts, followed by the familiar voice on the loudspeaker. "Attention, all passengers. Dinner will be served in ten minutes. Please start making your way to the ship's cafeteria. The mess hall will remain open for one hour. That is all for now."

I joined the impassive procession as we made our way through the dim interior corridor. According to the announcer's earlier directions, the mess hall was just around the corner, not far beyond the women's community bathrooms.

Our line swelled again, as the men arriving from the opposite corridor merged with us. I expected families to rejoice at the reunion with their fathers and husbands, but other than young children latching onto their fathers' hands, there were few visible signs of emotion, and more unnerving silence.

Enticing aromas found me as we neared the cafeteria. Having not eaten since breakfast, I hoped the food being offered would trigger my appetite.

The entrance door had been propped open by a footstool, revealing a vast, utilitarian space with rows of rough-hewn wooden tables and long, backless benches—hardly inviting, but at least it was well lit. Once out of the claustrophobic corridor, I joined the long and winding serving line.

The offerings for our first night were a crusty piece of bread, which I hastily hid in my pocket, and a modest bowl of stringy beef stew interspersed with some small, boiled potatoes and an occasional carrot. Not seeing what I had done with my first slice of bread, another server farther down the line smiled and handed me a second. Happy to receive the coveted end piece, I hoped to be able to slather it with creamy butter. Although I felt a little guilty for having two pieces, I had learned long ago that it was important to squirrel away food whenever possible, to avoid the panic triggered by feeling hungry later. I told myself there was plenty of food here anyway, certainly enough to fill everyone's stomach and not leave anyone hungry.

Cradling my cafeteria tray, I searched among the crowded rows for a secluded place to sit. There was no privacy to be had anywhere. I squeezed in beside two unfriendly-looking women who did not speak to, let alone acknowledge, me.

I nibbled at my bread, my favorite comfort food, but I could only pick at my stew. Even though I hadn't eaten in nearly twelve hours, my hunger pangs had been stifled by anxiety and those horrid body smells. I told myself I must eat. For the last six years, having enough food was unpredictable. What was certain was that the food would run out. We ate when food was available, hungry or not.

I slowly began to relax, occupying myself with my nervous habit of using tiny pieces of bread to sop up drops of gravy. Thankfully, after a while, my appetite returned, and I guzzled down my stew. I wanted to return to line to get another helping but thought better of it, not knowing if that was a proper thing to do. Besides, it would draw unnecessary attention, and I didn't want that. Without any instructions as to what to do next, I pretended to still be eating, playing with the tiny piece of bread I had left.

As the last of my stew disappeared, I soon succumbed to my core trait: curiosity. My intense inquisitiveness had endured since childhood. It was the one thing that could overpower my inhibitions and my desire to remain unnoticed.

Cautiously scanning my surroundings, I caught sight of that beautiful young woman with the lavender scent. Immaculately made up, her shoulder-length blond hair gleaming, she had already changed into the outfit she had been admiring earlier.

Seated next to her was a striking gentleman who was a head taller than everyone around him. He, too, was impeccably groomed, wearing a white button-down shirt and dark-blue dress pants. He was blessed with curly, light-brown hair; his pleasant face bore the beginnings of deeply furrowed lines. Definitely older than his female companion. I tried to guess his age. *Maybe thirty?* I couldn't really tell. The war years had a habit of aging adults prematurely, while stunting us children.

How could they possibly keep their clothes so clean and free from wrinkles? I had not seen two people dressed in such posh, unsoiled clothes in years. Poised as if they were attending some dinner party, the two of them were completely mismatched with the rest of us on board.

From their easy interaction, I thought perhaps they were married. Trying to keep my low profile, I looked at their hands. They weren't wearing wedding rings, but that didn't mean anything. Many people had their rings and other jewelry confiscated by the Nazis or needed to exchange them for money or food. It was certainly possible they weren't married. They could be brother and sister, or maybe cousins.

Whatever their relationship, their pleasant chatting in the otherwise hushed mess hall attracted my attention. They were speaking German, though it was a little more formal than the everyday German I was familiar with. *But how could that be? I thought the consul officer said that only Jews and displaced non-German refugees could board this ship.* Maybe they were Austrian or Swiss, but they certainly didn't look like refugees. I couldn't help but continue eavesdropping. I knew it was rude of me, but they seemed to be the only ones in the room who were alive.

Just then, the young woman caught me watching them. I was mortified. *Now I've done it! Oh God, I'm so embarrassed. She must think that I am spying on her!* But she smiled at me and winked. Not knowing what to think, I gave a sheepish smile before looking down at my tray.

Having been found out, I felt the last twenty minutes of dinnertime drag on forever. Utterly embarrassed, I thought of leaving the mess hall to go back to my bunk, which would have been easy enough, but I was unsure what I was to do with my tray and dirty dishes. I felt silly about being unable to make such a simple decision, but I didn't want to further humiliate myself. I stayed put and didn't look up again until dinner was over.

Finally a bell rang, mercifully signaling the end of dinner hour, but no further instructions came through the loudspeaker. Some of the adults returned their trays to a dishwashing window, so I followed suit. After confirming that my extra piece of bread was still safely tucked away in my dress pocket, I breathed a sigh of relief upon seeing the young man and woman I had been observing leave before me.

Outside the mess hall, some passengers headed to the right instead of making the expected turn back to the sleeping quarters. Wanting to explore a bit, I followed them and soon arrived at a steep, wide, and rusty set of iron stairs marked OBSERVATION DECK LOOKOUTS. We made our way up, and I reached the next level a little out of breath.

My, the observation deck is enormous! A railing circled the entire front of the ship. With room for us to spread out, I could finally breathe again.

Although it was early summer, the North Sea winds blew chilly and unrestrained across the *Marine Flasher*'s upper level. Shivering, I half-blamed my mother for my discomfort. Mutti had said it would be stiflingly hot in New York and that I needed what little space there was left in my suitcase for other things—which I now knew were those horrible shoes. At least the air was fresh up here. As I looked for an open spot along the observation rails, the scent of lavender wafted over from somewhere nearby.

Oh, there they are again. The woman and man I had been spying upon during dinner had a pair of binoculars and were chatting and sharing the view. Pensive about the same sight, I watched as the gentleman pointed enthusiastically to the mouth of the harbor and the agitated sea beyond.

Away from the shelter of the harbor, whitecaps were tumbling over the dark waters. I bit my lip anxiously and pulled my kerchief down to hold my unruly hair in place against the wind.

I turned back toward the harbor but didn't find much relief. With the last of the supply crates loaded onto the ship, a couple of sailors were now retracting the boarding ramp, our last tether to the security of dry land.

HOOOOOOOOOONNNNNNKKKKKK.

HOOOOOOOOOONNNNNNKKKKKK.

My nerves were rattled again as two long blasts from the ship's horn announced that the *Marine Flasher* was preparing to leave port. I watched the two sailors toss the remaining mooring line onto the deck.

The ship's mighty engine cranked up, its giant propeller whipping a swath of foam to the rear. The *Flasher* began to move, ponderously at first, with clouds of acrid smoke billowing from its colossal smokestack. Positioning its bow north and west, the *Flasher* headed straight into the fetch of the increasing swells. As we picked up speed, spray from the waves splashed over the deck.

"Attention, all passengers. We are now leaving port. There will be a curfew at nine o'clock, when everyone will be expected to be back in the sleeping quarters. Again, a bell will signal when it's time to make your way to your bunks. Twenty minutes afterward, a second bell will signal lights-out. At nine thirty, the ship's interior lights will be darkened for the night, and all passengers must be secured in their bunks. That is all for now."

Behind me, the harbor's gray skyline stood in ruins, reminding me of what I could never forget. I wondered if Germany would ever be rebuilt. Maybe it would be left just the way it was, as a punishing testament to a senseless war.

Ahead of me, the clouds hung low, obscuring the line between the earth and the heavens and hiding all that lay beyond. Although I had waited my entire childhood for this moment, I couldn't shake my insecurity and fear. I could barely remember America. I hoped she would remember me.

Drawing a deep, calming breath, I made a promise to myself. *I will never look back again.*

FRIDAY EVENING, JULY 5, 1946

Entering the North Sea, 12 Miles Out of Port

The day had been overwhelming from the start—the heartbreaking scene at the embassy, my little sister's mournful pleading, that awful ride to the Port of Bremerhaven. And then to face the people aboard this depressing ship, their ghostly demeanors somehow reflecting the worst of what I had been through. I should have known better. Although the fighting was over, the casualties were everywhere.

I needed to withdraw into something soothing and familiar, and walking back to the sleeping quarters, all I wanted was to change into my nightclothes, maybe draw or write for a half hour, and then hopefully fall asleep. I had had enough for today.

Approaching my bunk, I saw something I hadn't really thought about until now—my bunkmate. She looked older than me, but guessing by her size and stance, maybe not too much older. It was hard to tell with her face turned away and her hair tucked beneath a plain, washed-out kerchief. She was unpacking her few belongings from a small, tattered burlap sack filled with holes.

Should I introduce myself or walk on by? She had not seen me yet. I could easily get past her without saying a word and head up the ladder to my bunk. But I could almost hear Mutti's voice admonishing me. *That would be rude, Rosel. We have to remain decent to other people. We don't know what they've been through.*

Yes, it would be impolite, but certainly no one would fault me for it. Not here, not in these times. We had all learned to pull into ourselves when the Nazis took over. Not that we wanted to; we felt we had to. No one knew for sure who was friend and who was foe. Lines were drawn even within families. Nazi informants were everywhere, ready to turn in their brother or sister or neighbor to the Gestapo, Hitler's secret police. It wasn't worth the risk to extend yourself, even for everyday courtesies and social exchanges.

I forced myself to say a quiet hello, but her face remained turned away, and she didn't answer. *Maybe she didn't hear me. Just as well*, I thought, as I climbed the ladder. I hadn't really wanted to speak to her, but Mutti was right—it was the decent thing to do.

Or maybe she can't understand my English? I had already heard so many different languages on board this ship: Polish, Finnish, French, English, German, and even more that I didn't recognize. But regardless of their home country, almost all Europeans knew the word *hello*. It was more likely that my bunkmate was respecting the war's unspoken rules and keeping to herself. I could hardly blame her.

Climbing awkwardly into my bed, I lost my balance and nearly tumbled off the open side, but no one seemed to notice. I knelt in the middle of my scratchy mattress, with my suitcase still tethered to me, which I dared not leave unattended on the deck below. My suitcase alone took up a good third of my sleeping space . . . *And I still have to find a spot for my day clothes up here!* I chuckled at that thought because my daytime clothes consisted of my blue dress, the one presentable outfit to my name. That dress needed to stay with me at all times, especially with the American money Mutti had given me sewn inside the hem.

I opened my suitcase and took out my nightclothes, toiletry bag, sketchbook, and pencils. After a few trial-and-error moments, I found a position that was tolerable. I could put my suitcase behind my head and prop myself up with the small pillow the ship had provided.

Lights-out was still some time off, and I did what I always did when I needed to get away from the world. I drew. I wanted to sketch something hopeful, befitting of my journey to America. I started with a hazy image of myself and was soon engrossed in my work, oblivious to my surroundings.

Art was like that for me. Even as a young child, I loved to draw wild-flowers and landscapes from the pretty eastern German countryside. My uncle Alfred, a well-known artist from Germany's Silesia region, had given me a set of colored pencils and pastels. My father always said I had his brother's artistic talent. It was the one skill I had truly enjoyed showing off, and I was proud to be compared to my favorite relative.

As I grew older, drawing became my way of coping, my reprieve from the countless unpredictable circumstances that came with war. In my mind, I could visit a beautiful lake or a flowering meadow whenever I got out my pastels. Art became my sanctuary, the last vestige of an early childhood in which I was still free and felt safe.

Time passed while I was drawing, but I couldn't tell how long. I had yet to see a clock anywhere on board. I scrutinized my work at arm's length. I had placed myself at the forefront, with Mutti and little Eleonore behind me, alongside Papa, whose image was fading into the background. Without planning to, I had re-created my send-off back at the American Embassy. The scene was still fresh in my mind, as was the hurt that came with it.

With a sudden roll of the ship, I slipped sideways across my bed, the raised lip of my bed frame stopping me from falling off. I shuddered at the thought of what the days ahead might bring. The open Atlantic would be dangerous, even aboard such a huge ship. I could easily drown out there if the ship foundered or I fell off the deck. *That is irrational and unlikely*, I told myself. *Be brave.* But since we had come to Germany, the unlikely had happened so many times that it had become almost impossible to soothe myself with self-assurances.

I figured that the first curfew bell would chime in a few minutes, so I put away my drawing supplies. Around the room, mothers were unabashedly getting ready for bed—right out in the open—with their children fussing about feeling sick to their stomachs in the rolling swell or having their nightgowns pulled too tightly over their heads.

I was self-conscious about so many things: my underdeveloped body, my malnourished appearance, my body odor, the worn-out clothes that announced how poor I was. The list felt endless and inescapable. There was no way I was going to change in front of other people.

Climbing back down the bunk's ladder, nightclothes and toiletry bag in hand, I resisted the urge to peek in on my bunkmate. Holding my head high, I left for the bathroom. There, I hoped to find a modicum of privacy.

In the corridor, the smell of vomit clung to the heavy air, bringing back more memories I had tried to lock away. To me, that stench signaled things far worse than seasickness: sirens in the dark of night, explosions, desperate screams for help, defeated cries, and death.

When I opened the lavatory door, the stench nearly doubled me over, and for a moment I thought I might faint. I breathed through my mouth to block the smell. I was disappointed to find little privacy in here, either. Distressed mothers held sick kids over toilets as the North Sea's waves periodically sent bodies careening against the walls. Trying desperately not to heave myself, I rushed to a stall that had just been vacated, and with shaking hands, I latched the door behind me.

I held my dress in my mouth, afraid to touch anything, and stepped into my frayed cotton pajamas. Patched numerous times, they itched against my dry, cracked skin. The salty sea air that permeated the *Flasher* had flared-up my eczema, yet another discomfort and embarrassment to add to my growing list.

Another roll of the ship sent me stumbling into the corner of the stall. *Dear God, is the entire trip going to be this miserable, without anywhere to be alone, the air choking me with these horrendous smells, my skin constantly itching, the ship and its incessant rocking tossing me about?*

A harsh knock on the door startled me back into the moment. *"Pośpiesz się!"*

I recognized the words as Polish and understood that the woman wanted me to hurry. There were many Poles living in Breslau, owing to its position near the Polish border and the frequent changes in the German-Polish borders through the generations. Although our family's everyday language was German, it contained numerous Polish words.

"Proszę! Please!" A mother and her small daughter were anxiously waiting when I left the stall. Our eyes met for an instant, but we said not a word. The little girl tightened her grip upon her mother's skirt as I brushed past them.

I was thinking about my separation from my family again as I made my way back to the sleeping quarters. I felt like I was on the verge of another anxiety attack, filling up with more worry than I could stand. At my bunk, I once again avoided eye contact with my bunkmate, thankful I had chosen my little corner space so I could at least pretend to be alone. As the first curfew bell rang, I draped my dress over the bed post and lowered myself into my crib-like bed.

I thought about writing a few words beneath my sketch to chronicle the day's events, but the gnawing angst in my stomach told me that was not a good idea. I already missed my family terribly. *How on earth will I make it through the next ten days?*

Then it hit me, as hard as a bully's punch to my gut. *Ten days? Who am I kidding? I might be separated from my family for years, or maybe my entire lifetime.*

The second bell chimed, mercifully interrupting my thoughts. *Lights-out, time for bed.* I decided to wait to write about my first impressions aboard the *Flasher* until tomorrow.

I noticed that the sea was becoming a little calmer with nightfall. I wondered if the strong winds that churned up the ocean by day would quiet down every night. Maybe with a good night's sleep and a fresh start in the morning, things would look and feel differently.

The last of the female passengers returned to our room as the room darkened. I felt strangely relieved when I saw the woman with the lavender scent among them. Chatting a little with her new companions, she had already brought a little life to our otherwise dreary sleeping quarters. I hoped I would be brave enough to introduce myself to her in the morning.

Exhausted from the long and tumultuous day, I sensed the familiar brown haze of my nighttime world calling to me. My dreams usually arrived like that, sepia-toned like some antique photograph. Soon asleep, I drifted into 1936 Germany, just after my sixth birthday.

I was sitting on our apartment balcony, gently stroking what I called my first pet and best friend at the time, Peter the Cat. He wasn't my cat, exactly; he lived outdoors and seemed to be taken care of by everybody in the building. He would come to me sometimes by climbing up the ivy trestles before tight-roping the rail between apartments. I had often asked Papa if I could bring him inside the apartment, even just for a few minutes, but he always said no. He and I were allergic to animal dander, as well as born with the unforgiving and constantly itching curse of eczema. Besides, money was in such short supply; we wouldn't be able to feed Peter the Cat anyway. It didn't bother me too much, as I could play with him each day out on the balcony, and I did so, regardless of my itchy skin. I was grateful to have a playmate.

Although our new home was only a modest, two-room apartment, the space seemed luxurious to me, and a major improvement over sleeping on the floors of my relatives' homes. Our living room windows overlooked the Hundsfelder Strasse, the bustling city avenue below. And the little balcony looked out upon a nicely kept courtyard where I could pick flowers for sketching and to arrange in pretty vases for Mutti.

After two years of squatting with various family members, Papa had found a good office job as a buyer for a textile factory. And just in the nick of time: Mutti would be having another baby at the end of December. Longing for a real playmate, I couldn't wait for my baby brother or sister to be born.

In the background I could hear my parents' voices as they made up the beds in our only bedroom. Papa sounded irritable and unhappy again. It troubled me that he had been sad a lot lately. I was beginning to worry that Papa's sadness was going to last forever.

My grandfather had quietly passed the month before, his heart finally giving way after two long years of illness. My parents had taken me to the funeral, the first I had been to in my young life. Everyone there was so quiet and unemotional. A stark casket stood as the centerpiece in a creepy room. The adults talked quietly among themselves, barely acknowledging my presence. No one had taken the time to comfort me or explain anything about death or grieving. The whole scene had been terribly confusing.

I watched the late-morning sun streak across the balcony, through our open living room windows, lighting up the floor inside. Though autumn was upon us, it was another beautiful day. The warm days were a precious gift, but it had been weeks since Papa had gone outside with me.

The breeze felt wonderful, and I wanted to walk down to the community gardens, where we could have a picnic and collect yellow-and-white *Gänseblümchen*. I thought that a bouquet of daisies would cheer Papa up. Saying goodbye to Peter the Cat with a scratch under his chin and a pat atop his head, I went back inside.

I wasted no time in pleading to go outside when Papa and Mutti emerged from the bedroom. I supposed they expected as much. I was always full of ideas about what activities we could do as a family.

"Mutti and Papa? It's nice outside again today. Can we go for a picnic?" I didn't wait for an answer. "We could go to the *Schrebergarten* and pick *Gänseblümchen*. Can we, please?"

Ever practical, my mother answered first. "Rosel, I would like that, but we had planned to clean today. Papa, what do you think?"

Papa said nothing, managing only a weak, half-hearted smile. At least I knew I had his attention. There had been many days since my grandfather's death where he seemed to just stare through Mutti and me.

I persisted, in my usual way, as if the decision had already been made. "Papa, you don't have to work today, and I can help Mutti make our picnic lunch. We can do housework tomorrow. So, when will you be ready to go?"

Papa agreed with me, as he often did. I was his spirited American girl, assertive and ready to take charge, so different from all the other children in the neighborhood. "Why, I think that is a lovely plan, Rosel." He smiled for what seemed like the first time in weeks, maybe months.

"Wonderful! So, we will all go. Papa, me, Mutti, and the little one." I pointed at the bulge in Mutti's abdomen, thinking I had made a clever joke.

Papa let out a loud laugh. I was overjoyed to see him happy, if only for an instant.

Now full of myself, I continued, delighted that I had orchestrated what would certainly be a festive outing and hopefully the end of Papa's sadness. "And we can have jam and butter sandwiches, the yummy kind that you make, Mutti. I can hardly wait. This is going to be such a fun day!"

For a fleeting moment, I partially awakened aboard the *Flasher*, smiling at my younger self in the dream. As the ship swayed gently in time with the softly rolling waves—a soothing lullaby of sorts—I felt myself drifting back to sleep, through the sepia haze to an age where the world still belonged to me.

SATURDAY, JULY 6, 1946

Off the Coast of The Netherlands, 170 Miles Out of Port

The first wake-up bell chimed, rousing me from the last of my pleasant dreams. Bolstered by a good night's sleep and the gentle sea, I awoke hungry on my first morning aboard the *Marine Flasher*.

It had been so long since I had been able to enjoy the simple pleasures of eating. For the past three years there had been little connection between feeling hungry and the availability of food. During the war years, even little children learned that it was pointless to complain about it. Being hungry fueled a different kind of despair, a slow, relentless grind that first sapped energy and then slowly wore away one's spirit. Chronic hunger had robbed children like me of normal development. Here I was, fifteen and a half years old, and I still looked barely twelve. I had not even started my period yet.

Hurrying my way down the ship's interior corridor, I was relieved to find the bathroom nearly empty and the stalls cleaned up. Getting up early might have its advantages.

I glanced at the shower area, seeking the privacy that had eluded me the night before. Only two women were washing inside the community shower. Although it had been several days since I had washed, I asked myself if it was worth the stress of feeling vulnerable and exposed. I didn't have any soap anyway. Maybe tomorrow I would brave the showers. Taking the first toilet stall I came to, I changed back into my blue dress, for a moment pondering how on earth I would keep it clean and fresh for the duration of our journey. What did it matter, though? It was all I had. Besides, it was obvious that all the other passengers were in a similar predicament.

Everyone, that is, except that intriguing young woman and her companion, whom I had watched in the mess hall. They were more fortunate than the rest of us. I wondered what their circumstances were, once again trying to find answers to all that did not make sense. *Where are they from? How did they end up aboard this ship? How did they manage to hang on to their wealth during the war?* I told myself that if I got the chance to meet them, I would tactfully investigate.

I stepped out of the stall and up to one of the sinks. I was too hungry to give my snarly hair a good brushing, so I hid it as best I could beneath one of my kerchiefs, while wondering what the day would bring. I told myself that I was off to a good start, that maybe the trials of yesterday were just a fluke, caused by the commotion of boarding and the turbulent seas. Things had quieted down substantially this morning. Maybe my journey would be manageable after all.

Satisfied that I had made myself at least presentable, I made a quick trip back to my bunk, climbing the ladder halfway so I could put my nightclothes and toiletry bag back on my mattress. Averting eye contact with the person who was still in the lower bunk, I told myself I would make another attempt to introduce myself later today. Right now I was anxious to see what would be served for breakfast. Maybe those tasty American pancakes Papa said I loved when we lived in New York City?

Arriving at the serving line, I searched for those pancakes and the delightful, sugar-sweet brown syrup that always came with them. To my disappointment, there weren't any. Still, they were serving one of my favorite foods, crusty rolls with butter and jam. My parents had called this kind of breakfast *Butterbrot mit Marmelade*. And they had my favorite—strawberry. Fighting off the urge to pocket all that I could, I placed two rolls on my tray, thinking that would not be nearly enough, even along with a bowl of oatmeal and some condensed milk. Before I left the line, I took one more roll, discreetly placing it inside my pocket as a snack for later.

While searching for a place to sit, I looked around for that interesting young woman from yesterday, hoping to find enough courage to sit next to her or at least introduce myself. But she was nowhere to be found. I did see the young man who had accompanied her last night. He was eating alone. Although I wanted to, I wasn't brave enough to say hello.

I squeezed in at the end of a table that was almost entirely taken up by one family: a mother, father, and three children, the oldest being a boy of about eight. Although they looked safe enough, they weren't exactly friendly. While the kids occasionally talked quietly among themselves, their parents barely said a word. Except for a quick glance from the oldest boy, no one bothered to even look at me, much less talk to me. No matter. They weren't speaking German anyway. It sounded like Russian or Ukrainian or some Slavic language other than Polish; I wasn't sure.

Keeping my eyes low and my head still, I surveyed my surroundings as best I could without being obvious. Although full of people, the cafeteria remained quiet, my shipmates persisting in their aloofness and stilted distance.

I could relate to such inhibition back in Europe. The Nazi takeover had taught all of us that to be conspicuous in any way was to attract trouble. Hitler and the tentacles of his Third Reich were everywhere, lurking even within families. Papa said the Nazis were threatened by anyone who stood out, that they preferred the company of mindless sheep. But here, aboard this ship, a year after the war had ended, why was there still a need for such behavior? We were bound for America, the land of the free. Couldn't these people see that they were no longer shackled? Why weren't they rejoicing? But then again, why wasn't I?

I finished my breakfast, making sure my extra roll was still secure in my pocket, and readied myself for a visit to the observation deck. I wondered what the day would have in store. What would there be for me to do? Without any friends, the only thing I could imagine was to gaze out at the open water and think.

Unfortunately, thinking was not something I wanted to do. The war had infiltrated every nook and cranny in my mind. Aside from thoughts of my family, there were few safe memories to turn to for comfort. And now, with my loved ones left behind, thinking about them had become painful too.

Happy to get out of that lifeless mess hall, I found my way to the noisy, rattling iron stairs that led "up top," to the observation deck. As I reached the upper deck, I could smell the salty water and taste it in the air. Soothed by a belly full of comfort food, I found a perch along the portside rail—what I had learned referred to the left side of the ship. As we moved against the wind, the smells of the past decade were missing out here.

I followed the frothy wake of the ship out to the horizon, finding it surprisingly relaxing to simply rest my gaze upon the open sea. This morning was a far cry from the angry sea and foreboding clouds of yesterday. The scene was like some beautiful painting, the gentle ripples shimmering in the morning light.

For a moment, I daydreamed about a hopeful new life away from the reminders of war. I imagined the sun's rays glistening off the silvery steel buildings of New York City, with the street traffic below providing a syncopated rhythm. I could picture myself standing on some bustling avenue, wearing a new gingham dress, proud to be among the lively and smiling throngs of people. *Yes, America is out there, alive, and waiting for me. I must stay hopeful.*

I took a deep breath of the sea air, exhaling forcefully, as if to clean out all vestiges of the war. I had not asked for what life had given me over the past ten years. *Did I even have a childhood?* I wasn't sure. I searched my mind for some answers.

I could only remember scattered pieces of my first three years. New York had been reduced to a hazy blur of fleeting images. I could see myself holding Papa's hand in the park, throwing breadcrumbs into a pond to feed the ducks. I recalled bits of the living room and bedroom of our small apartment in New York City. And sometimes I could picture the tall buildings of downtown Manhattan, their stately presence dominating the horizon all around me. I often worried if those precious few memories would fade from my memory altogether.

The rest of my childhood, after we came to Germany, was not in danger of being forgotten. I wanted to erase most of those memories, if I could. All that seemed to work, however, was to lock them away, as if in boxes hidden deep within the interior regions of my mind. I didn't feel completely safe with that strategy, but I had at least learned to live with it. At any rate, my old life was over now. I was on a ship bound for New York. I was going home.

I had never felt that I truly belonged in my parents' birth country, aside from that first year or two when everyone in my family welcomed me as a novelty. The German adults didn't seem to like my outspokenness or my tendency to challenge things that didn't seem honest or fair. I also took delight in telling adults, "I can do it myself," sloughing off their attempts to direct or teach me. They often scolded me while criticizing what they thought was my mother and father's lack of parenting and discipline. "You have to break her will; she is too headstrong," the other adults would say. "It is dangerous for her to think and act that way!" But I was bent on being me. Even as a young girl, I didn't want to waste time trying to remember to always be quiet and obedient, waiting on instructions from irritated and stern-looking adults.

By age six I was already insisting upon doing things normally reserved for much older children. I could knit and crochet and was learning how to sew under the tutelage of my *Tante*, Friedel. I had taught myself to draw, and I was already a proficient reader. Papa made sure to practice English with me, although as I grew older, I tended to think only in German. Told by my family that I was a clever girl, I would become frustrated and angry when things did not go as I imagined they should. And if simply told no, I would sometimes become furious. It made no sense to have to always check in with adults for permission to do things I was capable of and good at.

I was a happy child, at least at first, but I wasn't very social. Not that I didn't want to be. I longed to be liked, but I always had to be the one in control. When I tried to play with other kids, I often pretended that I was the mother, or even the grandmother, aloof and in charge, overseeing whatever activity we were engaged in. The other kids didn't like that. More than once I heard my hoped-for playmates say, "Rosel is too bossy to be my friend." Perhaps I deserved that, but it hurt nonetheless.

I didn't fully understand back then. I was just trying to be helpful, to get the other children to cooperate and be more organized. Our games would be more fun and fairer, I thought, if we had clear sets of rules to follow. But that was too much structure for my peers. They just wanted to play. I didn't quite realize that conflicts were a normal part of childhood. Frustrated with being shunned, I eventually came to believe I just didn't belong with kids my own age. I sought out the company of my parents, particularly my father, instead. He respected my need for order and fairness. Of course that was the case; he was the one who had taught me that.

A resounding single blast from the *Marine Flasher*'s horn interrupted my self-reflections. The *Flasher*'s horn calls were a relatively common occurrence, so much so that I no longer flinched when I heard them. I was starting to realize that each type of blast had a particular meaning—a direction or a warning—though I wasn't quite sure exactly what most of those were yet. I had already figured out a single blast meant we were turning left, as we had done so several times since we pulled out of port. In this case, turning left meant we were now heading west.

I pictured the map upon the wall of my primary school classroom. Owing my knowledge to my favorite class, geography, I knew heading west meant we would soon be entering the more protected waters of the English Channel. I watched expectantly as the ship's bow swung a full ninety degrees, away from the morning sun.

With the turn of the ship, I sensed something towering over us, occupying more and more space until it seemed to be blocking out part of the sky. Apprehensive, I looked up and lost my breath.

Oh mein Gott, my God! In an instant, I felt very small, completely humbled. Before me stood the most magnificent sight I had ever seen. Chalk-white limestone cliffs rose from the water, reflecting the soft rays of the early-morning sun in bluish crimson hues. They were so close I felt I could almost touch them.

I wanted to go below to collect my sketchpad and pencils but realized that doing so might result in me missing the experience altogether. Committing the sight of those crimson and blue cliffs to memory, I imagined how the sketch could be drawn in color.

Out the corner of my eye, I caught sight of a long shadow approaching on the deck beside me, followed by an engaging female voice.

"Beautiful, aren't they? The White Cliffs of Dover, I mean."

I turned slightly toward her. Although there were faint traces of a German accent, she sounded more American than anything else.

"They are pretty famous, you know." A tall, attractive, young woman in a blue-and-pink dress extended her hand to me. I stifled a gasp as our eyes met. *It's her!*

"Good morning! My name is Liesel." She took my hand, clasped it, and gently pulled me in. She introduced herself like an American would. A German introduction would have been much stiffer and more formal. My father had gone to great lengths to teach me the difference.

Intimidated by her forwardness, I couldn't respond right away. Apparently thinking I didn't understand her, she switched languages. "*Guten Morgen. Ich bin Liesel, und du? Sprichst du Englisch?*"

"*Ja, ich bin Rosemarie.* Forgive me. I was lost in my thoughts. I do know a little English from when I was younger. I am usually called Rosel for short."

She smiled but cocked her head a little, looking a bit confused. "Are you German, or maybe Polish, Rosel?"

Taken aback by her lack of inhibition, I paused for a moment.

"I am . . . American."

I felt like I needed to explain. Although the rules of war still nagged at me, I was eager for companionship and took the chance.

"I was born in New York City. But my parents and sister were born in Germany, in Breslau. They are not yet American citizens. Are you American too? You sound like it."

"No, I am like the members of your family. Not yet, but I will be soon! My mother is now applying to become an American citizen. She is waiting for us back home in New Jersey."

Back home in New Jersey? My eyes widened. Intrigued, I wanted to know more. Fortunately, she obliged.

"I am traveling with my older brother, Kurt. We were both born in Leipzig but grew up in America. We came back to Europe with my father when I was eight, to visit my father's family. My mother stayed back to tend to our house. She didn't want to risk . . ."

My thoughts drifted for a moment. *So, the young man is her brother, and they are German. And their mother is not an American citizen either, at least not yet.*

Unaware of the mental detours I was taking, Liesel continued. "We came back to visit my father's family in Leipzig and Berlin. We were only supposed to be gone for a few weeks, and then . . ."

It was hard to concentrate on what she was saying. My head was filling up with questions. *Why had they been allowed to return to America, when my own family had been denied? And where is their father? Is he aboard this ship too?*

Liesel went on, her voice becoming softer and more nostalgic. "That was long ago; it's been so many years. We were kids back then, and now . . . well, look at me."

I tried to keep the conversation flowing despite my wandering mind. "Leipzig? *Ja*, I know that place. We stayed there for a time, as refugees, on our way to Mecklenburg."

"Yes, my father's two sisters live there. I also had an uncle in Berlin, but he died in the war."

Still wondering how her family was able to board the *Flasher*, I fished for more information. "And your father is here with you, aboard this ship?"

Liesel's lips tightened, her expression suddenly strained. She stammered out, "My father . . . my father . . . didn't come back with us."

"Oh, I am sorry." *My big mouth!* I had inadvertently caused her pain. I wished I hadn't asked the question.

"It's all right." Liesel's face softened, and she hurriedly changed the subject. "How did you get stuck in Germany?"

"We came back to Germany to visit family, just like you. My grandfather was very sick, and my father wanted me to meet him while we still could."

My conscience jabbed at me. Papa and Mutti had often warned never to give away that much information to people I didn't know.

Feeling headstrong, I went on anyway. She seemed safe, and it felt good to talk openly with somebody. "We stayed longer than we thought we would, until my grandfather passed away."

Liesel looked interested, so I continued. "When Hitler closed off the borders, we weren't allowed to return home. We had ocean liner tickets to return to New York, but we weren't allowed to use them."

"*Ja-ja*, it was nearly the same with us. That Hitler . . . he was a madman from the very beginning."

I nodded, thinking once again that my father should have recognized the danger before we left New York.

Liesel continued, her eyes brightening again. "I am so glad we are going back to America. Finally! Look at us! After all these years."

I was amazed that someone like Liesel—so sophisticated and cultured—seemed to be enjoying my company.

"So, you came to Germany sometime in the 1920s?" I was probing for her age now.

Liesel laughed. "How old do you think I am? We came over in 1936, in the summer. You know, when the Olympics were going on."

I did the math inside my head. *She came over when she was eight, and that was in 1936. That would make her only seventeen or eighteen right now? That can't be. She's got to be much older than that, well into her twenties. I must have gotten something wrong.*

Before I could ask her to confirm her age, Liesel changed the subject again. "So, are you going to get off the ship this evening, in France?"

My stomach dropped. *France? Get off the ship?* Unwanted worries arose. *Have I been misled yet again? Where are we actually going?* I tried to maintain my composure, but my heart was racing.

Struggling with the thought that I might end up in another refugee camp, I hesitated before asking, "Why . . . why would we get off the ship? Aren't we going to New York?"

Liesel picked up on my trepidation. "No, no, Rosel. Please, my new friend, do not fret! I'm sorry if I alarmed you. Our ship is stopping in Le Havre for supplies and to pick up more passengers. The sailor I was talking to said we could go ashore for a few hours, while we are docked."

Liesel must have noticed my face relax, and she continued. "I was thinking about having a proper dinner and maybe a haircut, if I can find a hair salon that's open. Kurt doesn't want to go. Would you like to come with me instead?"

"I don't know. I'm not really sure." As unsettling as the ship was, it still felt like the safest place to be. I was already worrying that leaving the ship would land me in trouble with some unknown authority. And if that didn't happen, I could easily imagine the *Flasher* departing without me.

"Come on, Rosel, it will be fun. France is a free country once again. The Americans are there. We'll be fine. It will be an adventure!"

I cast about for an excuse, any excuse. "But I have nothing, just a little money my mother gave me that I will need in New York." Now I knew that I had revealed too much. I fought the urge to feel for the modest fold of money hidden in my dress hem.

Liesel smiled. "Do not worry about money, Rosel. I have plenty for the two of us."

SATURDAY NIGHT, JULY 6, 1946

Docked at Le Havre, France

The first bell rang, announcing that it was time to get ready for bed. Feeling a little emboldened, careful not to disturb my newly styled hair, I ignored my bashfulness and quietly changed into my nightclothes at the back of my bunk.

Climbing up and over the ladder, I crawled into my bed, smiling when I lowered myself down this time without a hitch. Hanging my dress over the post next to where I would lay my head, I remained mindful of the need to keep my money safe and secret.

I still hadn't interacted with the woman who rested beneath me. I had caught a glimpse of her face on my way to the ladder, but our eyes did not meet. She looked older than my first impression, with long, straight hair streaked with gray and white, her skin pale and anemic looking. But her face still looked youthful. I wondered if we would ever converse. She seemed content to keep to herself, like me, like nearly everyone else on board. Well, everyone besides Liesel.

With a few minutes left before the second bell would chime, I reached into the outside pocket of my dress and took out a small package wrapped in brown parchment paper. Although I had planned to save it for tomorrow, I knew I couldn't wait that long. Unwrapping its contents, my mouth began to water. *Maybe I will have just a little bite.* I wondered if I should share it with my neighbor below, but I chickened out. This was my quiet time to be alone each evening, anyway.

I hadn't had chocolate in nearly ten years. Although it was expensive, owing to the shortages left by the war, Liesel had bought it for me during our time in Le Havre. Popping a small piece into my mouth, savoring every second as it melted, I took a moment to relive my adventure going ashore.

Liesel and I had a strangely wonderful time walking the streets of Le Havre, though I stuck to her side like some lost, insecure puppy. Le Havre surprised me, but then again, it didn't. I expected a city resembling the Paris I had once heard about, but I should have known better. Le Havre looked more like the decimated German cities I had seen in the last days of the war. The port and business district had been heavily bombed. Craters and piles of debris marred the streets. Toppled streetlamps framed the mess, their glass blown out by the explosions, the poles lined up along the curbs to await repair.

Unlike most of Germany, however, there was life and activity in the streets of Le Havre. It seemed as if the city was trying hard to find itself again as a once happy place.

A few families were out strolling in the early summer air. Happy French music and alluring aromas wafted their way into the streets from a handful of small, family restaurants. There were American soldiers everywhere, smiling and dare I say flirting with us, tipping their caps as we walked by. I didn't know how to handle that, but Liesel did, exuding what seemed to be boundless friendliness and confidence.

Liesel paid for everything during our three-hour outing: a fashionable haircut, a splendid dinner and dessert, and the chocolate I was now so happily munching on. The restaurant we chose contained a little salon run by the innkeeper's daughter in the back. While we waited for dinner, Liesel had her hair done up like I imagined some American movie star would. I had my snarly curls washed thoroughly for the first time in months, my long locks now shaped "to show more of my face," as the hairdresser put it. Liesel said afterward that I looked pretty, though that embarrassed me.

I had my first full glass of wine and savored a dish called *escalope de veau*, a breaded beef cutlet with a mushroom cream sauce, along with tarragon-herbed potatoes, some crusty French bread, and lots of sumptuous fresh butter. Although we were stuffed, Liesel insisted we have dessert, French *quatre-quart*, a type of pound cake, smothered in fresh strawberries and rosewater syrup. Simply divine, and so much of it! Although I thought I didn't deserve it, I felt like royalty with my new friend as my host.

Liesel's generosity and lavish splurging had been eye-opening. Sitting on my bunk, greedily breaking off a much larger piece of chocolate, I wondered where she got so much money. Not only did she have enough cash but she also didn't think twice about spending it. Did she come from a wealthy German family? But how could that be plausible? Everyone in my world had lost their money and most of their possessions during the war. The Nazis had confiscated everything.

I had also noticed that most of her cash was in American bills. That money was coveted more than any of the European denominations, as it was the only money people in Europe had any faith in. Could her mother have sent it all the way from America? That seemed unlikely as well, with the broken mail and financial systems caused by the war. All mail was opened and inspected once it reached Germany. Mailing money in an envelope was like flushing it down the toilet.

Just the thought of having so much money was foreign to me. The most I had ever seen my parents spend was on food for the Christmas holidays, when luxuries such as *Bratwurst*, *Spaetzle* served with *Braune Butter*, *Sauerbraten*, pickled red cabbage, and crusty rye bread with homemade butter became our holiday fare. Beyond that once-a-year indulgence, money was only allocated for badly needed necessities. We often couldn't even afford to buy soap.

Someday I will have enough money to not worry about it so much. I will work hard in America to earn it and share part of it with my family. I drifted a million miles away with my thoughts, picturing myself once again as some successful clothing designer at a big fashion store in New York City.

Guilt interrupted my fantasies, as it often tended to do with me. Here I was, thinking only of myself, selfishly devouring the precious dark chocolate Liesel had bought for me. *Such kindness. And yet that comment she made about her father earlier . . . she looked very distressed.* The pain in her voice and the look of anguish on her face—it was all too familiar.

What could have happened? Why had her father been left behind? Maybe he was still a German citizen, like my parents, and would be allowed to return to America at a later date. I hoped she might feel safe enough to eventually tell me. I could be trusted with that, especially after what had happened to my father.

I told myself that it was rude for me to stick my nose in her business, even if the meddling was only happening inside my head. Glancing at Liesel across the room, laying out what looked like her next change of clothes from her suitcase, I decided to just let things be.

The second bell rang, and soon the room grew dark. I closed my eyes as the calm sea rhythmically cradled me, beckoning me toward my dreams. I imagined the stars shining down upon the ship, guiding us all, carrying each of us to our individual destinies. I remembered what Papa had said to me countless times before. *"Rosel, the angels are always about us, and if one's heart is open and kind, they will provide you with the guidance and help you need."*

My father had often confided his beliefs in me when I was growing up. I didn't understand most of what he said when I was younger, with his talk of guardian angels and divine purpose. But I remembered his words, placing them in my heart, just because he was so passionate about it. As I grew older, it was finally starting to make more sense.

I had felt the presence of angels many times in my life. They would show themselves as a warm shiver that ran from head to toe and back up my spine again. When I felt that sensation, I knew I was not only safe but also on the right course.

I had not yet felt the aura of my angels aboard the *Marine Flasher*. For a split second, I worried that they had been left behind, back in war-torn Germany.

As I slipped into sleep, my conscience started bothering me. I had selfishly eaten all my chocolate, including the piece I was going to share with my bunkmate.

In familiar bronze-tinted hues, my dream landed me once again in Breslau. It was still 1936, toward the end of what I came to believe was our last safe year. It was Christmastime and snowing.

Papa and I were walking down the wintry avenue to get to the *Strassenbahn*, the electric trolley or streetcar. Minutes before, he had picked me up from my aunt Friedel's, or *Tante* Friedel, as we called her. I had been staying with her for a few days over the holidays while my parents were away at the hospital, preparing for the birth of my new brother or sister. I imagined that having a new sibling was going to be the greatest holiday gift imaginable. I had been praying for months that the baby would be born on Christmas.

Tante Friedel had done quite well to distract me during my parents' several-day absence. Never married, and without children, she treated me like the child she never had. While my parents were at the hospital, I was showered with presents, my most prized gift being a sewing kit I had hinted at all year long. I helped my aunt make wonderful meals just for the two of us, including sugar-sprinkled, lemony crepes filled with jam for breakfast and roasted goose with *Klösse*, or potato dumplings, for Christmas Eve dinner.

Although it was now a couple of days after the holiday, it still felt like Christmas to me, walking with Papa down to the streetcar stop. Prancing along, playfully kicking my feet through the snow, I was having a hard time being patient. I wondered why Papa hadn't said anything about the baby yet. Maybe he and Mutti wanted to surprise me when we got home.

The clickity-clack of the *Strassenbahn* slowed as it approached our boarding stop. The electric vehicles always fascinated me, with all the sparks flying from the long tether that connected to the power line above the streetcar. It was crowded inside the car today, as people had returned to work after their holiday, but Papa was able to find a spot for us near the back, where I could look out the window. He probably thought looking at all the Christmas lights lining the streets of Breslau would distract me until we got home.

Minutes after boarding, seated snugly next to Papa, I began badgering him to give up the surprise. My strategy was to act as if I already knew.

"Papa, I am so very, very excited! And I know it's a girl. Oh please, can I hold her as soon as we get home? Please, may I, Papa, please?"

My father's answer wouldn't come soon enough for me. I kept talking to wear him down.

"I already know, Papa. It is written all over your face!" As was typical, I took impish delight in figuring things out before I was told.

"Always spending your time questioning everything." Papa smiled, putting up no resistance. "You guessed correctly, Rosel. You now have a beautiful baby sister, born on Christmas Day, just like you wanted. We have named her Eleonore."

I smiled gleefully. "I knew it, Papa, I knew it!" Trying to make a joke, I giggled. "I promise to be ever so careful and not drop her on the floor."

Papa chuckled, indulging my attempt to be funny. "Of course you can hold her. Just be careful."

Papa looked down at me sitting alongside him, placed his arm around my shoulder. He had such a confident presence. "Baby Eleonore will be glad to meet you, but remember, she is a newborn and needs lots of sleep. She will probably be asleep when we get home, so we will need to be quiet."

I held my forefinger to my mouth and whispered with a smile. "Oh . . . okay . . . shhhh . . . I'll make sure you don't say a word, Papa." Used to my playful irreverence, he just shook his head and smirked.

I already had a strong, unspoken bond with my baby sister. I had been imagining for months what she looked like and how we would play together. I couldn't picture her as being anything but the cute little play-mate I had always wanted.

The rhythmic noise of the streetcar slowed as it came to its last stop on the far eastern side of Breslau. Clasping my hands tightly, Papa propelled me through the air as I jumped from the top of the streetcar's steps to the ground.

"Whee! That was fun, Papa!" Extending my hands outward, I wanted more.

"Papa, do it again. Jump me one more time!" Taking both my hands, Papa sent me whirling through the air in a circle around him. It felt like I was flying!

Holding hands, happily churning up the fresh snow, we headed home on the busy avenue that twinkled in its holiday grandeur. The city streets seemed magical, my joy boundless.

But in the blink of an eye, everything changed. Up ahead, lurking in the hazy dreamscape, an ominous, middle-aged woman emerged, wearing a long, gray trench coat. Looking almost like a uniform, her drab attire was punctuated by a bright red-and-black swastika stickpin on her lapel, the telltale sign of Nazi Party loyalty. As the menacing figure came closer, I recognized her. It was *Frau* Schmidt, my first-grade homeroom teacher.

With her hair pulled back into a tight bun, Frau Schmidt's face was always framed by harsh lines. She was older than my other teachers and, unlike them, very mean. She had piercing eyes and an intimidating voice. I had been afraid of her right from the start of the school year, imagining she had the power to see through me and into my secret thoughts. She must have lived nearby, as I had seen her on our avenue after school several times before. Once I even hid when I saw her approaching.

Noticing my father and me, Frau Schmidt paused and enthusiastically greeted us, raising and then outstretching her right hand. "Happy New Year. *Heil* Hitler!"

With nowhere to hide, I stopped in my tracks. Mechanically and obediently, as was expected from all schoolchildren in Germany, I extended my right arm and responded, "*Heil* Hitler."

Clutching my hand tightly, Papa looked down at me, instead of at my teacher. Quickening our pace, he pulled me past her without saying a single word.

Once away from the encounter, I looked up to study his face. I felt I had displeased him, as if I had done something wrong. "Papa, why didn't you . . . ?"

My father started another conversation to avoid my question and its ugly answer. "Mutti and baby Eleonore are going to be so happy to see you, Rosel. We are almost home."

In my bed aboard the *Marine Flasher*, I awakened for a moment, feeling a little scared. It was still nighttime, much too early to get up. Although I knew I had had a nightmare, my dream had evaporated as quickly as it had appeared. I could remember only bits and pieces.

Anxious, I looked for Liesel across the darkened room, the ship's nightlights casting just enough glow to faintly illuminate the lower bunks. She wasn't in her bed.

Where is she? Disconcerted and restless, I closed my eyes and tried to fall back asleep.

SUNDAY JULY 7, 1946

Leaving the English Channel, Near Falmouth, England

The faint and haunting melody of a clarinet floated through the air, calling me as I stirred in my bunk. The sound seemed far away, off in the distance. Still lingering in the twilight state between reality and dreams, I wasn't sure if it was real. As I rubbed my eyes, the world around me gradually emerged in greater clarity and in color, confirming that I was indeed awake.

The music persisted. I followed the melody in my head as it floated through the sleeping quarters. The clarinet's song had a melancholy feel about it. Wistful and nostalgic, it somehow reminded me of the past, though I didn't know why.

Still groggy, I looked around. The room was mostly cleared out of passengers, and the ship's day lights were on. It was apparently later in the morning than I thought. I had overslept.

Liesel's neatly made bed reminded me that I had awakened last night and seen her bunk empty. As it came back to me, I remembered having a nightmare and being unable to fall back to sleep. *Where had she gone at such a late hour, in the darkness?*

Probably she had to use the lavatory and had gone down to the community bathrooms. But I had remained awake and restless for what seemed like hours after my bad dream, and she hadn't returned.

I told myself not to make too much of it. Liesel seemed fearless and adventurous. Certainly the darkened ship wouldn't bother her like it did me. Maybe she simply couldn't sleep and had gone up to the observation deck for some fresh air or to look out at the stars.

That wasn't such a farfetched idea. Papa had once said the deck of a ship was a good place to be alone at night. Having been a deckhand for an international merchant ship as a young man, he told me that far out at sea, the stars felt so close at night that you could almost touch them. Alone with the heavens, he said that one could talk to God and the angels up there. Maybe Liesel had discovered the same.

Being aboard a commercial trade vessel was how Papa had discovered America in the first place. His ship made runs between northwest Europe and the southeast coast of the United States in the early 1920s, well before I was born and prior to his emigration from Germany to America. His ship had often docked in various ports in Georgia and South Carolina to pick up timber and textile supplies for the return trip to Europe. He would walk the streets of Savannah, Beaufort, and Charleston while docked, taking in the sights of what he called a booming and friendly country.

Papa had told me he formed his first ideas of freedom in America, even though he said that not everyone in America was yet free. Women had only recently gained the right to vote, and many Black people still lived in squalor, often a stone's throw from the distinguished white mansions they had helped build. But America was different than other countries, Papa said. In America, freedom was expected—one's God-given right. Americans had built that concept so deeply into the fabric of their culture that they were ready to fight, and even die, for it.

Breaking into my thoughts again, the clarinet's entrancing song seemed to be trying to lead me somewhere.

Where is that wonderful music coming from? Maybe if I hurry, I will be able to find out. With my curiosity mounting, I climbed down the bunk ladder, noticing that my bunkmate's bed was empty. Realizing how late I must have slept, I hastened my way down to the community bathrooms.

I was surprised to find the women's lavatories empty. *Oh no, what if I missed breakfast?* Anxious again about not having access to food, I had to remind myself where I was. The two daily meals aboard the *Flasher* were both predictable and ample. And I had noticed yesterday that between breakfast and dinner, they had placed leftover rolls, jam, and cheese just outside the mess hall door, so passengers would always have at least a snack if they got hungry during the day.

With nobody in the shower stalls, I thought I'd better take the opportunity to wash up. But where would I hang my blue dress? Other passengers had washed some of their clothes, and drying garments were draped over makeshift clotheslines made from discarded packing twine attached to pipes and fixtures.

Shaking my head a little, I perused the odd assortment of belongings hanging above the sinks. Well-worn socks, fraying underwear, torn stockings, and patched children's jumpers alternated on the sagging clotheslines. Weren't people worried that their clothes might be stolen? I could never trust leaving my outfit out like that, unattended. Sadly, war had introduced me to theft, even of such worn-out clothes as these. Even used personal toiletries like combs, toothbrushes, and remnants from bars of soap were fair game.

The motley display brought me back to the war and more memories I had tried so hard to leave behind. Maybe if I took a shower this morning, I could wash those thoughts away along with my stale body odor.

In the shower, I tried to get as clean as I could without any soap. Although the water was barely lukewarm, it still felt luxurious compared to what I was used to back in Germany. Drying myself off with one of the always damp and heavily bleached towels the ship provided daily, I stepped into my only clean change of undergarments and my increasingly wrinkled dress. I brushed my teeth, using a little bit of baking soda Mutti had enclosed in my toiletry bag. I thought about washing my second set of undergarments with some of the remaining soda, but immediately second-guessed myself. My meager supplies would have to last at least ten days.

There wasn't time to tend to anything more, anyway. The music was still summoning me, faint and somewhere off in the distance. I didn't want to miss out.

Like a magnet, the haunting melody found me out in the corridor, drawing me toward the iron stairwell that led up top. The musician was out there, somewhere on the upper deck.

Passing the mess hall, I was disappointed to find the entrance door already closed. I had missed breakfast. Fortunately, like yesterday, a spread of rolls, jam, and cheese had been left out for the taking. Relieved, I hastily made myself a jam sandwich for breakfast and a cheese sandwich for lunch. Wolfing down my breakfast while standing there, I put my cheese sandwich in my dress pocket for later. Glancing around to make sure I was still alone, I put two more rolls inside my pocket for safekeeping before making my way up the clanging iron stairs.

Stepping out onto the observation deck, I found a balmy summer sun playing hide-and-seek with billowing clouds. Ahead, just inside the wrap-around railing at the ship's bow, a small group of passengers stood with their backs to me, hiding the subject of their attention. As I moved closer, I caught a glimpse of him.

It was the same boy who had come to my aid in the boarding line. A young man of fourteen or fifteen years, I guessed, but so skinny like I was.

My oh my, how handsome he is! Allowing the music to wash over me, I studied him for a moment, trying to take in his essence, as if I was going to prepare a drawing. His playing seemed effortless. I watched as he raised his clarinet, eyes closed, his instrument a natural extension of his body. His music seemed to touch all my feelings at once, sorrow, loneliness, longing, hope and joy. Smitten with his fluidity and grace, I felt an instant attraction.

I wondered where he was from. His complexion was more olive in tone than I was typically accustomed to in eastern Germany; his thick, nearly black hair framing sharp and striking facial lines. Was he Bulgarian? Armenian? My mother had some relatives from southern Europe, near the Black Sea, with features similar to his. Mutti said we had some Roma blood in our lineage. I used to tell my playmates about that, feeling that it made me even more special, along with my American citizenship. But when the war and the purges came, I was told never to talk about that part of our heritage again.

The young soloist's music sounded exotic, unlike any of the German marches or Austrian waltzes I had grown familiar with during my childhood. It felt free from constraint, deeply emotional—and yet forbidden. Hitler had banned this kind of music and the impromptu gatherings it drew. Such displays were considered a threat to the Fatherland.

Feeling uneasy as a result, as if I was in trouble for merely listening, I silently reassured myself. *The war is over now. I am far away from that wretched country. Adolf Hitler is dead, and the nightmare has ended.*

The clarinetist's powerful notes called me back to the moment. I wanted to include myself within his group of onlookers, but I wasn't sure that I belonged. I took a few steps closer, squeezing between two older men with beards and intriguing black hats. I had forgotten about those hats after the years of war. I had seen them before in Breslau, when some of the shop owners were opening their stores on my way to school.

Transfixed, I was mesmerized by the musician's charisma and the mystique of his song. Lost amid feelings that had been suppressed for so long, the musician's mournful notes seemed to be reminding me that I could feel again.

I had not allowed myself to feel much of anything over the last several years. *To feel* was not my friend anymore. I had lost that companion years before, on that dreadful morning when my father was ordered off to war. After that day, I had not been able to cry, not even shed a solitary tear. Blocking out all pain and sorrow, I had told myself to only look forward, even at the expense of being forever numb.

Pain and grief lingered within me, however, always trying to take me back to my past. I had tried my best to squelch those feelings, to barricade them in the far recesses of my mind. There were so many things I never wanted to feel or think about again. And now, with no warning, the soloist's song was threatening to set those memories free.

Before I could sink into sorrow, the young man's solo abruptly changed course. Leaving their mournful foundations, his notes now a rousing ascent, my mood lifted as quickly as it had nearly slipped into despair. Bursting upward, toward the heavens, his song seemed to foretell that a hopeful future was waiting out there, somewhere.

Where might his music take me; is it even safe to go with him?

As the clarinetist's song came back to earth, I felt the weight of the world returning too. Finished playing, he nodded to his onlookers and gently, almost lovingly, put his instrument back into its purple, felt-lined case. I hoped he would play again, later today or maybe tomorrow.

Leaning on the observation deck railing, I watched the sun turn red and then sink into the evening haze. Nearly a whole day had gone by since the musician's stirring concert this morning. Feeling inspired after the experience, I had gone below and retrieved my sketchbook and pencils. Returning to the observation deck, I had spent the day deep in thought, alternately sketching scenes and writing short vignettes drawn from memories of my childhood. I had forgotten so much until the musician's song reclaimed them. Calling the little stories and their accompanying sketches "my parables," I pictured myself sharing them one day with many young children gathered round, each vignette hopefully teaching them a simple but important life lesson.

I had not spoken at all with Liesel today, though I had seen her up on the deck a couple of times, talking to the sailors and to some mothers with their children. Her magnetism seemed to touch everyone she came into contact with. And that made me jealous, which I knew was a crazy notion. I had just met her! I reminded myself I could not always count on the company of other people, that I would need to get by on my own. I was beginning to see how needy I was. Had the war done that to me too?

I had seen Liesel at dinner, along with Kurt. They had smiled and waved enthusiastically for me to come over and join them at their table, and Kurt had even stood up to motion that there was a spot for me to sit down. But the mess hall was crowded, and I would have had to press through too many people to reach them. I had gestured to her about the crowd and then settled for a table nearby, with its usual cast of defeated souls.

HOOOOOOOOOONNNNNNKKKKKK. A shrill blast from the ship's horn catapulted me back to the moment, releasing me from self-absorption and letting passengers know that a sharp turn was coming. The sun would be going down within the hour. I decided I had done enough drawing and writing for the day and gathered my things to go back to the bunk room.

As the ship made its turn toward the unprotected water of the open Atlantic, I was surprised to hear one of the sailors holler from the stern.

"Farewell, Dorset, farewell, Falmouth!" His voice carried far across the calm strait. I wondered if he could be heard along the shore.

Two short toots from the Dorset lighthouse foghorn let me know the answer. A distant voice answered back. "Fare thee well, *Marine Flasher*. Safe travels to America!"

Looking out over the vast expanse of water now ahead, I contemplated how far the horizon had to stretch before we would be able to see America. A nearly forgotten memory flashed through my mind, taking me all the way back to when I was three. For an instant, I could clearly see New

York City's sky-high silver buildings glittering in the late-day sun over Central Park.

As the memory took hold, a powerful shiver ran up and down my spine. A cautious smile soon broke out into an unrestrained grin.

My angels, you did come with me! It had been so long I almost didn't recognize them.

It's time! The perfect time!

I sprinted along the ship's railing, back down the iron stairs, and through the narrow corridors to my sleeping quarters below. Smiling at my bunkmate as I passed by, I was happy to see that this time she smiled back. Hurriedly climbing the ladder to reach my bunk, I frantically opened the latches on my suitcase. Trembling, I could barely contain all the emotion coursing through me.

I spoke aloud, happily, for anyone to hear. "Come with me, you two; your time is drawing to an end!" Grasping my old, tired companions in my left hand, I headed down the ladder, jumping the last rung. Racing back through the corridor, I paused at the staircase to catch my breath before huffing my way back up to the observation deck.

Upon reaching the upper deck lookout, I stopped, deflated. Scores of people had gathered along the rails to watch the sunset.

No. Not here. There are far too many people. I must do this alone.

I knew from talking to Liesel that there was another, much smaller lookout at the stern of the ship, but I would have to go back through the ship's interior to get there. I had never gone down the opposite corridor before, as that was where the sailors' quarters were located. I wasn't sure if passengers were even allowed to go down there, but there was no time for self-doubt or second-guessing. Racing against the sunset, I had to be brave. My destiny was at stake.

Clamoring back down the iron stairs, I turned left instead of right, and headed along the unfamiliar, dimly lit corridor. I passed a few sailors along the way, but they merely smiled and nodded without stopping me. *It must be okay for me to be down here.*

The sailors' corridor seemed to go on forever. At last I came to another set of rusty stairs that presumably led up to the rear lookout. Scampering up the stairs with my two tagalongs in hand, I found myself up on the rear observation deck. The noise was nearly unbearable, with the ship's engine running full tilt and the loud, thrashing wake from the propeller.

The deafening noise on the small observation deck brought with it so many fears, the biggest being my fear of becoming dizzy and somehow falling into the turbulent water—I didn't know how to swim very well. If anything happened to me up here, no one would ever know about it. Summoning the strength of my angels, I bit down on my bottom lip and got on with my task.

To my left was a small building, more like a room, with a metal door marked MECHANICS' QUARTERS. To my right, a narrow footpath and rail led to a small, half-moon shaped lookout, with only enough room for one or two people. Above me bellowed the *Marine Flasher's* intimidating smokestack. As tall as a farm silo, it belched out a steady stream of thick black smoke against the crimson sky.

I could barely think over the deafening sounds. Holding tight to the railing, I followed the walkway, my legs nearly bucking as I worked my way to the rear lookout.

Positioning myself on the small stoop overhanging the sea, I fought to steady my wobbling legs. Even behind the reinforced rail, standing over the churning ocean water required the attention of every cell in my body. There was no one to tell me to be careful, much less save me if I stumbled. *If I become dizzy and fall in, I will surely drown.*

I told myself not to succumb to my childhood fears. I held my old shoes with both hands, as far out over the rail as I could. I considered looking up and taking one last look at the war-ravaged lands behind me. And then I remembered my promise. *Never look back.*

I focused on the swirling water of the ship's wake, speaking forcefully to hear myself over the roar of the engine and the massive propeller below me.

"Goodbye forever, my tired, old marching shoes. I have a new destiny calling. I do not need your service anymore."

I tossed the shoes overboard and watched them disappear into the foam, creating their own vortex before fading from view. Exhaling the demons of war, I took a few steps backward until I felt safe. Overcome with an exiled emotion that felt like joy, I took a deep breath and said quietly, "I will make it through all this. My angels, you will see to it."

Racing back through the interior of the ship, I felt my burdens lifting amidst waves of exhilaration. Wanting now to catch the sunset, I found my way to the stairs leading to the main observation deck. Reaching the ship's majestic bow, standing tall and surrounded by my fellow passengers, I saw there was nothing but open water ahead. For a few minutes, I forgot all about the war and my family left behind. And in that moment, an epiphany found me: I felt grateful I had been granted passage aboard the *Marine Flasher*.

Mutti had been right. I needed to get rid of those shoes myself. Memories of my troubled past would undoubtedly fade now that those old marching shoes and their wartime ghosts lay at the bottom of the English Channel.

As the *Marine Flasher* headed out into the mighty Atlantic, the horizon didn't seem so endless. New York Harbor, with its beckoning torch signaling freedom, safety, and a new life, was waiting for me on the other side. Papa's little American girl was indeed going home.

I couldn't get there fast enough.

SUNDAY NIGHT, JULY 7, 1946

At Sea, 120 Miles off the Coast of Ireland

My Dearest Family,

As I write this note aboard the SS Marine Flasher, *my journey to America and a new life has begun. When you read this, you will know that I have arrived home, for I will be mailing my letter from New York. Oh how I long for that day!*

More to come soon, but for now, know that I am safe, encouraged, and determined to make a new way for myself in America. One day, you will join me there. Try to stay hopeful, as I know that day is coming.

Please do not worry; my angels are here with me. My love to all of you.

Herzlich,
Rosel

PS: Mutti, you will be happy to know my old marching shoes are now at the bottom of the English Channel!

I thought of sketching the Statue of Liberty to enclose with the letter, but the second nighttime bell warned that I wouldn't have enough time to finish something so elaborate. I couldn't remember exactly what the statue looked like anyway or what hand the torch was held in. Determined to sketch something in the few minutes of light I had left, I had to think of something simpler. I chuckled to myself, knowing that my subject was no longer available to model for me. With my old shoes and their cast of ghosts now banished to the bottom of the sea, I would have to draw them from memory.

Absorbed in my sketch, it seemed like mere seconds before the ship's lights dimmed for the overnight. Satisfied that my modest picture was mostly done, I packed up my drawing supplies and tucked them under my pillow.

Exhausted from the long day, I soon drifted off to sleep, leaving the vestiges of today's events in my wake. While I slept, my other world, the shadowy realm of my dreams, awakened.

As my bronze-tinged dreamscape came into view, I found myself inside my family's apartment in Breslau. Almost nine years old, I was standing at the second-story window of our living room, looking down at the avenue below. I called for my little sister, now three years of age, to come join me.

"Look, Eleonore, a parade! *Komm schnell, Komm schnell!* Look at all the people down there. All of our neighbors are celebrating. I can see Dieter, Gretchen, Wolf, and Angelika. They are giving pretty flowers to the soldiers." My energetic sister ran to my side, her eyes wide with excitement.

Trying to match Eleonore's excitement, I continued, "And look, *mein Liebchen*. Those are our colors. *Schwarz, Weiss, Rot.* Don't the men in their uniforms look handsome? Look how tall and proud they are! See how they are all marching together, in such close step with one another? So precise and in perfect time. They must have had a lot of practice. And their uniforms, neat and fresh-looking, with their fancy helmets. Look how polished their boots are, Eleonore. You can see the shine even from way up here!"

Smitten with the excitement and neighborhood camaraderie, I wanted so badly to join the festive parade. There was a celebration going on outside, and we were missing it!

With Papa busy taking inventory at work, I would only have to get permission from our mother. "Mutti, is it a holiday today? Everyone is so cheerful and excited. I want to go outside to be with our friends. May I go, please?" I looked over at Mutti, expecting a quick yes to my reasonable request.

"Me too, me too! I want to go," Eleonore chimed in, feeding off my enthusiasm, as I knew she would. With pressure coming from both of us, our mother would certainly let us go down to the festivities.

I didn't wait for Mutti to answer. "You can come outside with me, Eleonore. Hurry. Go get your shoes."

Mutti looked out our partially opened front room window. We could hear a rousing German march punctuated by snare drums. Strangely, our mother did not seem happy with the sight. I watched her shake her head and turn away, a pained look upon her face.

Too absorbed in the moment to pay much attention to Mutti's distress, I didn't want to miss out on the grand spectacle. "Come on, let's all go down to the street. It looks like such a celebration, and we don't want to miss another minute of it! Okay, Mutti?"

"I don't know, Rosel. Papa is not here right now. Maybe we will just watch from up here, *ja*?" Our mother's voice lacked enthusiasm, and I was baffled as to why.

Persisting, I was determined to wear our mother down. "Please, please, Mutti! Why can't we go? I want to give those soldiers some flowers! Eleonore and I can pick some before the men all go by."

"I said no, Rosel. Your papa would not approve."

"But everyone is down there, Mutti. Please?"

"No! I already said no; your father is not here." I was taken aback by my mother's forceful response; such a sudden flash of anger usually came from my father.

Mutti came to the window and placed her hands lightly on both of our shoulders. "I am sorry, *meine Mädchen*."

Intensely disappointed, I couldn't understand why we couldn't join in the fun. It made no sense.

As we watched the regiments of soldiers and military vehicles march by, Mutti drew my sister and me in close to her sides. A swastika-emblazoned flag of the Third Reich unfurled from a second-story shop window across the street, spotlit by the late-summer sun. The crowd cheered wildly as the *Schwarz, Weiss, Rot* proclaimed the dawn of a new era.

The sun soon ducked behind a layer of heavy, gray clouds. A storm was moving in.

Mutti rapped her fingers nervously against the windowsill. The bold cadence of the military march forced its way through the open window and into our living room.

"*Dear God*," Mutti whispered, tears trickling down her cheeks, as the sudden awareness found her. "They are heading for Poland." It would be the last time I ever saw my mother cry.

The sound of my own frantic scream wakened me. Disoriented and clammy with sweat, I slowly became aware of where I was. I had experienced a nightmare. Vivid and horrible dreams were yet another curse of the war. I had grown to expect them back in Germany, but here, aboard the *Flasher*, as we were propelled to safety in America?

Lying in my bunk aboard the *Marine Flasher*, my eyes fixed upon the pipes that made up the ceiling, a chilling question crept into my mind.

What if my ghosts had not been sunk to the bottom of the English Channel?

MONDAY JULY 8, 1946

At Sea, 370 Miles off the Coast of Ireland

Alone, picking at my oatmeal inside the mess hall, my mind wandered. I missed my little sister, Eleonore. Except for school, I had never been very far away from her before. Although I usually acted annoyed by her and I relentlessly complained to Mutti that she was following me around too much, Eleonore had been my devoted sidekick since she had learned to walk.

"Please, Rosel, take me with you!" Those words haunted me. I couldn't help but think that I had abandoned her.

Eleonore had been christened after American First Lady Eleanor Roosevelt, in subtle and clever defiance of Adolf Hitler and the Third Reich. In many ways, she was a symbol of, and a tribute to, our family's identity. Feisty and opinionated, she was already living up to her namesake. I often thought she was bent only on bothering me with her playful chatter and aggravating barrage of questions. But in reality, she was sweet, thoughtful, loyal, and most of all, unwavering in her adoration of me. Separated from her now, I began to see how badly I had sometimes treated her.

Breaking a roll open to put jam on it, I remembered the time Eleonore was given a sandwich by an elderly woman in Leipzig, when we were homeless refugees after the war. The woman had noticed my sister picking through the rubble of one of the city's decimated streets. She had kindly offered her a treat, *Butterbrot mit Marmelade*, a strawberry jam and butter sandwich. Just eight years old at the time, Eleonore had bravely asked if she could have a second sandwich for me. The woman obliged, and moments later Eleonore skipped over to me to share our favorite comfort food. Sitting together, happily eating our sandwiches on a jagged slab of concrete, the scene would remain etched in my memory for the rest of my life.

I took it upon myself to mother Eleonore from a very early age. I had her help me with household chores as soon as she was able, starting with simple tasks such as setting the dinner table and giving Peter the Cat some scraps out on the balcony. As she grew older, I would help teach her laundry and cooking skills, and I'd play school with her. Although fueled by love, my expectations for Eleonore were often intense and demanding, like my father's expectations for me. She would sometimes break down and cry when she wasn't able to perform at the unrealistic level I expected of her. I always seemed to be defending myself to my parents, explaining that I wasn't picking on her—I was trying to teach her the "right way" of doing things. Without knowing, perhaps I was mirroring the harsh culture of the adult world going on all around me.

Would I ever be able to make amends to Eleonore? Was it too late? A terrible notion struck me, a thought so despairing that I could barely hold it in my mind. *What if I never get the chance to tell her how I really feel about her?*

I finished what I could of my oatmeal porridge and wrapped my jam sandwich in a napkin before putting it inside my dress pocket for later. Wondering if I would ever conquer my food insecurities, I told my sadness to leave me alone for the day, and I headed for the observation deck.

I passed Kurt, coming back down the observation deck stairs, a book in his hand. I glanced at the title, which was in English. *Moby Dick.* I had heard about that intimidating-looking book once before in school, when my primary teacher held it high in my English class, as an example of what we might read some day if we studied hard and our English became good enough.

"*Wie geht's*, Rosel!" Kurt's sociability and enthusiasm were no less infectious than Liesel's.

"*Guten Morgan*, Kurt." I tried to sound as boisterous as Kurt, but it just didn't come out the same.

Kurt didn't slow down, continuing to walk by as if preoccupied and on a mission. Perhaps sensing he could be perceived as impolite, he turned toward me after already passing by.

"It's my reading time," holding out his book. "I will see you perhaps at dinner, *ja?*"

"*Ja-ja*, Kurt, I will talk to you later. Enjoy yourself."

And with a quick turn, he was gone. *I wonder where he goes off to read?* Maybe back to his bunk, I supposed.

Another warm, humid day greeted me up top, and I wondered if this was what it would feel like each day if I lived in the tropics. I soon spotted Liesel nearby, chatting with the mother of three young children. She smiled enthusiastically when she saw me and excused herself to come join me.

"Good morning, Rosel!" Liesel's contagious zeal was not only expected but just what I needed. As usual, she was dressed for a gala, wearing a yellow sundress; shiny, round-toed black shoes; deep-red lipstick; and white sunglasses. I was still more than a little intimidated by Liesel's polished appearance and mannerisms. She looked and acted nothing like the young women that I was accustomed to back in Germany. To me, Liesel was like some American celebrity or movie star.

"Good morning to you too, Liesel! I didn't see you earlier—you know, in the mess hall." Although I didn't want to appear obvious, I was already prying for more information. Her unexplained whereabouts were fast becoming a mystery that I wanted to solve.

She waved me off and averted her eyes. "Oh. You must have missed me; I was up early and was one of the first in line."

That's funny. I was one of the first too, and I didn't see her. Although I had caught her off guard, I dared not speak my thoughts aloud.

As usual, Liesel was quick to change the subject when she needed to. "It's a beautiful summer's day, isn't it? New York is getting closer by the minute. I am so excited I can hardly stand it."

Having seen Liesel shift gears like this before, I told myself to just let my question go.

"Kurt and I haven't seen our mother for so long; it's hard to believe these last ten years are finally coming to an end." She laughed a little and forced a smile. But her eyes betrayed her, as she fought back a tear. "I hope she will still recognize us."

I felt for her. The idea of going a decade without seeing my family felt like more than I could ever bear.

I was still baffled as to how Liesel and Kurt had been granted passage aboard the *Flasher*, with parents who were both German citizens. Perhaps it was because her mother had not gone back to Germany with them? Maybe they bribed their way on board, with all that money Liesel carried. I banished that thought and all of its implications. I shouldn't think the worst, nor be resentful of Liesel and Kurt's good fortune.

Interrupting my thoughts, Liesel went on. "Who will be waiting for you, Rosel?"

Now I was the one caught off guard. I didn't have an entirely truthful answer at the ready. My parents had never heard back from the Wagners. Although deeply worried about my reception, I didn't want to expose any more fears to Liesel.

"My aunt and her husband. They will take me in. They live in Queens, on Long Island in New York. I will get a job there and save all the money for my family's return."

Liesel looked concerned. "Rosel, how old are you?"

"*Ja*, I know, I look very young, like I'm eleven or twelve. But I'm actually fifteen."

"Fifteen?" Liesel looked astonished. "Rosel, in America it will be hard to find work until you are at least sixteen, and probably older than that. They have laws as to what age you have to be to work various jobs. You could never pass for older."

The familiar dread and panic hung over me like a cloud of shattered expectations. My vibrant image of myself as one of New York City's opportunistic young workers started fading. "But I must have a job. I will need money to bring my family home."

Liesel reassured me. "Well, my dutiful friend, do not worry yourself too much. You could get a job babysitting or something like that until you are older. Many younger people do that before they go to work for a business of some kind. It will all work out, you will see."

Barely pausing for a breath, Liesel continued in an encouraging tone. "You know, being a babysitter might be just the thing. You could earn enough money and still go to school. And then someday, you could attend a big American university." She briefly put her arm around me, trying her best to provide some comfort. I wanted to welcome her hug but felt myself stiffen and tense up instead.

My mind was running rampant. I hadn't attended school in almost two years. Fears of being caught in a bombing raid or a poisonous gas attack or of being abducted by soldiers had kept Eleonore and me close to Mutti. In America I would probably be far behind where I should be in the classroom. And my English was not as good as it once was. I had forgotten much of it after Papa left with the People's Army. All my thoughts were in German now. I would certainly face language difficulties in an American school.

Badly needing more reassurance, I said, "Liesel, I'm worried that I am so far behind in school. I don't know how I will manage all that I need to do." As the words left my mouth, I couldn't believe what I had just done. Back in Germany, showing vulnerability like this would have been an unforgiveable transgression.

Unfazed, Liesel responded, her optimism unflappable. "You know, after you start working as a babysitter, you will gain enough experience to find employment as an au pair, when you get older."

Her eyes brightened as she went on. "Then you will be able to afford college and still earn all the money you will need for your family. But it will take some time. You must be patient, something I've noticed you are not very good at." Liesel winked at me and laughed.

"An au pair?" Remaining serious, I knew that I had heard this term before but had long forgotten what it meant.

"Yes. That's sort of a live-in babysitter for a family. It's like being a nanny. You help take care of young children while their parents work. They do it a lot in America. It's a way you can keep working while you attend school and later college."

It came back to me. My great-aunt Emilia had been an au pair for a wealthy family when she first came to America. And I thought Mutti had told me she had been one too, for a brief while before I was born, although I wasn't sure I was remembering correctly.

Taking a deep breath, I felt myself relax. *"Ja,* an au pair sounds like something I could do, and good experience too. And going to a university, well, that's what I always wanted to do."

For years before the war, I had seen Papa go off to the University of Breslau in the evenings, after work, taking classes in religion and philosophy. Papa talked of college for me as if it were a given. He said I could be whatever I wanted to be, back home in America. Some days I dreamed of becoming a nurse, other times a dress designer or a teacher, maybe even an artist like Uncle Alfred. On my best days, I felt I could do all of it. I would just have to work hard enough.

Before I could tell Liesel about my aspirations, two sailors approached us from behind, carrying an oversized and apparently heavy wooden crate. Liesel tugged at my hand, pulling me with her, in order to get out of their path. The younger sailor smiled at her in a strangely familiar sort of way.

Putting the bulky container down close to us, it landed with a thud, causing me to flinch. As the two sailors began transferring canned goods from the container onto nearby loading pallets, they chatted, occasionally glancing over in our direction. Gauging their accents, I thought they were both American.

The older man, his face weathered and creased, spoke first. When he raised his voice, he reminded me of Papa. "Those Germans wanted to rule the world, and now so much of it is in ruins. All because of them. Murderers. Those damn murderers can burn in hell forever, if you ask me."

The younger sailor nodded but remained silent, still trading glances with Liesel. The older sailor continued, his voice filling with more and more intensity and anger, just like my father during one of his outbursts.

"Why we didn't wipe them from the face of the earth I will never know. Should have dropped the A-bomb on them too. And now we're letting some of them come to America, and on this ship?"

I didn't need to look at him directly; I just knew he was talking about me. I could feel my face flushing, the older sailor's words like daggers plunging into my heart.

Liesel could see my distress. "Rosel, are you all right?"

I was not all right.

"What is the matter, my friend?"

I didn't want to answer, but this had been bothering me for years. I turned my back to the sailors and spoke in a near whisper. "Liesel, do you think all Germans are to blame? I mean . . . is that what most Americans think?"

Before Liesel could reply, I blurted out the rest of my thought. "I am not a Nazi, nor one of their sympathizers. I am just a child . . . well, I was." In my mind, the Nazis were the enemy, not the ordinary German people. The Nazis were an armed gang that took over the country by storm. People had no choice.

Liesel's voice grew uncharacteristically quiet and vulnerable. "I know, Rosel. But a lot of people think Germans are all Nazis. We must get used to people judging. When you think about it, can you really blame them for feeling that way?"

I didn't want to hear that answer, especially coming from my own mouth, and I expected Liesel to provide me with more assurances. Instead, she pressed me for an answer. "Well . . . can you?"

I ducked my head sheepishly and was unable to reply. When I glanced up again, Liesel was waiting, eyebrows raised, expecting an answer. I felt defeated, filled with shame about my family's heritage. Again I thought of my accent.

"I know you are right, Liesel," I said quietly, still repeating my negative thoughts.

In Germany, I was secretly proud to know that I was an American. I wanted America to win the war, and I cheered in my heart when they did. Now that I was returning to New York, my accent would be a dead giveaway. I was branded. No one would ever believe I was an American.

I couldn't say the rest of my thought out loud. *I am going to be painted as the enemy, in my own country.*

MONDAY NIGHT, JULY 8, 1946

At Sea, 600 Miles Southwest of Ireland

Lying in my bunk again, trying to block out all the distressing thoughts coming at me, I was unable to shake off what that American sailor had said earlier in the day. *"Why we didn't wipe them from the face of the earth I will never know."* I couldn't get those words out of my head. He was talking about the Nazis for sure, but why would he include all Germans? My family hated the Nazis from the start. If anything, my father was a freedom fighter, believing in the equality of all people. He despised war, and he loathed Hitler and his detestable gang of bullies. How could that sailor accuse Papa, Mutti, little Eleonore, and me? We were not the enemy. *How could we all be painted with such a broad brush?*

The first bell chimed, telling me to try to settle in for the night. Thirty more minutes until lights-out.

With my nightmares resurfacing regularly, I didn't dare fall asleep awash in such questions. Searching for safe things to think about, I drifted to my early years of school and the joy and security I once felt there.

I used to love school. As a young girl, I couldn't wait to jump out of bed in the morning to get ready for class. I took such delight in being part of the colorful, bustling classrooms and learning new and interesting things. I discovered that I was really good at math, as well as literary composition and geography. I would hurry home every day to tell Papa and Mutti all about it.

School was where most of my friends were too. Although I had become proficient in German, I used to tell them in English that I was American, taking great pride when they gathered around to ask me questions about my nationality and my birthplace. I loved to describe what I could remember of New York City, watching my schoolmates' eyes widen when I told them of the incredible buildings that touched the sky.

I looked up to my teachers back then, almost as much as I did to my parents. Not only kind, they seemed genuinely interested in me. During my early primary school years, most of my instructors were young, in their twenties or early thirties. They encouraged us to ask questions in class when we didn't understand something, and there was little fear of making a mistake. *"Mistakes are how we learn,"* I remember one of my teachers telling us. I was always at the ready to raise my hand, eager to participate.

Frau Schmidt, my homeroom teacher, was the only teacher I didn't like during my early years of school. She was the exception—much older and with a harsh, critical voice that set her apart from my other teachers. Anxiety overwhelmed me when she approached and then towered over my desk, her voice stern and her expression usually angry. Fortunately, my homeroom class, the first of the day, always passed quickly. Once we had taken attendance, recited our allegiance to Hitler, and listened to our daily current events updates, I would fly out of Frau Schmidt's classroom, excited about the things I was going to learn that day.

The second bell soon chimed aboard the *Flasher*—lights-out was imminent. I hoped to carry only pleasant school memories into my nighttime world. But as the ship's lights dimmed, I found myself pulled elsewhere, unwillingly. My other school memories were waiting there, the ones that took me to places I did not ever want to return to.

Caught up in the onset of a dream, I drifted through its surreal brown-and-bronze-tinged haze until I found myself back at my primary school. Floating through the school corridors, passing wispy ghosts of children, I landed in the second row of my fourth-grade classroom, during the year when everything changed.

Before me was *Fräulein* Hertz, the last of my favorite teachers. Young and vibrant, perhaps in her middle twenties, she taught geography, one of my favorite subjects. I used to take great pride in seeing the world map at the front of her class, particularly pleased to note the size of the United States, which dwarfed all the European countries. America seemed to me the center of the world. I remembered when I could point to New York City, proudly telling the class where I was born. But not anymore. America was one of Germany's enemies now.

One by one, all my other young teachers had left the school over the past couple of years. We were told they had gone off to support Hitler and his push to make Germany great again. Men and teenage boys went off to war; women did volunteer work for the military or Nazi-controlled social organizations and public works. Factories were booming in Germany, but it wasn't because the economic depression was over and trade had resumed. I didn't quite see it yet, because of my young age, although the signs were everywhere. A war machine was being built in our midst.

Waiting excitedly in my seat, I was anxious to show my teacher I had come prepared.

"Okay, children, my young scholars. Who can tell me the countries that border Germany to the west?"

Raising my hand to answer, I knew the five countries. I was good at geography.

Before I could answer, however, the class was interrupted.

Without bothering to knock, two German officers, one middle-aged and the other no more than nineteen or twenty, opened the door and entered our room. Wearing gray-brown uniforms with armbands boasting a bold-red swastika, they needed no introduction, nor did they provide one. They were from the SS, the Schutzstaffel, Hitler's intelligence unit.

The older officer was in charge. He spoke first, his voice piercing and cold. "Fräulein Hertz?"

"Yes, I am Fräulein Hertz . . ."

The officer in charge had a skull stitched on the front of his hat, and it moved with him as he handed my teacher a document. "We are here for these children. You will kindly call them up to the front so we can escort them to their transport."

"Escort them to their transport? What is this about? Where are the authorizations from their parents?" Our teacher looked dumbfounded.

"That is none of your concern." The officer's stern reply made clear that he expected no debate and no more questions.

Fräulein Hertz persisted. "It is my concern. These children are in my charge."

"These children belong to the *Reich*. Please call them up."

"What? Where is your authority to take them?" My teacher's shocked face also exuded worry, her youthful face now punctuated with forced lines.

"My dear Fräulein, you wouldn't want to be cited for resistance, would you? Now please call them up to the front of the class."

Fräulein Hertz looked down on the sheet of paper she had been handed moments before. Her hands began shaking as she read from what looked like a typed list. "Viktor, Jakob . . . please come up . . . Seth, you too . . ." Looking bewildered, the three children dutifully came up and stood before the class.

With feigned kindness and a smile that didn't reach his eyes, the older officer spoke to my classmates standing before him, "Children, you will please remain silent and come with us. Your parents are waiting for you."

The room was unnaturally quiet, and my classmates appeared frozen in time.

I felt my airway constrict and a rush of anxiety overtake me. My heart pounded. I couldn't seem to get enough air.

Finally, one of the three boys mustered up enough courage to ask a question, despite the officer's directive to remain quiet. "Where are you taking us, sir?"

With a sweeping arm, the older officer herded him to his side. Forcing another fake smile, he bent down to my classmate's eye level. "And what is your name, young man?"

"Jakob. Jakob Steinway. I am the son of Isaiah and Hannah Steinway."

"You have no need to worry, my boy. "The officer laughed humorlessly. "You are going on vacation with your parents."

"A vacation? But it's the middle of the school year. What about the other—"

The younger officer cut him off. "Fräulein Hertz, I believe there is one more name on your list. A girl."

Oh my God, oh dear God, no! Breathing rapidly, I was so afraid to move and call attention to myself that I thought I might lose control of my bladder.

★   ★   ★

I jerked wide-awake in my bed aboard the *Marine Flasher*. Pinned by fear, I lay there with my eyes open, a prisoner in the darkness. *That boy in my dream, Jakob . . . he seemed so familiar. I know his face, but from where?* As bits and pieces of memories tumbled through my mind, I felt my nighttime specters trying to emerge, only this time while I was awake.

Fully conscious, feeling scared and restless, my mind frantically searched for the memory of Jakob. I finally found him at the Breslau *Hauptbahnhof*, the city's central train station, where I had seen him once before. My mind must have transplanted him inside my dream, to remind me.

It was in July 1940, when I was still nine years old. I was on a summer trip with my mother and now three-year-old sister to visit Papa's sister, my *Tante*, Johanna, in Berlin for a couple of weeks. The war had broken out but hadn't reached German soil yet. While waiting to board our train in Breslau, I saw something strange. An eastbound train was coming into the station, carrying hundreds of people packed like animals into open cars used for livestock. As the train slowed, I saw a boy about my age standing near the outer wall of one of the filthy cars. Around him were scores of disheveled people with blank looks on their faces. The boy had a palm-sized yellow Star of David sewn onto the front of his dirty, blue coat. As their train came to a stop, he saw me and waved impassively. I instinctively waved back.

I knew what that star meant. It was common knowledge even among primary school students. The Nazis had ordered all Jewish people to sew those yellow stars on their clothes and paint them on their businesses, so they could be easily identified and their shops and businesses boycotted.

What are they doing in there, in those dirty cars used for pigs and cattle? Where are they going? I needed to ask Mutti. But amid the bustle of boarding, this was not the time. I could ask her once we were settled in our seats.

The passenger car of our westbound train was congested. As we pushed and bumped our way down the aisle, nearly all the seats were already taken. Toward the back, we squeezed in alongside a man who was about Papa's age. He was seated at the window, smelling of alcohol, pork sausage, and body odor. I wanted to look out the window, but I didn't want to look at him.

"Die Juden gehen auf Ferien." The man laughed and nudged me as he pointed through the window at the cattle car containing the boy I had seen. Again he prodded me and smiled, his crooked, yellowed teeth momentarily exposed, expecting me to join in his amusement.

"The Jews go on vacation." The words screamed evil no matter what language they were spoken in.

★   ★   ★

The remaining hours before dawn passed fitfully for me aboard the *Marine Flasher*. Afraid to return to sleep, other memories streamed back, an unwelcome encore to my terrifying dream.

I remembered my young playmate, Adam, from when I was five, the Jewish boy the neighbors said I wasn't supposed to play with, the boy Papa had said needed to be rescued.

Then that horrible night in November, when I was eight, when I awakened in the dead of night to the clatter of men shouting, followed by screams, breaking glass, and anguished crying. I thought it was a scary dream, and I covered my head with my pillow, trying to drown it out. But the next morning, Papa and Mutti kept me home from school. When I went outside to play, I saw broken glass strewn all along the avenue in front of our apartment building.

Papa said I was too young to understand what happened, but a few nights later, eavesdropping when I was supposed to be asleep, I overheard Papa telling Mutti that a number of shops had been broken into along Hundsfelder Strasse. A number of Jewish men had been killed, others arrested, defending their own stores. Papa said they were calling the riot against the Jews *Kristallnacht*, the Night of Broken Glass. I heard him say that the police had just stood by and watched as it happened.

I curled up in the corner of my bunk, a scared little girl who needed her Papa. Try as I might to make them stop, more images streamed through my mind, each one a clue as to what had really happened in Hitler's Germany. My parents had tried so desperately to shield me from what was going on all around us, but the Nazi poison had seeped inside me anyway.

After what seemed like hours, the ship's day lights finally came on, and the torrent of memories stopped. I wondered if I could ever feel safe closing my eyes aboard the *Flasher* again.

TUESDAY, JULY 9, 1946

900 Miles Southwest of Ireland

Sitting up top on my bunk, I was glad morning had mercifully arrived. I wondered if I was losing control of my mind. The pleasant dreams of my first nights aboard the *Flasher* seemed far away now, perhaps no longer retrievable. Taking their place, the worst of my childhood was being unlocked at night, against my will. I felt like a helpless puppet, commandeered by some malevolent force to act out macabre little plays drawn up from all the disturbing scenes from my life.

Needing something to distract me, I looked across the room for my friend, but Liesel's bunk was empty again. It once again appeared as if her bed had not even been slept in.

Liesel was an enigma. I thought of her frequently, searching my mind for answers to explain her whereabouts at odd hours of the night. *Where does she go under cover of darkness?* I had not seen her asleep in her bunk since the first night.

I could already see that underneath her outgoing façade, Liesel was a very self-protective person. Adept at changing the subject of conversation, she rarely revealed anything that might make her appear vulnerable or distressed. I could sometimes sense sadness in her eyes, a festering hurt that she could not or would not express. That time I had asked about her father, she had seemed close to breaking down. But what right did I have to question anything about her? I wouldn't want anyone digging around in my experiences.

The ship's bell signaled the start of the breakfast hour, interrupting my thoughts. I heard my bunkmate stir beneath me. Grabbing my dress from the bedpost, I considered introducing myself as I passed by. Other than that first failed attempt, I had not made any effort to speak to her since our voyage began. Feeling a twinge of guilt, I reminded myself she had not made any effort to talk to me either. Still, it seemed rather callous or at least impolite to continue acting as if she didn't exist down there, only an arm's length or two away from me.

As I stepped off the bunk's ladder, I glanced over at her. Her back was to me as she tied her hair back. "Excuse me. My name is Rosemarie. How are you doing today?"

No response. Maybe she didn't hear me. I tried again, this time in German. "*Hallo, wie geht es dir?*"

The woman turned, revealing her tired but youthful face, her eyes sunken and rimmed by dark circles. Evidently, she had not been sleeping well either. Not saying a word, she only shook her head despondently before turning her back and finishing her hair.

At least I had tried. I didn't know what to think of her headshake, but I wasn't going to start obsessing about her too. She was just another phantom aboard the *Flasher*. Although there was undoubtedly a person in there, somewhere beneath her troubles, I had enough to worry about just taking care of myself. I walked away, berating myself for being callous.

Hurrying through the corridor with my dress in hand, I noticed that my only outfit was not only embarrassingly wrinkled but also starting to smell. I pledged to wash it for the first time later today, when I got ready for bed. I would have to use the baking soda reserved for brushing my teeth. That odor emanating from under the sleeves would soon become offensive. I could hang the dress from my bunks bedpost to dry overnight, careful not to dampen the hemline and its secret stash of money.

The bathroom was crowded this morning when I opened the door. Children wriggled and whined at different corners of the room, each in a different language, as mothers tried their best to make them look presentable. Uncomfortable with all the people, I skipped the showers and hastily put on my dress, taking a quick peek in the mirror. My hair was still nicely styled after our salon visit in Le Havre. I pictured myself winking at my reflection, like Liesel would, but then thought that would be self-indulgent and refrained. Collecting my nightclothes and toiletry bag, I hurried back to my bunk, tossing my little drawstring bag and nightclothes onto my bed before heading down to breakfast.

Upon entering the mess hall, I scanned the crowded room but found neither Liesel nor Kurt. After filling my tray with a bowl of wheat porridge, some condensed milk, and an orange, I chose the nearest table that had enough space for me to squeeze in. Although increasingly desperate to talk to somebody, I once again found myself sitting among ghosts. I didn't even bother trying to catch anyone's eye anymore, looking for an opening to speak or even a welcoming smile. It was pointless.

Although I had been hungry earlier, I couldn't finish all I had placed on my tray. I was getting used to having enough food available for everyone. Finding that meals came in predictable fashion, my food insecurity was lessening. But as I carried my tray to the dishwashing window, I put the orange in my pocket as insurance for later.

Making my way up the now familiar iron stairs, I set off to find my lone bastion of security aboard the *Marine Flasher*. Upon reaching the upper deck, I soon spotted her, down at the far end of the observation overlook. Wearing a bright-pink dress with white lace, she was laughing with some of the sailors, even poking one of them playfully on his chest. The sight would have drawn scornful looks back in Germany, but Liesel didn't seem to care.

Feeling the need for companionship after the trials of yesterday, I wanted Liesel all to myself today but already knew that was a ridiculous idea. Here I was, just my third day after meeting her, and I was already picturing Liesel as a best friend for life. I had even imagined her living close to me on some flower-lined street in New York City. I knew I was going way too fast, living inside such fairy tales, but I still had trouble restraining myself.

Liesel already seemed to have developed many relationships aboard the *Marine Flasher*, each tugging at her, all seeking her company. Was I really that special to her? Each day I had watched her talk with other passengers, from the little children whose parents used her as a babysitter, to young adults who leaned on her poise and optimism and the enamored sailors who flirted with her while they were working. Liesel also had her brother, Kurt. I had never seen her alone, and I presumed she was never lonely.

I told myself I should make other friends aboard the *Flasher*, though it seemed that there was no one besides Liesel I would be able to relate to. The few teenagers I'd seen were always in the company of their younger siblings or parents. I thought of that handsome and intriguing young clarinetist, but I was so uncomfortable around boys my age. The war had robbed me of that stage in development entirely. I had never had even a crush on a boy. I wouldn't know what to do if I did.

Being far out to sea emphasized my sense of isolation and loneliness. With no hints of land or other ships, there was little to distract me or divert my attention. The ocean was a vast expanse of emptiness stretching endlessly in all directions, today overcast by gray clouds.

Oh, my angels, would you help me, please? I must make some other friends aboard this ship besides Liesel. I cannot be clinging to her every day like an annoying little tagalong or some insecure puppy lapping at her heels.

Searching the length of the ship, determined to overcome my shyness, I noticed a boy far down the railing ahead of me. As he stood alone, staring out to sea, a faded blue cap kept his long, slightly unkempt hair in place against the blustery ocean breeze.

It was the young musician. Seeing him alone and without his clarinet, I hadn't recognized him at first.

He seemed like he might be a safe person to approach, kind and gentle. Right from the start, there was something special about him, almost spellbinding. He played his clarinet in a way that evoked such feeling in me.

Should I introduce myself? On a ship full of refugees, I was uncertain how to go about it. *Do I speak in English or German? Should I be formal or informal?* He had spoken to me in English before, and back in the boarding line, he had appeared anything but formal. Although nervous, I decided to take a chance. I didn't want to spend another day aboard the *Flasher* alone.

The walk along the ship's railing seemed uncomfortably long. My legs wobbled a bit as I got closer. Finally reaching him, I chose to introduce myself in English.

"Good morning. My name is Rosemarie, Rosel for short." I smiled bashfully and rushed on. "I almost didn't recognize you without your clarinet."

Continuing to stare out across the open water, the young musician didn't respond. *Maybe he doesn't fully understand me.*

"Oh . . . I'm sorry. You spoke English with me the other day, so I thought—"

"I speak English all right, I suppose," he said flatly, still not acknowledging my presence with his eyes. "And a little German too, if you are wondering."

It didn't feel like my introduction was going very well. He seemed uncomfortable with me. I worried that I was being intrusive, but I pressed on. "What is your name, may I ask?"

The young musician returned only silence.

"You are quite popular here with your engaging concerts." I tried smiling again, anxious to connect in any way I could. But he wasn't even looking at me.

At last he spoke, saying only, "My name is David."

"David, it's nice to meet you. Where are you from?"

After a long pause, he answered me in a nearly soundless monotone. "Nowhere. I am from nowhere."

David's emotionless demeanor caused an eerie chill to run through my body. His voice, flat and lifeless, was completely unlike his music.

"Excuse me, David. I didn't quite hear you. Where are you from?"

"Nowhere. I am not from any place worth remembering."

"You are from nowhere? How can that be? Everyone is from somewhere."

"Not anymore."

I didn't know how to respond. Was he being hostile or merely self-protective? He had been so friendly and compassionate when I had first met him in the boarding line. Had I offended him somehow? I felt the need to apologize.

"I am sorry, I didn't mean to . . ."

He finally turned toward me, but I couldn't finish my sentence. A surge of anguish rose from my stomach. Looking at him, I saw something I was ill prepared for.

I saw the cold, detached face of a soul adrift. I had seen that absent and vacant look before, on my father's face. For a moment, I couldn't breathe. Like with Papa, it was as if I was looking right through David.

Unnerved, I took a step back, stumbling over my words. "Well, I, I hope we . . . maybe we can talk again some time soon."

Silent and disconnected, his eyes hollow and dark, David turned back to the sea.

Unable to respond myself, I wanted to run, but there was nowhere to run to.

TUESDAY NIGHT, JULY 9, 1946

1,100 Miles Southwest of Ireland

Sitting on my bed, dejected after my failed encounter with David earlier in the day, I couldn't shake his unsettling facial expression from my head. I tried to sketch him, but the uneasy presence now attached to his image impeded me. I could only draw him from a distance, with his back turned. I soon put my pencils and sketchpad away, my botched introduction repeating like some broken record, over and over in my mind.

David had looked as if he was not even present within his body, his spirit detached and adrift. Baffled, I was unable to reconcile his behavior today with that of our first encounter, in the boarding line. And when he played his clarinet, he seemed so self-assured, commanding the complete attention of his audience. The person I had tried to talk to today seemed entirely different—beaten, withdrawn, barely able to speak. It almost seemed as if he were two different people.

I wondered if I had done anything to trigger David's pain, like I had inadvertently done with Liesel. I blamed myself as I searched for explanations.

Was it my accent? As I thought about it some more, that made sense. Maybe he thought I was German and one of the enemies, like that sailor had implied. *I hate my accent. I hate it! I wish I sounded American.* Some people did seem to think Germans were all Nazis. Like Liesel had said, could I really blame them?

I had to find a way to make things right. I prayed for the chance to tell David that I was an American, born in New York.

As the ship dimmed its lights for the night, shadows crept in. Once again, I could feel my nighttime puppeteers lurking, poised for my arrival. They might as well be demons, I thought. I could be in for a long, fitful night.

★   ★   ★

"People of Germany! You have been suffering for too long! You have not been able to find work, your children have gone hungry, your German pride and strength have been replaced with fear and cowardice! Rise up, my German nation! It is time to restore your rightful position as the world's master race."

The words of Adolf Hitler, der Führer, as we now had to call him, rang discordantly in my head. Tonight's dream had landed me at the streetcar stop, just steps from our apartment building along Hundsfelder Strasse— sometime in April, I supposed, guessing from the bright new leaves on the trees. Springtime was the start of the school year throughout Germany. I was ten years old in 1941 and on my way to secondary school.

Papa and Mutti had allowed me to take the streetcar, the *Strassenbahn*, all by myself. Papa and I had practiced the route many times during my month-long school recess. Although there was a war going on, it hardly appeared like it in Breslau or anywhere else in eastern Germany. It didn't seem real to me yet. The way German radio broadcasts described it, it sounded more like some far-away chess game.

"The superiority of the German people and their mighty will shall be restored! The time has come to reclaim German greatness as leaders of the world. We must seize our moment and choose our own destiny!"

The angry and evocative words of Adolf Hitler continued to blare from a loudspeaker positioned atop the tall, blue-tiled kiosk. The kiosks, which looked like decorative towers, were a common sight along German city avenues. They were typically placed at regular intervals, one for each neighborhood and streetcar stop.

"We must take back what is rightfully ours from our enemies! They have stolen our country from us, trying to bring us to our knees, to destroy our proud culture and heritage. People of Germany, no more! No more, I tell you! We will once again be proud to be German. We will bow our heads to no one!"

Papa said the powerful speakers had been positioned years ago, before we had come to Germany, to announce public events, farmers' market days, holidays, and festivals. He said music used to play from them too, colorful folk songs to usher in a holiday, a festival, or a harvest event. Now the loudspeakers were being used to spread only what Hitler's *Reich* wanted us to know. And the only songs that played from them were the harsh-sounding military marches that introduced blistering, hate-filled speeches.

Standing alone at the streetcar stop in the chilly morning air, yet another provocative message blared at me. I had already had more than my fill of it.

"Germany for Germans! The Jews have appropriated our wealth, the imperialists have taken our land . . ."

I had been bombarded with these speeches for as long as I could remember. With the loudspeaker just a few steps from our apartment, I had heard the fiery rhetoric nearly every time I went outside to play or walk to school. The announcements were inescapable. The words of der Führer and his Reichsministers came on at all hours of the day, and often well into the evening.

I watched as the streetcar came down the avenue, clanging along the tracks, a trail of sparks flying from its long tether to the electricity line. I remembered being afraid of the sparks as a little girl, worried that they would set fire to the car we rode in. Older and wiser now, I shook my head, realizing how naïve and innocent I once was.

I pulled my leather school satchel up over my shoulder; it would be heavy with books when I returned home later today. As the streetcar pulled to a noisy stop, I looked behind to see that the boarding spot had filled up with other secondary students from my neighborhood. I recognized most of them. Missing, however, were several of my old friends. I knew what had happened, with the purges going on, but I tried to keep from thinking about it. Both Mutti and Papa had said we were powerless to do anything about it, anyway.

The passenger car door swung open. Climbing aboard, I handed the conductor the change Mutti had given me for the fare. Looking down the aisle for a good place to sit, I was happy to find a window seat just behind the conductor. For some reason, I felt safer up there.

"We must rid our nation of the foreign invaders and reclaim the lands that were stolen from us! The Jews are stealing our wealth! The Communists have taken our jobs! German workers and German families have been the ones who have suffered. Too long! Too long, people of Germany!"

School was three stops away. As the conductor closed the door, the angry announcements faded for the moment. I knew they would resume when the door opened for its next stop.

Hitler's lies had been spreading for years, like a plague. It appeared to me that most people in Germany had become infected. Desperate to regain better economic conditions and a sense of pride, people were quick to believe anything that explained their misery or lessened their fear. Papa had told me that many of the older Germans remembered the Great War, two decades before. That war left the country in economic shambles, the vast Austro-Hungarian and German Empires dismantled. Germany's rule stripped from the continent, borders repartitioned by British, French, and American victors to be a fraction of what they once were. As the empires had been taken apart, so had German pride and identity as a world power.

The streetcar pulled into the next stop, and the doors flew open, admitting a few more of my schoolmates.

"The people of Germany must repel the threats to the Fatherland! The French, British, and American imperialists will not keep their boots pressed against our throats any longer. We have had enough! It is time, people of Germany. We must destroy the threats! Remove the Jews! Expel the foreigners! Make haste, people of Germany; we have had enough!"

I was beginning to see the country more clearly as I grew older. An air of hate and contempt for anything not perceived to be purely German was taking hold—just the way the Nazis had planned it. People were quick to blame anything and anyone for the country's economic woes and lost identity. Anyone except themselves.

I could feel the hate in our neighborhood, within our apartment building, even inside my school. I saw it in the way people looked at each other, unsure and uncertain, peering at each other's faces for signs of threat. Without being able to question anything out in the open, we increasingly lived in a troubled world built upon lies and half-truths. It was becoming hard to tell what was real anymore, and what information could be trusted.

"The Jews are working with the imperialists to overthrow Germany! They have infected every industry, every store, even our political structures. They have collaborated with the Americans, the British, and the French aggressors! No more! We will eradicate them like vermin . . ."

The rambling propaganda stopped as the conductor pulled on his lever to close the door, heading for the last stop before we would arrive at my school.

Looking out the window, worrying about so many things, I thought about how wicked it had all become. Even us children were now being dragged into the Nazi pollution. Over the past couple of years, more of my friends and their families had disappeared, often without warning. The children the Nazis called "impure," the ones they branded as threats, had been removed with their families by the police. We didn't ask why anymore. To ask questions would put our own families in harm's way.

I had trouble seeing how those children, my old friends, constituted any sort of threat. I remembered that when I was younger, I didn't even know that my playmates were Jews or Poles or Romani, the people the Germans called Gypsies. I saw them as being just children like me, with innocent faces, playful smiles, and welcoming eyes. Now we were being told to not only avoid them, but to hate them. The Nazis wanted only *Aryan* children, full-blooded Germans, to lead the nation forward.

It wasn't hard for me to understand that with my American citizenship, I would soon be counted as one of his threats. But I was fluent in German, complete with a Silesian accent. Blond and blue-eyed, I fit the Nazi bill, as long as they never learned I was an American.

The streetcar slowed and then stopped. Five or six more students were waiting to board, along with a few adults who presumably were going off to work. The factories were humming again in Germany, giving credence to the belief that Germany was on the move, its power and economic vigor restored.

As the driver flung open the door, the last of the morning's propaganda drifted in, along with the new passengers.

"We have reclaimed our lands to the east and to the south. Poland, Austria, and the Republic of Slovakia have now been returned to the rightful auspices of the Fatherland. Our mighty Wehrmacht has marched with lightening speed into Denmark and Norway to the north, and the Low Countries, Holland, Belgium, and Luxembourg, to the west. France is falling, without as much as a whimper. All are in awe of the powerful German Army and the crushing airstrikes of our powerful *Blitzkrieg*! There has been little fighting and few casualties, for the people within these lands have welcomed us as liberators!"

Liberators? How can people succumb to such blatant lies? I wanted to scream out as people boarded the streetcar. Everything was so routine and business as usual. Can't anyone see what is happening?

"Keep your heads high and be proud that you are German, as we stake our claim as the most superior race on earth. The renaissance of our glorious empire is within our reach. People of Germany, take heed, for our destiny is calling us. *Heil* Hitler!"

The words from the loudspeaker faded again as the door closed. I heard the crackle of sparks as the streetcar headed for my school.

The sound of muffled, plaintive crying from somewhere below me caused me to stir in my bed aboard the *Flasher*. I tried to force my eyes open, but I was too deep in sleep to escape. Tumbling back into my hazy nighttime realm, I apparently had skipped ahead in time. The trees lining my secondary schoolyard had all turned red, signaling that it must have been fall.

I found myself near the basketball courts, gossiping with a few girl-friends during our morning recess break. My new school shoes, given to me for my birthday, finally gave away the date. It was still 1941, late in October or early November.

Through the shadowy dreamscape, two figures came into view, strutting purposefully across our school playground. They were older than me, perhaps about seventeen, much closer to adulthood than childhood. My girlfriends scattered like mice as the two BDM leaders neared.

They had come only for me, and I knew why.

I had been avoiding their organization for some time now. The Hitler Youth was a Nazi program disguised as a club for German children and teens. There was a branch for girls, the Bund Deutscher Mädel, or BDM, and a separate branch for boys, called the Hitlerjugend. I had been a member once, back when I believed it was harmless. It seemed like fun at first, a place where I could build friendships, participate in athletics, and enjoy making crafts to raise money for poor German children. Many of my friends belonged. I used to proudly say I belonged too, before my eyes had opened.

I had not signed up this year, afraid that being a member would lead to the discovery that I was an American. I had envisioned such detection would lead to my parents' arrest and to Eleonore's and my removal from our home. My sister would be placed in a Nazi-sponsored foster home. I knew such homes existed, as Hitler had bragged that he was importing blond, blue-eyed children from Scandinavia for placement in German homes. To boost the *Aryan* population, he said, so the next generation would have fewer dark-haired children.

As the two BDM leaders reached me, my stomach gave its first gurgle of warning. Wearing crisply pressed, identical white blouses and dark-blue skirts, the two girls greeted me with feigned smiles and politeness.

"Rosel, may we speak with you for a few minutes? We are with the German League of Girls, the Bund Deutscher Mädel, the BDM, as most of our members call it. I am Helga, and this is Gisela. You are now eleven years of age, *ja*?"

"*Ja.*" Already knowing I had done something wrong, I braced myself as they inched closer.

Helga continued. "We are welcoming young German girls ready to shape the future of the Fatherland. There will be a gathering of our members later today, after school. We expect that you will attend, ready to join us."

After nearly two years of evading them, I had been cornered. I pushed down the dread and nausea and offered up my first excuse. "I am busy this week. I have my studies. I am sorry, I cannot go." It was hard to catch my breath between words, giving away my failed attempt to remain composed.

Helga went on, without missing a beat. "Do not worry—we will make sure you still have plenty of time for your studies."

Her next response seemed well scripted. "As I am sure you know, der Führer has made it mandatory for young German boys and girls to attend our programs."

Gisela now chimed in, in precise lock step. "We heard that you are one of the top students in your class. You performed quite well on your *Lyceum*, Rosel. Your homeroom teacher said you excel in academics and stand out as a superb athlete and a competent seamstress. Those are qualities we favor."

Shifting my stance, trying to hide my fear, I was mercifully saved when the school bell sounded, indicating that our morning recess was over.

"I am sorry. The bell. I need to go."

"You will not leave until we are finished" was Helga's curt reply.

"But our recess is over, and my next teacher is waiting."

Helga started laughing. "We are the BDM. Your teacher will wait for us."

Gisela jumped in. "Your homeroom teacher did say you are a bit headstrong. Maybe that is not so good for the classroom, but it is good for leadership, *ja*?"

My face flushed with fear. I tried to steady my legs.

Helga continued, "Der Führer wants strong, capable young women like you to help lead the BDM. We will train you for a leadership role within the BDM—"

Gisela finished Helga's sentence: "—like we were trained when we were younger." She took a step in, deliberately invading my space.

I dared not speak my thoughts, keeping them to myself. If I talked back, my parents would be blamed for my insolence and then reported to the SS or the Gestapo.

Helga resumed, feeding off my fear. "So. It is already decided. All that is required is your attendance later today and simple background checks of your parents' and grandparents' identities. You must be pure German. Not even one drop of Jewish, Gypsy, or Polish blood can be tolerated." Helga paused, scanning my face for reaction. I held my breath, careful to remain expressionless, while my heart raced.

"I am sure your family will check out. You look like you are from good stock, well on your way to becoming a beautiful *Aryan* woman." Helga turned toward Gisela and nodded.

"Thank you. I'm sorry, but I cannot attend today." I was out of excuses that were safe. I worried they would see my face flush, although maybe that was what they wanted. And at that thought, I felt my head was going to explode with fear and anger.

"You would not want to disappoint your parents, now, would you?" Gisela's artificial politeness was turning into outright intimidation.

Gisela answered her own question. "Of course not. You do not need to worry, Rosel. We are simply recognizing your talents and your leadership potential. Your parents will be so happy and proud of you for joining and becoming a leader among your peers."

I remained silent.

"We meet every Tuesday and Thursday afternoons right here, in your school activity center. We have our field events on Saturdays, once a month. It is really quite fun. You will compete in athletics and learn how to be the ideal homemaker, how to raise children of the *Reich*, and how to be a proper, upstanding German woman."

Get away from me! I will never be what you expect from me. I am an American! I wanted to scream at them to go away, maybe even hit them in the mouths. But I remained quiet. It was too dangerous. I had heard that the secret police were putting people in prisons and starving them for such insolence.

The second school bell rang, signaling it was time for class to begin. "Please excuse me now. I am already late and must return to my classroom." I turned toward the school building, but I knew the bell would not rescue me.

As I tried to walk away, the two teens took my arms, one girl on each side. Helga finalized the one-sided conversation, pressing down on my forearm as she spoke. "So, we will see you later today, after school."

I quickened my pace, thinking hard about breaking free of them and running. Sensing my panic, the wolves closed in for the kill. "Now Rosel, we do not want any trouble for you or your parents. Your mother and father will understand. And your little sister—Eleonore, I think her name is—she will idolize you as a BDM leader."

I stopped immediately, nearly ready to surrender. *How do they know I have a little sister named Eleonore? She is not even in school yet.*

Gisela moved as close as she could get, her acrid breath now upon my face. "So, it is crystal clear and settled. We will see you at the school activity center at three o'clock. Do not be late. As you know, precision and timeliness are most important to der Führer. *Heil* Hitler!"

I raised my hand in a halfhearted return salute, knowing the consequences if I didn't.

After raised salutes, the two BDM leaders walked away, their heads high, arrogant and confident that they had successfully fulfilled their mission.

I tossed back and forth on my bunk, silently screaming in frustration and fear. Trapped inside my own ghoulish theater and unable to fully awaken, I found myself dropped into one more shadowy corner of my dream world.

Inside my mathematics classroom, my last class of the day, another stern figure stood over me. The sharp rap of her ruler landed forcefully upon my desk, a centimeter or two from my fingers.

Looking up, I saw the irritated face of *Frau* Richtenhoff. The oldest of the replacement teachers, she appeared well into her sixties, making her older than both my grandmothers. I thought her cold and exacting, far too mean to be anyone's grandmother. A shiny-red swastika pin on her black lapel confirmed her allegiance to a madman.

"Rosemarie, you are one of my top students, but you always seem lost in daydreams. Where do you go inside your mind? Nothing can be as important as what we are learning in this classroom."

The unwanted attention forced a mixture of embarrassment, fear, and anger within me. I looked up at my teacher's unyielding face and then down again.

"Rosemarie, eyes forward we require your full attention."

"I am sorry, Frau Richtenhoff; it will not happen again." My words left my mouth with a hint of sarcasm and defiance.

I heard my classmates murmuring at what I had done. Once reprimanded, we were not supposed to talk at all, much less talk back.

"You will be respectful, Rosemarie, like a proper child of the *Reich*. You will listen and be a fitting example to your classmates."

Frau Richtenhoff wasted no time with niceties or small talk. "As planned, class, we will go right to our mathematics exam this morning. I expect all of you to pay close attention and demonstrate your skills."

Thankfully, she had taken her eyes off me and stepped back to the front of the class. Exhaling a quiet sigh of relief, I glanced over at one of my friends, Ingrid, sitting across from me. She winked and smirked a little, first making sure Frau Richtenhoff wasn't looking. I smiled and rolled my eyes in response. Our glances said it all. *She is so mean.*

"And as a reminder, the Bund Deutscher Mädel will meet today after school. Students are to report to the activities room promptly after class. I remind you that attendance is required by order of der Führer."

Pulling open the sliding doors that hid the blackboard, Frau Richtenhoff revealed a series of mathematics problems composed in chalk.

My eyes quickly scanned the three rows of problems. They were relatively easy—at least for me. I smirked inside my head as I copied them down. Doing the best in my class would be the best revenge.

"Now children—proud, competent young women of the Fatherland— here is your exam. Take out a piece of blank paper and copy problems one through twenty-five. Raise your hand when you have finished, all eyes on me, ready for my next directive. Do not begin solving any problems until I say so."

Silent and without complaint, my classmates copied their exam problems. Within a few minutes, all hands were raised, mine included, the class dutifully waiting for the next instruction.

"Yes, very good. I see that you are all attentive, even Rosemarie." As her penetrating glance reached me, I imagined she could see my underlying irritation with her.

"You have forty-five minutes to finish, not one second longer. Show all of your work and be sure to keep your eyes fixed only upon your own paper. When you have finished, put your head down, keeping your answers covered. Now, begin."

Despite my public shaming, I was not anxious about the exam. Working through it effortlessly, confident in my abilities, I finished well ahead of my classmates. I put my head down, and soon my thoughts returned to the wolves' threats about the BDM meeting this afternoon.

Worried, I pictured myself in the activity room with the rest of my peers. To start the meeting, I would have to declare German citizenship, announcing that I had no Jewish, Gypsy, Polish, or foreign blood. Next, I would have to swear allegiance to Adolf Hitler and his *Reich* and cap that off with a salute and a resounding "*Heil* Hitler!"

Truthful declarations of my citizenship would certainly lead to an investigation of my family, with all of its known and unknown consequences. But what did it matter? If I attended today, the government would be doing a background check on my parents and grandparents anyway. We would surely be discovered. And if I refused to attend outright, the BDM leaders would tip off the secret police. There was no way out. It was not hard to imagine Gestapo officers waiting for me at our apartment after school, my parents already in handcuffs, my little sister screaming and crying while being carted away to a Nazi-aligned foster home.

Our examination ended when Frau Richtenhoff announced, "Time!" As we passed our completed exams to the front, I saw the apprehensive looks on the faces of most of my classmates. To do poorly on an exam meant not only humiliation in the classroom and a change in your seating assignment but also near-certain corporal punishment at home.

Those consequences seemed pale, however, given what was about to happen to me.

As we lined up and marched out of our classroom, I followed my girlfriends toward the activity center. Many of them were chatting happily about making crafts for Easter fundraising. I stayed a couple of paces behind them, uncertain as to what I was going to do. The anxiety in my throat threatened to choke me, as my legs became unsteady.

I spotted Helga outside of the activity center, tacking a red-and-black poster to the entrance door as our group approached. Engrossed in her duties, she was the spitting image of the smiling girl on the poster, her hair pulled back in tightly braided, sandy-blond pigtails. A bold, black caption under the girl's image read, *ALLE KINDER GEHÖREN UNS*, "All Children Belong to Us." A prominent red swastika and the smiling, almost paternal face of Adolf Hitler filled the background.

Things had become all too clear. I could no longer trust the words of teachers, my peers, or anyone other than my parents. Flinging my heavy leather *Ranzen* over my shoulder, I slowed to allow my girlfriends to walk ahead, and then I abruptly broke away. Walking fast, I soon started running. Maintaining my pace until I was completely out of breath, I did not slow down until well outside the school grounds.

Stopping under a tree along the avenue to catch my breath, I looked around to make sure no one was nearby. Forming my self-affirming words, I knew I needed to say them out loud.

"I am Rosemarie Katarina Ingeborg Lengsfeld. I am not one of your sheep. I am an American, and I hope Mr. Roosevelt blasts your 'glorious' Führer to kingdom come!"

WEDNESDAY, JULY 10, 1946

1,400 Miles Southwest of Ireland

I wanted to trust the ocean and the ship carrying me home. Gazing out over the endless water from my perch along the observation deck, I welcomed another calm morning at sea. Rocking ever so slightly with the sway of the ship, I felt soothed by the gentle rhythm and safe within the light of day.

The early-morning sun danced off the water as the *Marine Flasher* continued westward. I thought of my old marching shoes resting at the bottom of the English Channel and hoped that they might now provide a home for hermit crabs. I had always loved hermit crabs and the way those little creatures adapted to a harsh and changing world. They borrowed whatever they could find for a home. Like me, they lived their lives carrying histories not their own upon their backs, peeking out now and again when it was safe.

I felt the ocean breeze stiffen, watching the water's surface begin to ripple in turn. My mind continued to wander, taking its familiar course from one worry to another. There never seemed to be any shortage of things to fret about. I landed on one of the anxieties I had not thought of for a while, the Wagners. It remained completely uncertain if they would be there to meet me when the *Marine Flasher* arrived in New York Harbor.

The Wagners had been a last-ditch attempt to make it appear that we had a sponsoring family back home. Although I had never met Mr.

Wagner, listening in on my parents' conversations did not give me a very flattering opinion of him. I overheard that he was a womanizer, greedy and selfish, and a politician who was completely full of himself. I had also heard that his wife, my mother's sister and my aunt Verna, never wanted to have children.

Then there was that other bit of information that nagged at me—more details I wasn't supposed to have. Late one night, Mutti had told Papa that Mrs. Wagner had had a medical procedure done to end a pregnancy they didn't want. That shocking knowledge had cemented my less-than-positive feelings about them.

Although any number of harmless reasons might explain their lack of response to Mutti's letter, I focused on the most negative of all. *What if they don't want me? What if they see me as just another burden?* After all, if they could end an unwanted pregnancy, they could certainly terminate my placement with them without a second thought.

Looking out at the slowly building waves upon the ocean's surface, I felt the curse of my constant anxiety pressing down on me. Rising winds pushed the waves along, causing the ship to bounce a bit. Although the waves made me nervous, increasing now in height and frequency, this was a near-daily event that occurred when the winds picked up in the afternoon. I shook my head, chiding myself for creating yet another thing to worry about. But was I? The way my mind created scenarios, we were now so far out to sea that any rescue would be impossible, and drowning was a real possibility. War had come before I had learned to swim.

Fortunately, before I could work myself up into another useless panic, I heard the now familiar song of the clarinet, its penetrating notes lifting me skyward.

Looking down the length of the ship's railing, I could see David playing before a small group of onlookers. He had begun his morning serenade. Like his entourage, I had come to expect it each day.

I could see that his eyes were closed, lips pursed, at one with his instrument. No longer a ghostly caricature, he was again the vibrant soul I had admired. Lifting his clarinet skyward, he and his music seemed ready to transport me, and anyone else willing, to a place far from strife and worry.

I thought back to my attempt to talk to him the day before. If only I could get the chance to explain who I really was, an American citizen, born in New York. Maybe then he would talk to me.

Still caught up in David's music, my day brightened when I saw Liesel approaching. She spoke excitedly as she came up alongside me.

"My dear friend Rosel, how are you doing this fine day? We-are-getting-clo-ser!" Her bouncy, singsong voice always seemed filled with genuine happiness and optimism, eager to reach the future.

My mind still on David, I answered as attentively as I could. "Good morning Liesel. *Ja*, we are about halfway there, I think." Even to my ear, my voice sounded disinterested; I couldn't take my eyes off the captivating young soloist.

Liesel took note of my distraction. "He plays wonderfully, doesn't he? He reminds me that the world can be beautiful again."

Preoccupied, I smiled weakly in agreement. For perhaps the first time aboard the *Flasher*, Liesel was not the center of my attention.

I should have expected what came next. Not one to just stand still and watch, Liesel reached out and took my hand. "Come on. Let's join him."

I tensed and held back.

"Come on, Rosel, don't be so stuffy!"

Pulling us closer to the performance, Liesel soon gave in to my reluctance and released my arm. Working her way through the tight half-circle of David's entourage, dancing a bit as she went, she emerged right in front of him.

I wanted to join her, but I couldn't let myself go. Although it might have been irrational, I thought I would get in trouble. I could already hear the BDM echoes inside my head. *"Now, Rosel, you know our rules. You wouldn't want your family to be reported, now, would you?"*

Clapping in time to the music, Liesel looked back and waved for me to come closer. But I stayed safely behind, at the circle's perimeter, content to just be an observer. Studying David's beautifully chiseled face, at one with his clarinet, I had not given up trying to be his friend.

And then, the unexpected happened. For a moment, David's eyes met mine, and he nodded. *Could it be? Was that meant for me?* Elated, my emotions again followed his notes upward.

Then it dawned on me. *What if he needs his clarinet to express himself, to feel whole? Maybe this is the one thing the war could not take from him?*

I waited until David looked in my direction again, and nodded back at him with a smile. His eyes met mine, returning a smile as he drew a breath. *Oh, thank heaven! Perhaps I will get another chance with him.*

As David's notes meandered back down to earth, another unexpected reaction occurred within me, a feeling so strong it stirred my whole body. *He is simply irresistible. So handsome! And his song, strong and compelling—it's like he can summon a passageway to the heavens.*

Reflecting for an instant, I wondered, *Is this what it is like to have a crush on a boy?*

WEDNESDAY NIGHT, JULY 10, 1946

1,600 Miles Southwest of Ireland

My one and only dress hung from the bedpost of my bunk, dripping a little onto the deck below. I had finally washed it in the bathroom sink before bed, ringing it out as best I could, careful not to dampen the small fold of money sewn into the hem. I told myself my dress would be dry by morning, but who was I kidding? Nothing seemed fully dry this far out at sea.

Although I wanted to bask in my hopeful feelings about David as I sat in bed, sketchbook and pencil in hand, night was approaching, and someone else was on my mind. My father.

I tried to draw Papa as I wanted to remember him, before the war, the vibrant man who stood for noble ideals and believed in guardian angels. But that image wouldn't come.

I never had an easy time of it when it came to my father. As a child, I so badly wanted to idolize him. Always attentive to me, Papa was my rock and my protector. He understood me. He encouraged me to learn and to explore as many new pursuits as I wanted. Strong and courageous, he was the one person in my life who wasn't afraid to stand up to any injustice or bigotry. I wanted to be his prodigy, his bold and virtuous oldest daughter. Papa's proud American girl.

But there was another side to him too, that part with the terrible temper I was afraid of. Inexplicably and without warning, he could become volatile, bent on punishing me for the smallest of mistakes. At times, he seemed close to teetering out of control.

Sadly, Papa's angry outbursts shaped some of my earliest memories. His temper had been a problem for me long before the war, before we traveled to Germany. As early as age three, I could clearly remember his explosive episodes, his face intense and red with anger, his hand or belt primed to lash out at me if I did something wrong or spoke after being told to be quiet.

Questions nagged at me well into my teenage years, as his rages continued regardless of our circumstances. Papa's mood swings never made sense to me. Why would someone who championed and adored me like Papa did still choose to aim his fury at me? How could a man with such lofty principals, one I cherished and so admired, turn into someone scary, a stranger who ranted uncontrollably? Compounding my confusion, it appeared that I was his only target. Mutti had only to tolerate his bad moods; Papa never raised his voice to her, much less laid a hand upon her. And he never treated my little sister so severely.

As I grew older, I learned to adapt to his unstable moods, at least the best I could. Often I stayed away from him, hoping and waiting for his anger to pass. Other times I tried to please him, cajoling him to smile or laugh, so I would know things were okay again. But sometimes I found myself caught right in the middle of one of his rages, unable to escape.

Searching for answers, I had asked Mutti about it a few times when I was younger. Usually my mother would just brush it off, saying he was being grumpy and that it would pass. It wasn't the business of children in German families to question their parents' behavior.

A few years later, when I was about nine or ten, right around the time the war started, I asked her again. This time she had given me a clue. She admitted to me that Papa could be "cruel," using that word for the first time, and that he had experienced fits of rage since he was a teenager. She had said something about the Great War and how it had devastated my father and his family. I listen closely as she explained, recalling references to this war in my classrooms and in Hitler's fiery speeches.

At thirteen, a few years too young to be drafted, Papa had seen his father and older brother marched off to fight the Russians along the eastern front. They were presumed dead after two years without any contact, but in 1918 they both found their way home, lucky to have survived. The family's joy at their return was soon tempered, if not replaced, by the shock of their condition. Psychologically and physically beaten down, both his brother and father were mere shells of the people they once were, their spirits broken by fear and bitterness, their bodies now suffering from constant tremors resulting from exposure to poisonous gas attacks.

That was all Mutti would share on that day. I was too young, she said. "Maybe someday your papa will tell you more." She was right, of course. I couldn't picture what actual war was like.

The first bell resonated through the *Flasher*. With the second bell and lights-out only minutes away, I tried to turn off my thoughts of Papa, not wanting to take such difficult feelings with me on my nighttime journey. But I couldn't disengage, the happy times with Papa mixing with his episodes of cruelty. Helpless to stop it, my train of memories rolled on, taking me back to one incident that I couldn't erase no matter how hard I tried. I had never talked about it with anyone, not even Mutti.

It had happened just before we left for Germany, so I would have been three, possibly three and a half years old. We were living in our small apartment in New York City, where Papa worked as the handyman for the ten or twelve apartments our building housed. I had found Papa's watch one day lying out on the kitchen table where he had been cleaning it. I had tried to wind it like I had seen him do countless times, curious about how it worked. Although I had often been told never to touch his watch, I had given in to the urge, just this once.

My father exploded with fury when he entered the room and saw me playing with his prized timepiece. There was no time to even say I was sorry, that I had forgotten the rule. Enraged, he took me by the hand to our family bedroom. Bending me over his knee, he gave me a severe spanking. But that was not the worst of it. Pointing to my cherished stuffed animal on my bed, my "little Huggy," as I called it, Papa spoke the words I had yet to forget. "Rosel, take your Huggy. We're going for a walk."

I soon found out where we were headed. My heart pounded as he marched me down the stairs to the building's basement. I made no sound as we trudged down the steps, hoping that in the quiet Papa might still change his mind. Reaching the building's incinerator, only now would I begin to cry, as my father stoked the fire.

"Please, Papa, no!" I trembled as my eyes filled with tears. "I am very sorry I took your watch. Please, Papa, not my Huggy. Please!"

"Maybe you will finally learn not to disobey me." Pulling Huggy from my arms while I screamed, he tossed my precious little bear into the blazing furnace. I fell to the floor, sobbing uncontrollably. Seconds later, all that remained of my beloved Huggy was a pile of ashes and some smoke that went up and out the chimney.

The second bell chimed aboard the *Flasher*, and with it came the inevitable darkness of the overnight. Defeated, still struggling with thoughts of my complicated father, I put my sketchpad and pencil under my pillow to keep them near to me. What Papa had done seemed unforgivable, in my child's mind—tantamount to murder.

I fought against sleep, unable to find any answers. I prayed that my angels would help me find the strength to release my burden, to make peace with my father, and to find a way to forgive him.

Flung through time and space as my dream world took hold, I found myself inside our Breslau apartment. There I was, standing just outside the bedroom door, my breath visible in the frigid air. Mutti had said the winter of 1945 was the coldest she could ever remember. Our small, charcoal-fueled *Kachelofen*, or tiled oven, only managed to heat the front room of our home.

I peered through the partially open bedroom door, unseen by my parents. I saw my father laying out his warmest winter clothes across the bed.

Looking frail, tired, and well beyond his forty-two years, Papa seemed nervous and fretful, almost like a frightened little boy. I had never seen him look like that before.

I eavesdropped on my parents' conversation, still out of sight behind the door. Mutti was telling Papa he had no choice, the risk was too great if he didn't comply. And then something about him being drafted into the Volkssturm, the German People's Army. My father protested that he did not want to fight for something that didn't make sense to him; risking his life for fanatical ideas he didn't believe in. I could hear Mutti, her voice heavy with fear and worry, trying to make sense out of the senseless situation.

"*Mein Schatz*, I am sorry, but you must go. This is an order from der Führer. If you refuse, the Gestapo or his SS men will find you."

"Hilde, if I am sent to the front, I will have no chance."

"You have no chance if you do not go. The SS will execute you for insubordination and then come for us."

Mutti's warning expressed a grim fact that had been circulating in our community. Refusing to join the Volkssturm could mean on-the-spot execution of the traitor and retaliation against the family by the Schutzstaffel, or SS. We had all heard stories of what the SS had done to even elderly men who had refused to be part of the People's Army. Their bodies were hung, gruesome and lifeless, from city lampposts for all to see.

Still listening and out of sight, I watched my mother pick up a single-page letter from the nightstand. It had arrived by courier only yesterday from the Reich Chancellery in Berlin. Breathing as quietly as I could, I translated Mutti's words as best I could inside my head as Mutti read his orders aloud.

"*Herr* Herman Max Fritz Lengsfeld, by order of der Führer, the Supreme Leader, you are hereby required to enlist in the People's Army, effective immediately. It is an honor to serve the glorious *Reich* and participate in the mighty victory that will soon be at hand . . ."

After reading through what anyone could see was propaganda, Mutti paused after reading the next line, looking up at Papa when she had finished. "Failure to abide by this order will result in the most severe of consequences."

For the first time in my life, I watched Papa begin to cry, nearly silently. I strained to hear his ravaged voice. "Lies. All lies. Hilde, I've told you many times how my brother and father returned from the first war."

Mutti read the rest of what might as well have been Papa's death sentence. He was to report immediately, with nothing more than the clothes on his back, to a military compound set up at the end of the streetcar line across town. There, he would be given a military rifle and a yellow-and-black Volkssturm armband and be sworn into the German People's Army.

My legs began to tremble as reality set in. I watched my father remove a small black-and-white photograph from its ornate frame on the dresser. Our only family portrait, it had been taken in 1938, just before the war cast its ominous shadow upon us. Holding the cherished image before him, Papa smiled faintly before carefully placing it beneath the insole of his right shoe.

Mutti took Papa's right hand in hers. "Now, *mein Lieber*, you must be extremely careful. Do not take any unnecessary risks. Not for this war." She placed a tiny, glittering object into his cupped palm before closing his fingers around it. *It must be his birthstone!* I had heard the story of her giving him a diamond many years before, on his thirtieth birthday in New York. "Hold this close, Herman; it will keep you safe. We will see you again, *ja*, at the end of all this lunacy."

Clutching the tiny diamond, Papa's hands shook, and his tears welled again. He tried to give a directive to Mutti, but it came out as a question. "So, we will all take the streetcar down to the induction compound?" I was shocked by how unsure of himself he sounded. His composure and proud stature were faltering before my eyes.

"*Nein.* My dear Herman, we must say our goodbyes here. It is too cold outside for Eleonore. The girls shouldn't go through this anyway; it will be too much for them."

Papa simply nodded.

Unable to keep quiet any longer, I burst through the bedroom doorway. "Papa, I will go with you on the streetcar!"

"Rosel, were you spying on us? You were supposed to be reading with Eleonore!" There was anger in my father's voice, the one emotion he wasn't afraid to express. Soon eight-year-old Eleonore trailed in from the apartment's only other room.

"Papa, why is everyone being so sad and grumpy? What's going on, Mutti? Why is Papa laying out all his warm clothes? Where are we going?" Eleonore's questions came in rapid fire, at the worst possible moment.

Exasperated, Mutti ignored her and looked directly at me. "*Nein*, my brave Rosel, *nein*." In her eyes, I could see that her decision had been made. "We will have no more discussion of this. *Nicht mehr*, enough! We will say our goodbyes here."

Silent, Papa glanced at me before dropping his gaze to the floor.

"I will go with my papa! I must go! I know how to get back; I have taken the streetcar many times before." Papa may have been defeated, but I was not. "I am fourteen now. When will you let me grow up, Mutti? I can do it."

The distress in Papa's face drained away, if only for a moment. "Hilde, let Rosel go with me. She will be all right. She knows the way."

Mutti wasted no time in cutting him off. "*Nein*! I do not want Rosel out there alone with all this upheaval going on. It is dangerous on the streets. People are acting irrationally. She could be abducted! And it's too cold. I'm sorry, Herman, *no*." With an outstretched arm, Mutti reached for Eleonore, pulling her in and holding her close.

I continued my plea. "Mutti, I must go, I must! Do not worry—my angels will be with me to keep me safe." There was no doubt in my mind. I was too old to be treated as a child any longer.

My father smiled faintly at me, his obstinate daughter. "Hilde, I beg of you. Listen to her. Rosel is not a child anymore. We can trust her to stay safe. She will be all right."

"*Nein*, Herman. It's too dangerous out there, and there's too much commotion, too many frantic people. She will be taken advantage of."

"Hilde, please. She can take care of herself." Papa stood up straighter. "You must respect my wishes. I am still the father."

Papa had played his trump card. Holding tight to Eleonore, Mutti let out a long, frustrated sigh. Papa was still head of the household, and he made the decisions.

I hurried to get my things together. Amid so much tension and unspoken sadness, no one said a word. The war was no longer a civics lesson in class or some faraway chess game where we were told that the Germans were always winning.

I knew the odds Papa would soon be facing. Over the past four years, nearly all of the remaining vestiges of my childhood innocence had been shattered. The world wasn't safe anymore. The adults around me were no longer my rocks, providing security; they were as lost and frightened as I was.

And death kept creeping closer and closer. Many fathers and older brothers of my classmates had been killed during the last year alone. Our neighbor's oldest son had recently had his leg blown off in battle along the western front.

Papa went into the bathroom with two sets of winter clothes, presumably to layer them for extra warmth. He came out some minutes later, trembling, not from cold but from fear.

I found the hat, scarf, and mittens I had knitted over Christmas and put them on. My mother handed me some change for the streetcar fare. Taking in a deep breath, I prepared myself for what I thought would likely be the last time I would ever be with my father.

"I'm ready, Papa. We can go now."

...Thrust forward in time by my nighttime puppeteers, I saw that Papa and I were now approaching the entrance to the induction compound. Throngs of people, mostly women with older children, paced around anxiously just outside the complex. Times were desperate now. I could see it on the faces of everyone around me.

Through a crackling loudspeaker, a phonograph recording of Hitler and his Reichsführers told everyone to be confident, that Germany was winning the war and crushing its enemies.

"The Volkssturm will be a violent burst of fanatic rage against the invaders!" Hitler's voice was unmistakable. Seething and paranoid, barely in control of his own emotions, he once more proclaimed the superiority of the German people and the victorious destiny of the *Aryan* race.

But in scanning the faces of the disheveled people forming the enlistment line, I knew otherwise. Today's ragtag reinforcements looked nothing like the self-confident young soldiers I recalled from the military parade back when I was eight. These men and boys looked more like family members, weary and frightened, beaten long before being given a rifle by the Nazis. Most looked like grandfathers. And some were just boys, maybe even younger than me. Their beards hadn't even begun to come in yet.

After the men's brief oath of allegiance to Herr Hitler and the Fatherland, I watched in dismay as each of the inductees, my father among them, were given wooden rifles that looked obsolete even to my untrained eye. There were no uniforms, no heavy woolen coats to keep them warm, no helmets for even the most basic protection.

Sworn in for his suicide mission, Papa broke from the column of ragged soldiers to say his farewell. Wrapping his arms around me, he patted me twice on the back. Gently pushing himself off, he mustered his only words.

"Be careful on your way home, Rosel*chen*."

"I will, Papa, I will. I have my angels with me."

As I turned and started walking toward the streetcar stop, I looked back, raising my arm to wave to him. But Papa wasn't looking for me. I saw him though, his posture stooped, his face ashen, looking old, frail and brittle. I was all but certain I would never see him again.

Fighting back tears, I boarded the eastbound streetcar to head home. The car was packed with people rife with body odor, so I didn't mind having to stand outside on the overflow platform. Holding onto the frigid standing rail, I replayed Papa's last words to me. *"Be careful on your way home, Roselchen."*

The streetcar bell rang, signaling our impending departure. Holding tight, I watched the sparks crackle and fly from the electricity pole.

The war's ugly reality could no longer be downplayed, much less denied. I began to sob, giving up my years-long fight to hold back over-whelming sorrow.

As the car started moving, I could hear another *Strassenbahn* coming in on the opposite rail. Also crowded with passengers, the inbound street-car slowed as it approached its dock along the avenue.

Just then, I heard a young woman's voice. "Rosel, Rosel!"

I was surprised to see a familiar face in the crowd on the incoming streetcar's overflow stoop. It was Sonja, my old friend from secondary school, with her family. For an instant, we caught each other's eyes.

"Rosel! Where are you going all by yourself? What is the matter? Why are you crying?"

Before I could even think of how to respond, our streetcars slipped away from each other. Wiping away tears with my open palm, angry at the entire world, I told myself I would never cry again.

THURSDAY, JULY 11, 1946

1,100 Miles East of Newfoundland, Canada

I couldn't tell what time it was. It was still dark in the sleeping quarters, and the ship's interior night-lights were on. As I looked around, my roommates were still in their bunks, fast asleep. Once again, though, Liesel's bed was empty. I was used to that now, as the mystery of Liesel's whereabouts continued. I had run out of simple, reasonable explanations for her frequent absences. Those that remained I didn't want to think about.

Lying in my bunk, reeling from another round of bad dreams, my mind sought safe harbor. Despite my efforts to stay awake and out of the path of my nighttime torment, I felt myself drifting off again.

Without warning, the entire cabin rose with such velocity that my stomach tingled, then fell with a force so strong that it felt like a slab of concrete had been laid across my chest.

What on earth?

Then it happened again. The cabin vaulted and fell in a series of nauseating undulations. On the way up, I felt so light and unrestrained that I might become airborne—coming down, I was pinned by a force so strong and heavy that I couldn't move. The sensation was so strange and disorientating, like drifting in and out of one of my horrible dreams.

Dear God, will these nightmares never end? Haven't I suffered enough?

The unnerving rises and falls inside our quarters worsened. When my stomach began to churn, I wondered what realm of consciousness I was actually in. I had never felt sick inside a dream before.

My wild ride continued. Shrieks from women were accompanied by the piercing cries of young children. I had to hold fast to the bed frame's lip to keep myself from being flung off over the side.

This dream is so lifelike! Maybe if I can force a scream, I will be able to awaken myself.

The crushing weight upon my chest as we descended stifled any change of a scream escaping my mouth. Finally, the terrifying fall ended when we bottomed out and then began to rise again. Able to catch my breath on the way back up, this time I managed to scream aloud.

As my surroundings became clearer and my senses sharpened, I realized this was no dream. This nightmare was real.

Panic stricken, my eyes raced around the room, looking for clues as to what was happening. But before I could ascertain anything, the crushing weight returned, pinning me to my mattress, my arms and legs too weighted down to move a single muscle, my chest so heavy I could not draw even a shallow breath.

Another giganic rise and fall. And then another. The rolls seemed to be increasing in height and intensity. Consumed with panic and unable to breathe during the ship's plummets, I found myself gasping for air.

Then it came to me. *The ship must be sinking. We're all going to drown!*

I could not take in enough air to produce another scream. The room was in a free fall again, the weight upon my chest foretelling what drowning might feel like. I could not restrain my catastrophic thoughts. *Soon the walls of the ship will buckle, and water will come cascading in.*

Oh, my angels, my dear, sweet angels. You have helped me though so much. I don't want to die, not here, all alone and so far out to sea.

The force upon my chest threatened to crush me. The fall this time seemed endless, and I was certain that the ship would not rise again.

I clung to the lip of the bed frame for dear life, convinced that the end was near.

Mercifully, the oppressive weight lifted from me as the room elevated again. This time we rose with such speed my bunk could not hold me.

Airborne for a second, I was partially flung over the edge of the bunk, saved only by a collision with the corner wall that sent me careening back inside my bed frame.

My fear-addled mind spun wild and out of control, the thoughts streaming in like a runaway train. *There must be a hole torn into the side of the ship. Did we hit an iceberg? Or maybe we are under attack! Have we been hit by a torpedo?* Awash in familiar terror, a thought flashed that perhaps the war was not over.

I wanted to call out for Papa or Mutti, my fear momentarily tricking me into thinking I was a little girl. Recognizing that illusion, I searched for Liesel instead, but she wasn't in her bunk, her bedding undisturbed.

More rolls came, lifting the *Flasher* upward and then reeling it back down, one movement right after the other, now with terrifying regularity. In my mind, I saw a German U-boat or submarine hunting us as their prey, readying to fire again.

Consumed with panic, I heard myself cry out desperately as if outside of my body. "*Mein Gott! Nicht jetzt, nicht hier.* I don't want to drown!" My mind flashed back to a terrifying scene from my childhood, when I watched a little girl nearly drown in a lake. *Were my fears a premonition, forewarning that I was going to drown? Oh my God, is it now about to happen?*

Other scenes from my early childhood flew through my mind. Picking flowers in the meadows. Jumping off the last steps of the trolley with Papa holding my hands. Mutti and I reading together. My aunt teaching me how to sew. Christmas with *Tante* Friedel. Playing school with my baby sister. The images jumbled together, like a patchwork collection of old photographs, a desperately colliding summary of the most cherished moments in my life.

A classmate had once told me, during a school air raid drill, that when you are about to die, your entire life flashes before you. Was my life coming to an end, right here, right now, aboard the *Marine Flasher*?

Dear God, please, I am not ready. I am so afraid. Send my angels. Oh, please, send them now!

My time to plead with the heavens lasted only a split second. The *Flasher* continued to vault and plummet, over and over, in relentless succession. Screams and children's cries filled the air, reaching a level that was hopeless and increasingly desperate. I felt my stomach surrender to the constant thrashing and vomited all over my pillow.

Just then a clap of thunder pierced through the cries of the room and rattled off in the distance. Another followed, this one overhead. Loud and deafening, the boom shocked me out of my fearful vortex.

The loudspeaker followed, providing anything but reassurance.

"Attention, all passengers. This is your captain speaking. We are in the path of a major storm. Please secure yourselves and any children as best you can. For your own safety, do not, I repeat, do not attempt to leave your quarters."

As my thoughts became clearer, I realized that waves were tossing our ship. We were not under attack. We had not hit an iceberg. We were caught in a storm.

I tried to breathe deep and relax my tensed muscles, accepting the most likely explanation all along. But the comfort that followed my increased awareness lasted no more than a few seconds. The violent undulations of the ship had not abated. The waves had to be gigantic, certainly enough to roll us over.

The loudspeaker came on again, its message repeated, first in German and then in French. Like so often during the war, the warnings had come too late, after the threat was already upon us.

Waiting out the storm seemed to take an eternity. Hours must have passed as I lay on my back, my entire body exhausted by fear and heaving, my heavy arms clinging to each side of the bed's railing.

All I could do was pray.

In early afternoon, the powerful waves finally began to subside. I saw it as a miracle. My angels had saved me.

The loudspeaker crackled once again, followed by the calm voice of our captain. "Attention, all passengers and crew, the storm has now passed. We will soon be opening the ship's corridors and the observation deck. Please be careful of slippery surfaces. The normal dinner hour has been suspended. Bread, jam, and cheese will be made available in the mess hall. Thank you for your cooperation."

Despite the captain's encouraging words, there was no way I was going to leave the cabin. Words and sounds signaling the return of safety meant nothing to me. There were so many times during the war when I had been told I was safe—and wasn't.

I waited nervously for the next unforeseen assault upon my nervous system. Afraid to leave the imagined safety of my bunk, I watched two elderly women in our quarters with a bucket and mop begin cleaning up all the vomit splashed across the floor. Within an hour, the routines aboard the *Flasher* returned to normal. Most of the women and children in my sleeping quarters had left for some much-needed fresh air. I had watched my bunkmate join them, head down, her back turned to me. With the room still rocking with smaller, residual waves, I stubbornly remained in my bed, fending off the fear that refused to ease.

More time passed, my head clearing a little. From my position on my bunk, I worried for Liesel, who was nowhere to be seen during and after the storm. I considered searching for her, maybe even stopping at the mess hall for some *Butterbrot* and cheese along the way. I had not eaten anything since yesterday evening. Maybe I would find Liesel there. But my fear of being swept off the deck by an errant wave kept me from venturing out, and my unsettled stomach disagreed with thoughts that I should eat. Like so many times throughout the war, it was nearly impossible to feel hungry after fearing for my life.

Fear remained as my constant companion, and I had to constantly remind myself that the war was over. Fear of being abandoned, of being separated from loved ones, of being beaten down by war, of being homeless—all were still alive within me. And now, my fear of drowning had re-emerged. I knew now that none of my terrors, old or new, had vanquished or been left behind in Europe. I wondered if I would ever be able to shake them.

As I hunkered down in my bed, I remembered back to the time my drowning phobia had started. I was five, and Eleonore hadn't yet been born. My parents had taken me for a picnic by a lake on the outskirts of Breslau. It was a nice spring day, the first warm day of the year. While Papa and Mutti laid out a blanket and prepared for our lunch of potato salad and *Braunschweiger* sandwiches, I had gone down to the beach to look for treasures along the shore. I watched a young family like ours ready a rowboat at the nearby dock. I could still picture it, playing out now in slow motion.

As her parents lowered the rowboat, the cute little girl of maybe three had momentarily gone unnoticed. She had wandered to the edge of the dock and, unaware of the danger, had fallen into the cold, dark water. As the young child flailed helplessly about, I stood silent, frozen with panic, convinced she was about to drown before my eyes.

Thankfully, her alarmed father immediately jumped into the frigid water and pulled his daughter out. She was shivering and terrified, but safe. Papa rushed out with our picnic blanket to cover the girl. When they passed by me, I saw that her lips had turned blue.

After that experience, I promised myself I would talk to my parents about learning to swim, but I never got around to it. With all the upheaval in Germany, my longing for swimming lessons had been forgotten.

Now, ten years later, I found myself in the middle of the Atlantic, far from any possible rescue. I thought of how fragile we all were, aboard a ship that I now knew was vulnerable.

THURSDAY NIGHT, JULY 11, 1946

900 Miles East of Newfoundland, Canada

Finally, nighttime came again, mercifully ending a dreadful day. The storm over, the sea had returned to the gentle swells that were more familiar at night. Fresh linens and pillowcases had been placed outside our bunkroom entrance, allowing all of us to replace our urine and vomit-stained pillowcases and sheets. I was fortunate that my newly washed dress had landed inside the relative safety of my bunk, rather than on the filthy deck below. It was still clean, and free from the vestiges of fear that had splattered my pillow.

I was more grateful to have survived the storm, though I wondered if traveling through gales such as we did was a common occurrence for the crew. Why else would the ship's bed frames be constructed that way? Why else would the captain's voice be so calm at the peak of the storm?

As darkness encroached upon the *Flasher*, I waited and watched for Liesel as I tried to settle in for bed. I had not seen her since yesterday, at David's morning serenade. And she had not come into the sleeping quarters this evening, when the last of the passengers entered after the curfew bell. *Where was she during the storm? Where is she now?*

As I put worries for Liesel aside, my conscience reminded me of my bunkmate below. She too had been screaming in fear during the storm, without comfort or help from anyone.

It bothered me that I had not tried to come to her aid or at least attempted to comfort her after the storm had passed. Why had I allowed her to suffer through such a scary event alone? What was keeping me from merely extending a hand or a smile? Surely she had been as frightened as I was. Now, with the danger over and life aboard the *Flasher* returned to normal, I was too ashamed by my inattention to say anything to her.

I am no better than the other ghosts aboard this ship, I thought, sighing a bit. Had I been hypocritical to see myself as being different from the other reticent and injured souls making passage on the *Flasher*? I too remained chained to the war and its oppressive social norms. I was beginning to wonder if I would ever be able to free myself.

Utterly depleted by the events of the day, I did not hear the lights-out bell. I did, however, hear my bunkmate's hushed crying beneath me, punishing me one more time. Discouraged and feeling as though I had nothing left to give, I fell through the layers of my unconscious and plunged into sleep.

Caught within the tarnished imprints of my dream, I could see myself shivering as I packed up my battered suitcase in our only bedroom. The bitter, cold air, even inside our apartment, told me more of the particulars. It was February 1945, deep into the coldest winter anyone could recall. Papa was already gone, most likely somewhere along the eastern front, forced into a suicide mission by Adolf Hitler and his band of fanatics. Mutti was frantically telling me to get my suitcase packed so I could help my eight-year-old sister to collect her things.

I felt a twinge of anger for seemingly always having to be in charge of my little sister. Why couldn't Mutti finish packing her clothes? And what was of such importance today that we had to be in such a hurry?

I became distracted from my packing as I watched Mutti lay out some small silver serving pieces, along with her modest jewelry collection, to pack in her suitcase. Why? It reminded me of our occasional trips to the pawnshop before the war. Were we in need of money? Were we going to be gone for quite some time? I tried to make sense of what we were doing, not realizing that we were already in harm's way.

"*Schnell, schnell*, let's hurry up now, *ja*? Rosel, I need you to be ready first so you can help Eleonore."

"*Ja-ja*, Mutti. Okay. But where are we going? Why must we be in such a rush?

"Rosel, enough questions, just finish your packing and then help your sister pack up her *Ranzen*. Squeeze in as many of her clothes as you can, but make sure it's not too heavy for her to carry."

I rolled my eyes. A *Ranzen* was supposed to be heavy, as we carried all of our schoolbooks and supplies in them. I had been carrying mine for years, without complaint. No one ever worried about *me* having too much to carry.

"*Ja-ja*, Mutti," I replied flatly, slightly annoyed. I still had not yet fully grasped what the urgency was, but I knew a little of what was happening from eavesdropping. An hour before, Frau Krobott, our neighbor from down the hall, had rapped forcefully upon our door. She had come from the town square where there had been some sort of announcement over the loudspeakers . . . something about making Breslau a *festung*, the Nazis' word for a military fortress.

This was not the first time we were told Breslau would be made into a *festung*. Two summers before, when I was twelve, there had been a "strong suggestion" from the Nazi chancellery for all women and children to begin making plans to leave the city. We were told central Breslau was going to be turned into a military complex.

As usual, my mind started to wander and my packing slowed as I recalled the events of our last exodus from Breslau. My parents had arranged for Mutti, Eleonore, and me to move into my grandparents' home in Langenbielau, some fifty miles to the southwest, while Papa stayed in Breslau to work. The move had taken me to a new school and, thankfully, out of the clutches of the BDM in Breslau. I was so relieved to get away from those dreaded Bund Deutscher Mädel leaders that I put up no resistance to moving.

Although it had started out fine in our new home, we had to return to Breslau after just a couple months, at the insistence of Mutti's mother, whom we called *Omie*. Quite unexpectedly, my grandmother had turned on me. "I want that unruly child out of my house," she had said in a fit of exasperation. I had challenged her once too often when she asked me to stay home from school to help her with her chores and her tailoring business. In her eyes, I was paying too much attention to my studies and, by entertaining aspirations for higher education, getting too big for my britches. "Girls do not need to be so smart, nor practiced in subjects and fields reserved for men." That was the last straw for me. I was bent on making my grandmother miserable; and two months later Papa returned to take us back to Breslau.

"Rosel! What are you doing, daydreaming?" I was brought back to earth by Mutti's sharp words. "Finish packing and help your sister pack up her belongings. *Schnell!*"

My mother was overflowing with anxiety. I wondered why this departure seemed so much more frantic than the previous one.

While I went over to help Eleonore, *Frau* Krobott came back to our door, her boys in tow. With each dressed in multiple layers of clothing, her two youngest sons looked like overstuffed little ticks.

I could hear my mother talking with her. The German Army was preparing to make a stand in Breslau. Hitler had formally declared our city a German military fortress, ready to defend against the Bolshevik invaders from the east and the British and American invaders to the west. The last inhabitants of Breslau, almost exclusively women, children, and a few elderly men, had been ordered to leave immediately with only what they could carry.

Frau Krobott continued by saying that with the Wehrmacht, the collective German armed forces, moving in, we had to leave most of our food and charcoal behind, to help the cause. Although very few families had a vehicle, the order proclaimed that all streetcars, private vehicles, and motorbikes belonged to the *Reich* now, to be appropriated for military use. Only the trains would remain as modes of public transportation. Nearly everyone would have to walk to the *Hauptbahnhof* in order to get out of the city. Frau Krobott said it was going to be mass chaos.

"Rosel, Rosel! Are you and Eleonore ready yet? *Pass auf!* I need your full attention. It's past time to go. We must leave while the trains are still running." Far from the strong decision-maker my father had always been, Mutti seemed barely able to hold herself together.

I needed Papa to take charge. I wondered where he was and what he might be doing. I had heard the stories going around. There were many possibilities for my father's deployment, all involving the Bolsheviks, with virtually no chance for survival in any of the scenarios. He could be killed in battle with no helmet or artillery to protect him. Or ambushed by Cossack horsemen, whom we were told cut off units from behind, isolating the German regiments before slaughtering them. Perhaps Papa would be captured and intentionally starved to death in a prisoner of war camp or be executed on the spot by a Russian firing squad. But most likely his unit would freeze to death, having run out of supplies in the brutal eastern European winter. *Dear God, what chance is there for him?* The more I thought about it, the more hopeless everything seemed.

A sharp smack on the back of my head got my attention. "Rosel! I have told you several times, and I am not going to tell you again. Stop daydreaming! This is serious. Finish packing your sister's clothes. *Aber beeil dich.*"

I was shaken. My mother had never slapped me before. "*Es tut mir leid*, Mutti. I am very sorry."

While I hurried to stuff Eleonore's clothes inside her *Ranzen*, I could see Mutti's attention move toward the box of gas masks we had stored next to the front door. We had never used them, though we had practiced putting them on. Would we have to be carrying the cumbersome masks too?

Eleonore interrupted my thoughts. She spoke quickly, barely drawing breath between sentences, no doubt picking up on my mother's anxiety. I could tell she was frightened.

"But, Rosel, where are we going? Why is Mutti so upset with us? We didn't do anything wrong. I don't want to leave. It's too cold to go outside."

With my sister still a little girl, I skirted the ugly truth. "Well, I think we are going on a holiday, Eleonore." I chastised myself immediately after I said it. *Good God, I am no better than any of these adults, telling such a lie.* But it was too late. Eleonore had already taken what I had said to heart.

"A holiday?" Her face brightened at the thought. "Will Papa be there?" Eleonore looked deep into my eyes for an answer.

I looked away in shame, already knowing that what I said would come back to haunt me.

But Eleonore had more to complain about and didn't pursue an answer. Following Frau Krobatt's lead, Mutti had instructed both of us to wear three sets of clothes, one outfit right on top of the other, in an effort to both keep warm and carry more clothing with us. Uncomfortable and constricted by the bulkiness of her clothes, Eleonore started whining again.

"Mutti, why must I wear all these silly clothes? I can barely walk. It's too stuffy. What if I have to go to the bathroom?"

"I'm sorry, Eleonore, but you'll need all those clothes to stay warm. We have a long walk ahead of us." Our mother was not acting like we were going on a holiday. I braced myself for what was certain to come next from Eleonore's mouth.

"Rosel? You said we were going on a holiday!"

"Stop bickering, *meine zwei Mädchen*. Stop it now! This is not the time for complaining. It is time to go." Packing her well-thumbed Bible in my suitcase, Mutti's voice trembled, giving away what I thought was her complete lack of confidence.

"Eleonore, take your little doll, *ja*? And, Rosel, you take your gold cross, the one your aunt gave us. That will help keep all of us safe, including Papa. *Beeile dich*."

Eleonore retrieved her only toy, a plastic doll she had named Bridget. I pulled on Eleonore's *Ranzen* straps to tighten it against her back.

"What about Peter the Cat?" Eleonore remembered we were the ones feeding him. "Is he coming with us?"

Mutti looked surprised. Our neighborhood cat had not even crossed her mind.

"*Nein*. He is used to staying outside. He will be fine until we get back."

The truth was that there would be no one remaining behind to feed our community cat. Like everyone else, he would now have to fend for himself. I didn't question it. Mutti was already upset with me, and Eleonore seemed satisfied with her answer.

With our belongings packed and our suitcases filled to the brim, I wondered what we would do with gas masks. Everyone in Breslau had received one from the government, delivered right to our front doors.

"Mutti, what about the *Volksgasmasken*? There's no room left in our suitcases."

"Leave them then."

I was perplexed as to why Mutti did not see the need to bring them. The People's Gas Masks were designed to protect us from chemical attack. The government told us that our enemies might use mustard or chlorine gas on German troops and civilians, using their stockpiled, leftover supplies from the Great War. But the truth was, as Papa had told us, that chemical weapons had been invented first and unleashed by the Germans.

Glancing at the gas mask boxes along the wall, one for each of us, I remembered the strangely distant look on Papa's face when we had tried the masks on. Like some bizarre costume, they had given us the appearance of grasshopper-headed monsters. Eleonore had laughed, but Papa had looked horrified. A few days later, Papa took us permanently out of school, fearful that we could be exposed to the same deadly gases that had incapacitated his father and brother three decades before.

Sensing I was about to question her decision to leave the masks behind, Mutti answered, preemptively. "We are going to Dresden, where it is safe. There will not be any need for them."

I let it go. I had upset Mutti enough for today. "*Ja-ja*, just a last trip to the toilet, and then we can leave." Excusing myself for a moment, I put my suitcase by the front door.

"*Ja*, but make it fast." Mutti's urgency had not abated, even though we were now finally ready to leave.

Once I was inside the bathroom, however, my childhood curse of daydreaming found me again. Papa was out there somewhere along the eastern front, ill equipped to handle any kind of attack. After seeing our gas mask boxes, I could not stop thinking about him.

Within a minute or two, I could hear Mutti pacing outside the bathroom door, her demonstrative sighing soon replaced by a succession of sharp knocks.

"Come on, Rosel, come on. Stop dawdling! The train will be arriving at the *Hauptbahnhof* soon. We cannot miss it. It is the only way out of the city."

"*Ja-ja, ich komme.*" I finished washing my hands in the basin and rushed to dry them.

"I am ready now, Mutti. We can go." I helped my mother put Eleonore's mittens and winter cap on, tying it rather forcefully below her chin. She complained that everything was too tight.

Mutti locked the door behind us. We were off on another hasty and inadequately explained excursion, with no idea as to when we would be back. I hoped we might return by spring. My sister thought we would be returning in a few days, to take care of the cat.

Clamoring down the apartment stairs, suitcase bumping along, I bombarded our mother with questions. "So, Mutti, where are we going again? I see the neighbors are all leaving too. Is everyone going to the same place? And where is that? And why must we be in such a hurry?"

My mother gave me only curt answers. "Breslau is not going to be safe much longer. There will be fighting in our streets. There could be air attacks and bombing. We must leave by the government's orders." She paused momentarily, out of breath from anxiety. "We must get to Dresden."

I was stunned by what I heard. For the first time, the combat did not seem very far away. Fighting in our streets? Air attacks and bombing? The war was about to be directly upon us, its violence inside our neighborhood and on our doorstep.

Before I could ask any more questions, Mutti continued. "We will be traveling with Frau Krobott and her youngest sons to her sister's home in central Dresden."

I rolled my eyes, turning my head from Mutti's gaze. I had a lot of feelings about Frau Krobott. I was told by my parents to try my best to show respect toward her, but she usually seemed rather annoyed with me. She lived with her family down the hall, her husband and their four boys. Willy was seven, the youngest, and Brandt was nine. Her two older sons, Hans, eighteen, and Dieter, twenty, had been drafted into the German Army the year before. Dieter was now in a rehabilitation hospital somewhere in northern Germany after losing his right leg in battle outside of Hannover.

Frau Krobott's husband, Ulrich, an automobile mechanic, had been taken into the Volkssturm some weeks ago, just before Papa was drafted. He had volunteered to join as a mechanic, to avoid combat. It was likely that *Herr* Krobott was now helping to repair Panzer tanks and military trucks along the eastern front. I took solace that Papa might be with him. I imagined the two of them working together, repairing broken-down vehicles, far behind the dangers of the front line. In my mind, it was the only possibility that came to me where he might stand a prayer of a chance.

Reaching the ground floor of our apartment building, I saw Willy and Brandt waiting impatiently at the curb. Frau Krobott was pacing alongside of them, wringing her hands. The community kiosk was blaring out orders to leave the city immediately.

"Are you and your girls finally ready, Hilde? We are already later than we planned. There's no time for talking or questions from your children." She glanced at me, irritated if not outright angry. "We must hurry. No one knows how many trains will be running."

Cherub-faced, boisterous, and seemingly kind to everyone but me, Bette Krobott embodied traditional German motherhood much more than Mutti did. In better times, she had often invited our family over to bake bread and cookies to share, treating us like family. Although I thought I was respectful to her, I was apparently much too headstrong for her taste. Once she told my parents in front of me that I was not a good example for Eleonore and her two younger children. That embarrassed Mutti, but I thought it made Papa feel secretly proud.

All accounted for, each of us trapped inside multiple layers of clothing, our two families began to walk the several miles to the train station in below-zero cold. Still full of questions and opinions, I was having trouble understanding why our entire city was being herded to the same place.

Although our mothers had made clear that the children were to remain quiet, I didn't care. I was still going to ask the questions that I needed to. I was not a sheltered little girl anymore, innocent and blindly accepting, too young to figure things out.

I made sure Frau Krobott was within earshot of me when I launched my next query.

"I think this is a very bad idea, Mutti. I am sorry, but what makes you think Dresden is any safer than here?"

Eleonore looked perplexed. "But, Mutti, Rosel said we were going on a holiday. So, why does everyone look so worried?"

Frau Krobott raised her eyebrows at me and then looked disparagingly at my mother. I had deliberately disobeyed an adult's directive, and Mutti hadn't reprimanded me.

Mutti glared at me, holding her angry gaze for a long moment before turning back to my sister. "No, Eleonore. Rosel was wrong. We are not going on a vacation. We are going to a city called Dresden, so we can stay safe."

"So, we aren't going to see Papa?" Eleonore started to cry. "Rosel, you lied to me!"

With traditional German etiquette ignored and Mutti's authority fraying, Eleonore also began to challenge our mother's decision-making. "But why, Mutti, why? And what is Dresden? I don't know of any such place."

"Right now I want you and your sister to be respectful and just stay quiet." Try as she might, my mother's instructions lacked all the oomph that my father's authority held.

Eleonore persisted. "Won't Dresden be unsafe too? And how will Papa be able to find us? He won't know where we are anymore."

Frau Krobott interrupted with an attempt to reassure Eleonore and squelch me. She had grown all too familiar with my questioning and occasional insolence and how it spread like an infection to other children.

"Now, Eleonore, Dresden is a friendly city where we can be safe. It is not a military center, and there are very few soldiers there. It is a peaceful city of artists and musicians, so beautiful, like part of heaven itself, you will soon see. But right now, we need you and your big sister to be quiet and follow our instructions."

My sister started to relax, reassured and satisfied with the explanation. Noticing that Eleonore was responding favorably, Frau Krobott continued.

"We will be staying with my sister, Frau Meier. She has a splendid apartment with plenty of room. Your papa will be able to find us there; God will see to that, when this horrid war is over."

Although her reassurances worked on my sister, I didn't buy what Frau Krobott was saying for one minute. I could already see how arduous even the walk to the *Hauptbahnhof* was going to be.

Crowded with fleeing families, everyone hampered by the bitter cold, the streets of Breslau were full of desperate commotion. Most people were on foot, with a few farmers traveling by covered wagons and carts drawn by horses. German soldiers occasionally marched by, going in the opposite direction, noticeably tired but with their heads held high. Now and then, loud and intimidating Panzer tanks also passed, sputtering plumes of thick, oily smoke.

Tension hung in the frigid air all around us. With the storm clouds of war approaching, the adults walked with their heads down, ominously quiet. We children trudged along at their sides, cold, unwilling, and already hungry.

Walking, walking, and more walking. It seemed to take forever to get there. Two hours later, we arrived at the train station. Though we were exhausted, famished, and in need of toilets, there would be no time for any sort of break.

"Children, *mach schnell!*" Frau Krobott pressed us to make haste as we pushed through the crowded front entrance of the *Hauptbahnhof.* She joined a line to purchase tickets for our families, while Mutti sat with me and the other children on a nearby bench.

Frau Krobott returned out of breath. "Hilde, we must hurry. We must get in line right now. Everyone is leaving at the same time!"

"*Ja-ja.* Where are the tickets, Bette?"

Frau Krobott was still trying to catch her breath, overflowing with anxiety. "We don't need them . . . They told me the trains are no longer requiring tickets."

What madness, I thought. Without boarding tickets, order and discipline would surely break down. It would also mean the train cars would be packed, with everyone pushing and shoving for space.

Frau Krobott continued, her voice choppy and now filled with uncertainty. "We must take the next train heading west, toward Dresden. We have to catch it. No one knows if any more will be coming after that."

As we pushed our way into line, I overheard a nearby elderly man say that he guessed the Allied bombers would be coming from the north and west, paving the way for Bolshevik troops to try and take our city from the southeast. No one left in Breslau would be safe, military or civilian.

151

His words painted a troubling scene inside my head, one where Papa's Volkssturm regiment might be Breslau's first line of defense.

Frightened, Eleonore reached for my hand and held tight. Frau Krobott tried her best to remain in charge. "Hilde, gather your kids. Willy, Brandt, stay close to the group. We must stick together. Lock hands, now! The train will soon be here."

"Oh dear God . . . there it is . . ." Frau Krobott's own fear visibly escalated as the train came into view. The incoming train cars looked completely packed. People were hanging out over the railings.

Eleonore said what all of us were already thinking. "But, Mutti, what if there is no room left for us?"

I reached into my pocket for the cross my father had entrusted me with years before. Given to us by my *Tante* Johanna, it had once been blessed in a cathedral. I had been told repeatedly while growing up that this cross had the power to protect us. Praying with it now would not only keep us safe but perhaps keep Papa alive as well.

The sudden awareness slashed through me like a knife. There was no cross in my pocket. My last-minute trip to the toilet back at our apartment had sidetracked me from my most important task before leaving. I had left the gold cross behind, hidden in my bookcase back home.

I panicked as my stomach dropped. *Oh dear God, we are not protected. And it's completely my fault!* Without the divine power of that cross, I was certain Papa was going to die. Perhaps we would be next.

The crowd shoved and jostled forward as the train slowed and at last stopped in front of us. A long blast exhaled from its horn. "Hurry, line up. *Schnell!*" My mother's voice rose and shook with fear. With countless mothers in front of us pushing their children along, Mutti wasn't sure we would make it while there was still enough room. I remained frozen in place, worrying about my cross.

"Mutti, we have to go back to our apartment. We must go back to get the gold cross. I forgot it!"

"There is no time, Rosel. We cannot miss this train; it might be the last."

"But, Mutti, without our cross, we are not—"

Mutti shouted out of desperation. "Rosel, there is no time. There's no time! Be quiet and do as I say."

Evidently noting the distress and shock written all over my face, my mother softened her tone. "Rosel, please. We will someday be able to go back and retrieve it. I promise. Right now I need you to help me with Eleonore. It's going to be very crowded on the train."

Feeling responsible for the magnitude of our situation and the danger we were in, I was awash in guilt. "*Ich werde schon*, Mutti. I apologize. I will listen now. I promise."

★   ★   ★

Still deep in dream, I could now see the six of us climbing a steep staircase. Up and up it went, as far as my eyes could reach. A woman's kind voice was calling from the top, several flights above us.

"Come now, children, you are almost here. My apartment is on the fifth floor. I have your bedding all laid out. And some hot soup waiting for you, with freshly baked bread and butter!"

Frau Meier's welcome echoed its way down the stairwell. I continued climbing with Eleonore in tow, followed by the two Krobott boys, and then our mothers.

It had been a long, awful ride from Breslau to Dresden in the biting cold. With no more room in the passenger cars, we had to travel with scores of other desperate people in the open cattle cars being pulled at the back of the train. Sitting on straw used for stock animals, for hours I had to listen to the restless whines of children while their frightened mothers huddled next to them, all the while being choked by the stench of animal and human waste. I could still smell it on the straw that stuck to our clothes.

Although sections of the Dresden's railways had been bombed earlier the previous year, we were told its only military target, the Dresden *Hauptbahnhof*, was still functional, so we mercifully had only a short walk to Frau Meier's apartment in the central city. With our destination soon in sight, I couldn't help but take charge as we struggled our way to the stately apartment building and up the long flights of stairs.

"Come on, Eleonore, come on, Willy and Brandt, we are almost to the top! Come on, all of you. Frau Meier has hot soup with bread and butter.

I can smell it. Maybe we will get a nice hot bath too, I hope. We need to wash the smell off from that wretched cattle car."

At the top of the stairs, before us stood a short, round-faced woman with gray-and-white hair. About ten years older than Mutti and Frau Krobott, Frau Meier welcomed us with a big smile. "Come this way, *meine Kinder*; we can get washed up and then have some dinner. My door is open; just walk right in. There is hot water and soap in basins in the bathroom."

Frau Meier gave me a friendly smile. "Ah . . . you must be Rosel, Hilde's young woman, so brave and responsible. And you, *meine Liebchen*, you must be little Eleonore. Come in, come in, let's get you all clean and warmed up."

I liked Frau Meier right away. She had a calming, optimistic presence that my mother and Frau Krobott currently lacked. Married but without children, Frau Meier's retired sixty-three-year-old husband, Wolf, had been taken by the Volkssturm a couple of months before.

I felt myself relax in Frau Meier's presence. "Rosel, you take your sister and get cleaned up first; then it will be Willy and Brandt's turn. You must be quick because everyone needs to wash up. Dinner will be waiting as soon as all of you are done."

From the bathroom I could hear Mutti and Frau Krobott finally reaching the top of the stairs. Frau Meier ushered the last of our bedraggled unit inside. "*Willkommen*, please come right in!"

"Thank God for you, my sister." I heard Frau Krobott crying, releasing the stress of the past ten hours. Next I heard my mother's voice, depleted and exhausted. "Frau Meier, *danke, danke*! We are all so dirty, tired, and hungry. You are a godsend. *Vielen Dank*."

I kept washing. It didn't hurt that dinner had been made contingent upon finishing up in the bathroom. We had not eaten in over twelve hours.

After everyone had finished washing, Frau Meier seated us children on soft blankets she had laid down across the living room floor. We were soon given bowls of hot chicken soup and chunks of crusty rye bread with fresh, creamy butter. Besides that, there was a delicious array of *Liverwurst* and mustard sandwiches on dense *Pumpernickel* bread. I thought, *What a relief to finally have such good food, and enough to satisfy everyone's hunger. And Frau Meier said we could take as much as we wanted!*

The Meiers' apartment was roomy and luxurious by my family's standards. She had hot running water and full electricity, even in the evening. Dresden was like an oasis compared to Breslau, where electricity was sometimes cut and the water periodically turned off. Despite the difficult trek to the train station and that nauseating ride in the cattle car, I was glad that we had come here. The world actually did feel safer in Dresden. Most of the city seemed untouched by the war, and people here were friendlier. Maybe order and a sense of security could be restored for us after all.

With our bellies full, we curled up on the warm bedding. Sleep overtook Eleonore, Willy, and Brandt almost immediately, even though it was still early in the evening. I stayed up for a while, wanting to make sure my little sister felt safe and undisturbed but also thinking about Papa. Although exhausted, my mind was still buzzing. We had reached safety, but Papa was undoubtedly still in peril. I wondered if his regiment had indeed been called back to defend Breslau.

Believing that the children, including me, were all asleep, Frau Meier and our mothers gathered in the kitchen to hear the latest war-related broadcasts. A shortwave radio had been turned on, the volume barely loud enough for me to hear. Pretending to be asleep, I listened in, hoping for news that might pertain to my father along the front.

As Frau Meier moved the tuner across the radio dial, I was struck by the multitude of stations she passed through, and in so many languages, only some of which I understood. French, English, German, Dutch, and Russian competed for space on the dial. When she paused on a German-language broadcast, I could make out most of the words as the transmission alternately roared in and faded out.

"The glorious German Army, bolstered with fresh recruits from our brave and determined Volkssturm, is successfully fighting off the invading Bolsheviks to the south and east of the city of Breslau. Victory will soon be at hand! Their backward military is no match for our modern technology and the spirited resolve of the German people . . ." The broadcast faded out momentarily, then came booming back in so loud that Frau Meier had to quickly turn down the volume.

"And the American and British invaders have been stopped to the north and west of Berlin by our mighty Wehrmacht. The invaders are running out of supplies, their spirits crushed. All glory to the *Reich. Sieg heil!*"

Frau Meier resumed her spin across the radio dial, landing on a broadcast in English. "It is 2300 hours, Greenwich Mean Time, and this is the British Broadcasting Corporation, coming to you from London, England. Full report in thirty seconds, followed by a repeat message in German."

Peeking for a moment through squinted eyes, I watched Frau Meier gesture with her forefinger for the adults to be quiet as she fine-tuned her radio dial to the transmission. The scene reminded me that listening to BBC broadcasts brought considerable risk. To be caught listening to Allied radio transmissions carried the most severe of consequences, including certain arrest or even on-the-spot execution. Everyone knew that. The Nazis constantly warned us "not to inhale English lies."

Although my anxiety rose as I listened in, it was worth the risk. I needed to hear the reports from what I considered to be my side, the side of the Allies, the side of America and of the free world. That was the world my family still belonged to.

"British and American intelligence reports show the German Army in full retreat on numerous fronts. They are collapsing their forces around the major cities of Berlin to the north and Breslau to the east. Their battalions are fast running out of supplies and fuel. Many of their tanks are failing and have been discarded alongside the roads. Allied Soviet forces have been fortified along the eastern fronts, while American and British forces control the west. We have Hitler on the run. God save our king. This is the BBC, the voice of the free world, coming to you from London, England."

I heard Frau Krobott ask Frau Meier which version they should believe. Before she could answer, however, the BBC transmission returned, this time in German.

I knew which broadcast to believe. I was so excited I couldn't wait to hear it again. Focusing in on the crackling German language broadcast that came complete with a British accent, I felt chills run up and down my spine as the news replayed. "The Germans are retreating on numer-ous fronts."

I cheered inside my head at the hopeful news. I imagined my father listening to the BBC broadcast being blasted into the air from Allied loudspeakers along the front lines. I told myself that Papa's best chance for survival would be if Germany would hurry up and surrender.

I kept myself awake, hoping to hear more information. Frau Meier then said the words I had longed to hear. "Many people in Dresden secretly want the Americans to take the city. If they come here first, I don't think there will be much, if any, resistance."

How I wish that would happen! I would march proudly alongside the American soldiers, holding Eleonore's hand, finally able to shout out that I, too, was an American. I envisioned all of Dresden cheering as the Americans came in to liberate the city from Adolf Hitler and his evil Third Reich.

But my fantasy soon turned dark, my thoughts looping back to my father. Papa was in obvious peril, scared and unprotected. *Would he even fight?* Papa had once told me that no man had the right to take the life of another. I remembered a horrible truth, drilled into me by the kiosk announcements. *Papa will be executed if he is caught refusing to fire his rifle.* Once again, my conscience assaulted me for leaving that cross behind.

I finally fell asleep on Frau Meier's living room floor and was soon in the throes of a nightmare. Hiding in the bushes behind a farmhouse out in the countryside, I had a vague awareness that I was somewhere to the east of Breslau, possibly in Poland. A German officer had pulled three men from his own Volkssturm unit, herding them to a spot alongside the barn of an abandoned farmhouse.

I could see the faces of the men lined up against the barn's wall. Peer-ing through the bushes as the German soldiers aimed their guns at their own men, I watched helplessly as I recognized my father's face, rigid with fear.

"Cowardly traitors! Afraid to fire your weapons for the Fatherland? Say your prayers or call for your mothers!"

Bang! Bang! Bang-bang-bang!

No, Papa, no!

I bolted upright in my bed aboard the *Flasher.*

Bang! Bang-bang-bang!

Through the open door to the corridor, men were hammering nails into supply crates.

Bang-bang! Bang-bang-bang!

FRIDAY JULY 12, 1946

600 Miles East of Newfoundland, Canada

Rubbing my eyes, I tried to determine what realm I was really in. I wasn't sure of anything anymore. Stretching my arms out in front of me and then out to the sides, I became vaguely satisfied I was indeed awake. Ready or not, it was time to get up.

Stepping down my ladder, I made no effort to look in on my bunk-mate. Ignoring another of my daily reminders from my conscience, I told myself to stop making such a big deal of it. She was a stranger, one of throngs of nameless faces aboard this dreary ship.

For a moment I thought I remembered hearing her muffled sobs before I had drifted off to sleep last night. I had not cried in years, though there were countless times I wanted to. I felt strangely jealous of people who could still cry after the war ended. After all I had been through, the least that could have been left to me was the ability to weep, to properly grieve.

Fighting off my bad mood, I made my way down the corridor to the community bathrooms. I was surprised to find the lavatories clean and renewed. The rancid reminders of yesterday's storm had all been sanitized and bleached away. If only the wounds of war could be that easily sterilized. Happy to find the showers empty, and with my recently washed dress in my hand, I decided this would be as good a day as any to take a shower.

Stepping into the stall, I found the remnants of a bar of soap that had been left behind by someone else. Maybe my angels had seen to it that I had something to wash my hair with. My scalp had begun to itch these past few days. Itching was a sure sign of my other constant companions from the war. Lice. I prayed they had not come with me on my American journey, making an unwelcomed home in my thick, curly hair.

Mutti had taught me how to hunt for them with a small comb. Head lice. Body lice. And worst of all, pubic lice. *Schrecklich!* I shuddered at the thought of the repulsive little creatures crawling all over me. Working up a soapy lather with my palms, I washed my hair. Fortunately, just enough soap remained to wash the rest of me, including the filthy soles of my feet.

Luckily, I stopped itching after rinsing off. Drying off with one of the heavily bleached ship's towels, I hurriedly put on my undergarments so I could get my dress back on. Feeling decent for a change, I sniffed under my arms to make sure. Oh, what a luxury to be clean and fresh again. It instantly put me in a better mood. Instead of just tying it back, I braided my hair into pigtails and headed for breakfast.

The short cafeteria line suggested that most people were still feeling sick from yesterday's storm. I, too, was still queasy, but I reminded myself that I hadn't eaten in over a day. Intense hunger would soon catch up with me, and that feeling would surely trigger other, more difficult fears and memories. I would force myself to eat today, if I had to.

I glanced around the mess hall as I waited in the serving line; Liesel was again missing. It had become the norm, but it still bewildered me why she was almost never to be seen early in the mornings. Her bed was always made up when I awakened each day. And despite her being so meticulously groomed, I had yet to ever see Liesel primping for the day in the bathroom.

Liesel's excuses made less and less sense as time went by. It was almost as if she had a secret life. At first that seemed like a crazy thought, but it really wasn't so farfetched. Many people had secret lives during the war. It was virtually impossible to know anyone, especially adults, for who they really were. My father told the story of his once-trusted foreman who had turned in a fellow worker to the Gestapo, claiming he thought the worker was a Communist activist. My father said it hadn't been true, that the foreman really had wanted to ensure that the secret police would perceive him and his family as loyal Germans. "Fear brings out the worst in people," Papa told me. "Be wary, Rosel. There are wolves dressed as sheep all around us."

A steaming tray of hot oatmeal being brought to the serving line drew my attention to today's breakfast choices. My unsettled stomach chimed in, reminding me how upset it still was. Everything being offered today looked unappetizing anyway, from the oatmeal with condensed milk to the fried Spam that I recognized from American war rations. Even the *Butterbrot* and jam didn't interest me. I took my tray, barely aware of what I had placed on it, and sought a quiet place to sit. With the mess hall pretty empty today, that was finally possible.

Instead, I spotted Liesel's brother, Kurt, sitting in a corner across the room. *That's strange—how did I miss seeing him minutes before? How could he have gotten by me in line?* He motioned enthusiastically for me to come join him. I obliged, abandoning my desire to sit alone.

Giving me a genuine smile, Kurt spoke first. "*Wie geht's?* So good to see that you are all right."

"*Guten Morgen*, Kurt. I must have missed you in line." I set my tray on the table and sat down opposite him.

"No, you didn't. I skipped the breakfast line and just sat down." Kurt opened a brown waxed paper packet he was holding, revealing two big bars of chocolate. It was like watching a treasure being unearthed. He broke off a piece and happily popped it into his mouth.

Kurt didn't wait to completely swallow. He seemed upbeat, even more than usual, almost excited. "I feel lucky we are still alive today."

"*Ja*, that was terrifying yesterday. It felt as if the ship were a little toy being tossed all about."

Kurt seemed like he wanted to talk. "I heard one of the sailors say it was a tropical storm, maybe even strong enough to be a hurricane."

"A hurricane?" I had learned about them in school and had paid particular attention because they were an American phenomenon.

Kurt finally swallowed. "Yes, the sailors were saying they had to lock down the upper deck, as the waves were crashing over the observation area. They said some of the waves were over ten meters high. Think of it, Rosel—that's as tall as a three-story apartment building."

Dear God, we really could have drowned.

Breaking off a piece of chocolate, Kurt extended it to me, but I was momentarily caught up in unwanted imagery—being swept off the observation deck, flailing helplessly in the cold, dark water.

"Here, Rosel, would you like some? I'm still too sick from yesterday's storm to really eat much, but this chocolate is good. It's Swiss."

I smiled and nodded, readily extending my hand. He had given me a huge piece. It seemed a fitting reward for surviving the storm.

"*Danke schön*, Kurt. Did you save this all the way from Germany?"

"No, Liesel bought it in France. You know, when the two of you went ashore. It's really good, *ja?*"

I nodded, remembering the chocolate I had savored in my bunk.

Kurt spoke rapidly, relieved or anxious in the wake of the storm, I suspected, but I couldn't quite tell which. "*Ja, das ist wunderbar!* I am still too sick to eat anything else, but this is just perfect."

Encouraged by Kurt's willingness to talk, I took a risk and opened up a little. "It seemed many times like our ship might tip over. Everyone in our sleeping quarters was screaming. I was so scared. But no one offered any help or reassurances. How can people be so cold and distant in a time of such emergency?"

For a moment I thought I was really just talking about myself and how I had ignored my bunkmate crying below me. I felt the familiar twinge of returning guilt.

Kurt answered quickly, as if he had had the same thoughts many times over. "It's just the war, I think. No one trusts anyone or feels safe enough to share any real feelings. That's often true for me too. Everyone seems to have given up hope that things will work out for the better. It is almost as if we are all just waiting for the next disaster."

"You are right, Kurt. I've been alone too much, I think. I did look for Liesel when the storm hit early yesterday morning, but she wasn't in the sleeping quarters."

I scanned Kurt's face for some kind of answer. His smile faded, and he glanced down at his chocolate, silent and hesitating. I worried that I had crossed a privacy line. When he continued, he didn't meet my eyes, only reinforcing what he had said before, apparently wanting to steer the conversation elsewhere.

"*Ja*, the world has changed so much. People do not seem to trust even themselves. I think people wonder if they will be able to find a sense of hope and security again."

I paused for a moment, before taking one more risk.

"Even Liesel?"

"*Ja*, even my sister." Kurt caught himself, his brow furrowing a little. "You see how she covers it all up so well. But she is hurting badly too, like the rest of us." He was silent for a moment, shook his head, and then added in a softer voice, "I don't know what I would have done without her. After our father was killed, well, it was just the two of us." He sighed as he lowered his head, away from my gaze.

What? Their father is dead?

Kurt kept talking, as if he needed an outlet, but I was still stuck on his unexpected revelation. Liesel had never said anything about her father being killed.

"I am so sorry, Kurt, I didn't know. . ."

"I'm not surprised. Liesel never talks about it."

I leaned closer as he continued.

"We heard the sirens go off. Liesel wanted to go find our father, but I told her no. We had to respect what he made us promise to do if we were ever separated when the sirens blared. We went straight to the bomb shelter without him." Kurt's eyes dampened as his voice quivered.

"We waited for him, for hours, but he . . . he never came back." Now struggling, Kurt could barely get the words out. "The next day, we watched them pull his body out of the debris. Liesel blames herself, but it wasn't her fault."

I tried to smother my gasp by covering my mouth. I couldn't find a single word to even attempt a response. Wanting to say something kind, I found myself locked up inside my head.

Kurt wasn't finished. I couldn't tell whether he was speaking so openly because he felt safe with me or whether he just needed to hear himself say the words out loud.

"I thank God for my sister. In the last months of the war, many people in Leipzig starved or froze to death. I couldn't find any work, none. Not even removing rubble for a piece of bread. When the Russians came in after the war, it got even worse. The men were treated like slaves, the women as if they were servants—or worse. The Russians did that intentionally, so we would feel powerless. But I thank God for my sister. *Ja,* she found a way so we wouldn't starve, so we could survive."

Nearly speechless, I nodded slowly, not altogether sure what he meant. He appeared uncomfortable, as if he had shared too much.

Kurt abruptly started folding up the wrapper around his remaining piece of chocolate, making it clear he was done talking. "Well, that is enough talk of the war."

All I could say was, "I'm so sorry . . . I . . . ."

"Here, you take the rest." Kurt handed me his chocolate. "Let's leave the bad memories behind us. Like my father always said, 'We must look forward to what's ahead, to our life in America.'"

I attempted to summon a compassionate smile, some kind words to comfort him. But no more words came to me.

"Well. It was good to see you this morning, Rosel. I think I will go to my quiet place down the hall and do some reading. I have a secret retreat where I can disappear for a while. Maybe I will see you at dinner then, *ja?*"

"*Ja-ja.* I will see you later. Thank you for sharing your wonderful chocolate with me."

As Kurt turned and walked away, a few more pieces of the mystery had been left on the table before me. After hearing his heartbreaking story, one thing replayed over and over in my mind.

What did he mean, Liesel had found a way for them to survive?

At the top of the iron stairs, down at the far end of the ship, I spotted Liesel right away. She was hard to miss in her bright-yellow dress. Talking excitedly to one of the young sailors, I could see them both laughing, Liesel gesturing playfully, just inches from his chest.

Intrigued by Liesel's posturing, I thought I saw the sailor clasp Liesel's hand. From where I was standing, it looked as if she had taken something from his grasp.

What is that? My eyes must be deceiving me; I am too far away to see anything clearly.

But something had been exchanged. And it had looked like a wad of money.

164

I chastised myself for even thinking such a thing. Liesel was not some kind of loose woman, a *shiksa*.

I cringed as I remembered a regrettable incident back when I was nine and had joined a group of neighborhood kids taunting an unmarried mother. She had been out strolling with her baby boy, taking advantage of a nice warm day. "*Shiksa, shiksa, shiksa!*" We had sneered at her until she burst into tears and hurried away from us.

Looking back on it now, I felt such shame. Maybe those cruel words were still ringing in that young woman's head. What I had done was reprehensible. I had joined a taunting group of bullies just to feel like I belonged.

The familiar sound of the clarinet across the upper deck rescued me from my ugly memories. David's morning serenade had begun, and I was grateful for the distraction.

His entourage had grown in recent days. It appeared that a number of the passengers were now including David's spirited performances in their daily routines.

I moved closer, a few steps at a time. As his notes took their expected turn upward, a welcome shiver ran up and down my spine. Once again, his song had reached my heart.

David looked up, and his eyes seemed to smile at me just before he and his clarinet nodded in my direction. I felt my face flush. *Was that really meant for me?*

When David stopped for a moment to draw a breath, his quick smile confirmed his intention. Feeling my heart pound in joyful rhythm, I nodded back.

A tap on my forearm brought me back to earth. It was Liesel. I had not seen her walking up to me. "He sure is handsome. Maybe you should go talk to him when he's finished playing."

I blushed, but before I could say anything, she nudged me with her elbow. "I think maybe he likes you, Rosel." For a moment, Liesel was like some gossipy kid on the playground, egging her girlfriend on to flirt with a handsome, popular boy.

I leaned in so as not to be overheard. "*Ja*, I would like to. I tried the other day, Liesel, but he just stared off into space. He barely said a word."

"Maybe he couldn't . . ." Liesel bit her lip, as if deep in thought, before she finished her sentence. "Maybe he couldn't speak; I mean, perhaps it's too hard for him. Maybe he has to let his music talk for him."

I looked back at David and considered what she said.

Liesel went on. "I heard the Gestapo took him from his home. He is Jewish, you know."

Having my full attention now, she continued. "He is fourteen, and so skinny, just like you. He's all by himself, without a home to go to. I was told that there is a Jewish refugee program in New York that might be able to help him."

Liesel had a surprising amount of information about him. I wanted to find out more. "Did he have to leave his family behind?"

Liesel's long delay foretold her answer. She cleared her throat and said quietly, "His family is dead. They were killed by the Nazis."

Liesel continued, her voice raspier and more burdened now. "He was granted passage aboard the *Flasher* as a surviving Jew. I really hope he will find . . ."

I missed the last words of her sentence. Engrossed with David's fluidity and grace, I was captivated watching him become one with his own song. When the last notes faded, I realized I had drifted from our conversation.

"I'm sorry, Liesel, I was lost in David's music. What were you saying about him finding something?"

I turned toward her, but she wasn't there.

Turning in a circle, I spotted her many steps away, along the railing, covering her face with both palms.

"Liesel!" I ran to her side. "I'm sorry, I was so wrapped up in his playing. Are you okay? What is it?"

I tentatively put my arm around her, but she was detached and unresponsive. I gently rubbed her back.

Now looking out to sea with a vacant expression on her face, she finally spoke. In a barely audibly whisper, she said, "It's my fault my father is dead."

I felt her go limp inside my embrace. "Liesel, I . . . I am right here . . ." Holding her up, I thought she would drop to the deck if I let go.

"I asked him to go back into the store and get me some more chocolates, and then the bombing raid sirens came on, and he wasn't there, and . . . and . . ."

"Liesel, you mustn't feel like you had anything to do with your father's—"

She spoke over me, her voice harsh, "My own selfishness is to blame. I just had to have that chocolate."

I tightened my arms around her as she continued, her body stiffening against mine. "He's dead because of me!"

"Dear Liesel, it's not your fault."

"Please, Rosel, please. I can't forgive myself." She struggled within my embrace.

"Shhh, Liesel, my sweet friend, there was no way you could have known—"

"Rosel, please, stop, I beg of you! Do not pretend . . . There are things you should never, ever know about me!"

I held on tight, even as she was trying to push me away. Finally, I felt her surrender, her shoulders shaking as the sobs overtook her.

"It is all right, Liesel. You do not need to tell me anything more." Kurt's words came back to me then. "It wasn't your fault; it's just the war."

Huddling with my friend at the ship's railing, I could hear the notes from David's clarinet descending back to earth. He had played another song, but I hadn't even noticed. I saw him nod once to his audience and then put his clarinet away, ever so gently, inside its purple, felt-lined case.

Liesel and I stayed by each other's side the entire day. Talk eventually turned to her happier memories in America—childhood outings to the New Jersey shore, the beach boardwalks, the noisy summer traffic. I too tried to remember a little more of New York but couldn't. I had been so young. It was too long ago.

As the day wound down, I began to think about how much innocence had been stolen from us. Liesel, Kurt, David, and I were children when all of this started. And somewhere deep inside, underneath layers of pain none of us deserved, we still were.

I tried to keep the bitterness from consuming me.

FRIDAY NIGHT, JULY 12, 1946

250 Miles East of St. Johns, Newfoundland, Canada

Falling asleep peacefully no longer seemed possible. Fearing the return of the dream demons every time I closed my eyes now, I knew they would invade again tonight. I could already feel their presence on the edge of my consciousness, waiting. As I slipped from a world of color into brown and bronze shadows, fear and helplessness found me once again.

E E E E E E E E E E E E E E E E E E E E W W W W W W W W WUUUUUUUUUUUUUUUUUUUUUU.

E E E E E E E E E E E E E E E E E E E E W W W W W W W W WUUUUUUUUUUUUUUUUUUUUUUU.

Howling. Bone-chilling. The air raid sirens were going off.

Perhaps the most familiar sound of the war, it terrified all who heard it. Germans, Poles, British, Dutch, French, and Russians. Jews, Catholics, and Protestants. Children and adults. We were all held in its menacing grip.

E E E E E E E E E E E E E E E E E E E E W W W W W W W W WUUUUUUUUUUUUUUUUUUUUUUUU.

The dark sky lit up all over the city. Like a ferocious lightning storm, the unpredictable flashes cast long, eerie shadows across *Frau* Meier's living room floor. I knew what the flashes were and what was coming next. Vivid and bright, magnesium flares were being dropped by the hundreds, lighting up targets for the bombers trailing them. The Germans dubbed them *die Weihnachtsbäume*, or "the Christmas trees." God knows why.

E E E E E E E E E E E E E E E E E E E E W W W W W W W W WUUUUUUUUUUUUUUUUUUUUUU.

It wouldn't be long now. Although we had practiced bombing drills regularly in school, there could be no practice for this hellfire coming from the sky.

For an instant, Frau Meier's living room and kitchen were entirely illuminated, like it was daylight.

I screamed out. "Mutti, you said we were safe here!"

E E E E E E E E E E E E E E E E E E E E W W W W W W W W WUUUUUUUUUUUUUUUUUUUUUU.

Frau Meier shouted instructions before my mother or anyone else could respond. "Children! Hilde! Bette! Get up, right now! Put on your coats and shoes. *Schnell!*"

I started to ask Mutti where she put my clothes, but Frau Meier cut me off. "Damn it, Rosel, listen to me! *Sei schnell!* There is no time to get dressed. Just put on your coats. We must get to the bomb shelter across the street. No time for talking, children. Move!"

With my heart racing with adrenalin, I suddenly could think only of getting Eleonore to safety. "Hurry, my sister. Hurry now. There's no time for us to put on our day clothes, just our coats and shoes."

Unlocking and opening the front door, Frau Meier herded everyone into the staircase, already crowded with the building's residents. I nearly collided with Eleonore, who stopped short in front of me. Quiet and orderly, the people around us acted as if this was some sort of exercise. *What? Why aren't they hurrying?* Despite the sirens and the lights in the sky, for an instant I relaxed. *Could this be just a drill? Everyone is so calm; no one seems that alarmed.*

Eleonore rubbed her tired eyes as we made our way to the stairs. "What is happening, Rosel?"

Mutti answered before I could tell my sister anything. "There is no time for questions, girls. Move on down the stairs. *Mach schnell!* Let's go. There is not even a second to waste."

The crowd moved more quickly now. I could hear the drone of planes in the distance, approaching fast, followed by whistling sounds. What came next told me with certainty that this was no drill.

Explosions. Coming one right after the other, each one closer than the last. I had never heard that sound before. The bombs were screaming, and we ducked instinctively. The war had found us, in the supposedly safe city of Dresden.

Frau Meier led us to the bottom of the stairs and out into the street. Shouting orders, she shepherded us across the darkened avenue to the bomb shelter. "*Schnell, schnell.* Come on, children. Follow the people in front of you. Here, here you go, right down these steps. Get inside the bunker, all the way to the back. It is safe down there."

Following the flock, the people around us remained silent and orderly but moved quickly. None of this made any sense. Heart pounding, my words came out impetuously. "Frau Meier, you told us yesterday that—"

Her answer was a forceful push from behind and more orders. "No more talking, Rosel! Keep moving; go as far into the bunker as you can, put your head down, and cover yourself with your arms. Just do it!"

The explosions drew closer. Mutti pulled Eleonore in tight as we squeezed our way to the back of the shelter. An old community root cellar, it was cold and dank, with just a dirt floor. A single strand of lights hanging from the low ceiling cast an eerie, yellowish glow. Unfamiliar people crouched all around us. The sound of nearby explosions increased, each blast triggering more startle reactions among our ragged group.

I already knew there was no escape. Two or three more blasts and the explosions would be upon us. We stayed quiet, along with everyone else, waiting for the inevitable.

Eleonore's frightened little voice then spoke for everyone. "Mutti, are we going to die?"

As the whistling sounds escalated overhead, Frau Meier shouted over the roar of detonations. "Children, listen! Cover your head with your arms, like at school. Rosel, nestle in close to your mother and cover your sister with your body."

Frau Meier barked out her final directive. "Pray, children, pray!"

I felt Mutti push my head down, her hands trembling on top of me. Eleonore was below me, pressed into the dirt by the both of us.

Shaking uncontrollably, I felt the bombs detonate all around us. The dreadful noise drowned out everything. *Would death come quickly?*

With a crash, something huge hit the ground outside the shelter. Our space inside shook violently, and we were showered with concrete fragments and gray dust. *The roof is collapsing! Please, God, not like this, not like this!*

A second crash sent boards and planks falling everywhere. I could feel Mutti shudder on top of me. Closing my eyes, I prayed that our deaths would be painless.

An uncanny silence followed as the explosions paused. *Am I awake? Unconscious? Alive? Or am I dead?*

More time passed. Minutes? Hours? Unsure if I was alive, I wondered if time even existed anymore.

I opened my eyes when I heard my mother's voice, whispering unevenly. "My babies . . . my dear, sweet babies . . ."

Confused and trying to clear my throat from the dust, I found it hurt to try to talk. "Where . . . am I? Am I dead?"

Mutti stroked my dust filled hair. "Just concentrate on breathing, Rosel. We are all right."

Loosening her grip, my mother whispered, "We are in Dresden, Rosel. We are with Frau Meier and Frau Krobott. We have been in a bombing, but we are still alive."

I whispered back to Mutti, shaken, my disorientation lifting a little. "But who . . . ? Who bombed us? You said . . ."

My mother's answer came back devoid of all strength. "What does it matter?"

"No, Mutti, I want to know. Who?" I whispered back, furiously, "You and Frau Meier said we were safe here. All of you keep lying to us. You said the Americans and British want to save us. Frau Meier said we were in a city that the soldiers would leave alone."

Mutti lowered her head against mine, saying nothing, gently stroking my gritty hair.

Finally, the single, long blast of the all-clear siren sounded, followed by a collective sigh of relief from those around us. Some of the adults began to stand.

"Mutti, can we go outside?" Eleonore's innocent question only served to heighten the surreal scene going on around us.

"Eleonore, it's too . . ." Whatever Mutti said was drowned out. The air raid sirens began going off again, piercing the air, proving that absolutely nothing could be trusted anymore.

"Mutti, it's coming again! Mutti! I'm so scared. We need Papa to come save us."

My sister's cries reduced to barely audible whimpers as I gently pushed her head back down underneath me. Covering her completely, I could feel her body quaking under mine. "Shhhh . . . my beloved sister . . . this will all be over soon."

I braced myself for the inescapable blasts. We were lucky to withstand the first two rounds of attacks; could we survive a third?

As the sounds of explosions returned, we waited. We waited for God, for angels, for the madness to end. *Dear God, just let it all end. There is no more good left upon this earth.*

The explosions became louder for a few moments but then lessened in intensity as the blasts trailed off in the distance.

We had missed the third wave. We were still alive.

Afraid to leave the bunker, time felt suspended, frozen in the cold air. There was no way to tell how long we had remained underground. It felt like days. The adults brushed the dust from their clothes and their children—as if what had happened could somehow be removed. At some point, people began to clear away the planks and smaller chunks of concrete blocking the shelter entrance.

Uncertain about what was waiting just outside our bunker, we finally climbed through the rubble and emerged outside. We were completely unprepared for what we saw, smelled, and heard. As we froze in horror, I wasn't sure if we should be grateful for having survived.

We were in hell.

Our world was on fire.

An inferno had replaced the night's storm of explosions. The sound of crackling fire, of rushing wind, howled through canyons of rubble. I heard a man's voice crying out, "Put it out, put it out! I beg of you, please!! Put it out!"

The all-clear siren sounded again, the cruel lie that we were out of harm's way.

Mutti held our hands tightly as the three of us skirted the pile of debris at the mouth of the shelter. Her hands were ice cold, and we were all wheezing. It was very hard to breathe. It wasn't just the smoke and dust; it felt as if the fires were sucking all of the oxygen from the air.

Screams of agony warned me not to look, but I couldn't stop myself. The landscape surrounding us had been coated with some sort of oily substance. Most of it had ignited already, and soon the flames would reach everything left. Concrete, roads, buildings, stone, trees. Consuming everything good and everything bad, the firestorm burned relentlessly in every direction, as far as we could see. There was nothing anyone could do to put it out.

Climbing over mounds of rubble, we stopped in horror when we saw it. The size of a bathtub, it stood in our path, partially buried by debris. The bomb had not exploded. No one said a word, realizing how very close we had come to our deaths.

We worked our way precariously around the bomb, thinking all the while it could still explode. We eventually found the street, though it was barely recognizable anymore. I rubbed my eyes in a futile effort to erase what I saw: Dresden had been obliterated in all directions. A few untouched buildings stood out, Frau Meier's among them, desolate islands in a vast, smoldering wasteland.

I heard Frau Meier call from behind. "Head back, please . . . to my . . . to the apartment." Her once-strong voice was broken now, like everything else around us.

Making our way across the cratered street, more horror awaited us. They looked like charred logs from a fireplace—we had passed some of them before—but I hadn't realized what they were. Until now.

Mutti covered Eleonore's eyes, but she immediately pushed our mother's hand away.

Scores of bodies were strewn in the street amid smoldering debris. Most were so badly burned they could not even be identified as people. Arms and legs were missing.

And that smell. *Oh, dear heaven, the smell. What is that god-awful stench?* Overpowering, it was everywhere. I had never experienced a smell like that before, and it lodged within my lungs and within my brain.

We made our way back to Frau Meier's apartment, and as we entered, Frau Meier said something about a miracle. But this was no miracle. Even inside the apartment, I felt exposed, naked, utterly vulnerable. Burn victims coming in from the streets lined the hallway. Anguished cries filled the air. There was no refuge here.

I screamed myself awake aboard the *Marine Flasher*. I almost couldn't tell anymore what was real and what was a dream. The line had been breached, the one that had kept my past at bay and locked up in my subconscious. There were no more borders, no more walls, nothing left to hold back the memories.

With only two more days to go until our arrival in New York, I worried about what could happen if my demons weakened me enough. I had managed to lock the worst of the war memories away, but now I wasn't sure if my locks would hold. Was I about to lose my mind? How could I function in my new life with such horrific thoughts and images streaming through my mind? I had seen what the war had done to Papa. These were not ordinary nightmares. The bombings, the deaths, the homelessness, Papa's induction, the sickening hatred that infected the country—all were coming alive again within me.

I pleaded with the nighttime demons for mercy. *What is it that you want from me? Haven't I suffered enough? Why must you follow me to America?*

I waited for the answer, but none came.

SATURDAY, JULY 13, 1946

200 Miles South of Halifax, Nova Scotia, Canada

The iron stairs finished their syncopated song as I stepped out onto the upper deck. Depleted from my lack of peaceful sleep, I needed to find a refuge, or even just a reprieve out in the daylight. It felt like the demons were coming for me now, singling me out and inflicting more pain than I thought I could handle. I tried to tell myself they were just bad dreams, but I knew better. My demons were real events, vivid, punishing, and still very much alive within me.

Sticky and heavy, hot, muggy air hit me immediately. Certainly the warmest day of the trip—my dress clung uncomfortably to my skin. As I looked out from the portside rail, the forward motion of the ship created the only breeze, and the only refuge from the stifling heat. I wondered if this was what it was like to live in the tropics.

New York was undoubtedly getting close. I imagined it just beyond the horizon. I had overheard some sailors talking about how the storm had not held us up more than a half a day's travel. We would arrive this Monday, perhaps early in the afternoon.

The ocean was still, flat, and endless in all directions. It was hard to believe this was the same ocean that had pummeled and tossed us without mercy just a couple of days before. Summoning my mother's voice, I tried to feel grateful that I had made it this far. In my mind, it was a miracle I had survived the storm.

It was an even greater miracle that I had survived the war. My angels had certainly protected me, but I couldn't help but wonder how such senseless tragedy could happen when there were benevolent angels hovering about. Why had we been spared when so many other innocent people were not?

A single blast from the *Flasher's* horn announced our turn. As the ship's bow swung forty-five degrees toward the southwest, I wondered why the captain even bothered with the horn, so far out to sea.

What is that out over the far horizon? Land? That looks like land! I strained to make out shimmering columns of hazy blue-gray forms; they sort of looked like the cliffs I had seen across the English Channel the week before. Were we that close to land? No, that couldn't be. Or could it?

Liesel had told me that seabirds would be our first harbingers of land. I couldn't see any, but I kept searching. They had to be out there, somewhere along the shimmering horizon.

A gentle touch on my shoulder brought me back to the deck of the *Marine Flasher*. Turning happily, expecting Liesel, I startled when it wasn't her. Shivers ran up and down my spine.

It was David.

"Hello, Rosel. With an open palm, he gestured toward the horizon. "Those mirages are fascinating to me too, how the heat seems to make land out of the water. It is not real, of course, but it surely looks that way, don't you think?"

"Oh! Hello, David," I said, nervously tugging at my kerchief. "I . . . You surprised me. I was far away, lost in my thoughts again."

Despite his spindly appearance, he had such a powerful presence about him. Not nearly as sure of myself, I continued, careful not to say anything that might disrupt our developing rapport. "*Ja*, those mirages. For a minute I really thought that was land off in the distance. I was looking for the seabirds to tell us land was near." I gave an awkward little laugh. "I must really be desperate to get off this ship."

Inside, my thoughts were whirling. I knew I had to be careful with what I chose to talk about. I didn't want to ruin things with him a second time. I had to find a way to tell him I was an American.

David smiled again, this time less confidently, his voice quieting as he lowered his head a little. "I'm sorry I did not speak to you the other day."

Relieved by his apology, and noticing that he seemed nervous too, I relaxed a little. "That's okay. You looked preoccupied. I am that way myself a lot of the time."

"The truth is, Rosel, some days I just can't speak. Well, it's more like I don't want to speak, I guess. But it feels like I can't. I didn't mean to be rude to you."

David caught my eyes for a fleeting moment before he finished his thought. "All I seem to be able to do some days is play my clarinet."

"You play so beautifully." I brushed invisible specks off my dress, biding some time while I tried to find the right words. "I am so grateful for your playing aboard this ship. Your notes are like sweet little birds, carrying me up so high, away from the past, and bringing me hope again."

"That is kind of you. My grandfather gave this clarinet to me when I was very young. He started teaching me when I was seven. Now that seems like another lifetime ago."

David moved up along the ship's rail beside me. "Playing the clarinet is my family's tradition. My grandfather always said that music is a vehicle to carry our history, to embrace and lift our souls. The German soldiers would have taken my instrument from me when they came for us in 1941, but I hid it inside one of the walls of our old house. Miraculously, it was still there, years later, after the war ended."

I smiled up at him. My mind instantly took me to that cross Papa had entrusted me with back in Breslau, the one *Tante* Johanna had given to our family. We had not been able to go back and retrieve it after the war. But maybe it was still there, hidden in the secret compartment that Papa had built for me inside that old bookcase attached to our bedroom wall.

Feeling some connection with him, I saw my chance. "I am traveling alone, without my family. My only companions aboard this ship are my friend Liesel, her brother, and your music." I wasn't just flattering him; I meant it.

"I can be your friend, Rosel. I am all alone too."

"I . . . I'd like that, David." My mind battled inside my head. David actually seemed interested in me. But I was already beginning to feel the pain he was carrying. Filled with questions about him, I told myself to go slowly. Although Liesel had already given me some information, I didn't want him to know we had been talking about him.

"If you don't mind my asking, where are you from? When I talked with you the other day, you said you were from nowhere. But how can that be? Everyone is from somewhere."

David's jaw tightened. *Had I asked too much too soon?* He paused for a second or two, but then gave an audible sigh and continued.

"We lived in Lwow; that is on the border of Poland and the Ukraine. They tell me the city belongs to the Soviets now. The Russian and Ukrainian people in our community called it Lviv. That was our home, if you could call it that."

"Why do you say it that way? Home is home, isn't it?"

David went on, measuring each word carefully. "We lived there, but I'm not sure I'd call it home. We never really felt safe or even welcomed outside of our community—even though my family had been there for generations."

"Yes, I know. This war has been such a terrible thing. I still—"

"No, no. I'm sorry to interrupt you, Rosel, but I don't think you understand." David pointed down to the faded imprint of a star on his blue shirt. An image came to my mind of that boy at the *Hauptbahnhof* when I was nine, the one who had waved to me from the cattle car. He had a yellow Star of David similarly placed on his coat.

His head still turned away, David's voice began to strengthen, as if he needed to expel the memories. "During my childhood, I saw the Russians, the Ukrainians, and the Germans control Lwow. None of them wanted Jews living there. My grandfather told me that during the first *pogroms*, many Poles terrorized us, chasing us from our homes, pelting us with stones, trying to drive us out. That was right after the Great War had ended, but long before Hitler's war came."

"But why?"

"I don't know; it makes no sense. Our people were established there for hundreds of years. We were among the first people to settle there, along with the Poles, most of us coming many decades, even centuries before the Russians and Ukrainians arrived. And yet, when they moved in, we were the ones they said didn't belong."

A gust of wind blew my dress up against his pant leg. I took a small step back, still feeling the need to respect his space as he continued. "I was just eight when the Russians invaded, telling us they were taking back what was rightfully theirs. A few years later, the German Army came; they said the same thing."

David's nearly black, almond-shaped eyes seemed to reflect centuries of history. Drawn in, I was focused on his every word.

"We always had to be careful; we didn't make it known who we were in public, only behind our closed doors and at temple."

"You are Jewish?" I already knew the answer, but I wanted him to feel understood, and that I had compassion for him.

David turned back and looked at me. For an instant I saw the beautiful face that once belonged to him as a boy. But that image quickly faded, covered by an immense pain and sadness that seemed to be washing over him.

"Yes. I am the son of Anja and Arja Huvski. I had two younger brothers, Samuel and Joel." David's voice cracked at the word *had*, but he cleared his throat and composed himself.

"And you? You are German, Rosel? I have been wondering how you got aboard this ship then."

"I am not German. I am American." My words came out more timidly than I had expected.

David's face registered his surprise. "But you speak German perfectly, and you have what sounds to me like a German accent."

I felt myself reel. Once again, my accent had branded me. *Would David see me, or would he just see a German—one of the enemy?* My urgency to tell him I was an American born citizen was taking an unexpected turn. I sensed his pain building. Was I now fighting for the right to simply listen to him?

"I was born in New York, to German parents. We got trapped in Germany just before the war broke out. We had come back to see my grandfather, who was very ill with a heart condition. But when he passed on, it was too late to go back home. That madman Hitler had closed the borders." I made certain he knew what side I was on.

Not knowing where this would lead, I didn't wait for a reaction and barreled on. "I have been homeless with my family for over two years. The American Consulate let me board this ship because I was born in America."

David nodded understandingly, surprising me. I felt I could keep going, although I was confused by the pangs of guilt I was beginning to feel.

"I had to leave my family behind in Germany. I . . . I don't know if or when I will ever see them again. And I don't even know if I will have anyone to meet me when we land in New York Harbor."

David's eyes softly met mine. "You are very brave, Rosel. I sense you have been through a lot. I, too, must make my way in America by myself. I have no one there."

David's voice cracked again as he went on. "I am worried that I will not be accepted there, in New York, in America . . . or anywhere else in the world, really. I am afraid I might never find peace. Maybe it doesn't exist for Jews."

His words were heartbreaking. I tried my best to let him know he wasn't alone in his fears, but I was beginning to recognize that whatever I could say would be inadequate. "I'm worried too. That I won't be accepted, that people will think unkindly of me because of my accent. It brands me as something I am not. You thought I was German. So will everyone else, I'm afraid."

Saying nothing, David took a step back and stared down at his scuffed boots.

I studied his face for a cue on what to say next, but he remained quiet. I took another chance, trying to explain.

"The American sailors, well, some of them, seem to believe that all Germans are to blame for the war."

David looked up, sharply if not incredulously. I felt like he was staring directly into my soul. "Do you know what happened? I mean, during the war?"

"What do you mean? Of course I know; I was there." I was surprised at my unexpected defensiveness.

A long pause ensued. David looked pensive but not disconnected. He took his cap off and ran his hand through his hair as if he was trying very hard to decide what to say, or perhaps how to say it.

Wanting to fill the uncomfortable silence, I rushed to answer his question with what I thought was the undisputed truth. "The Nazis overran the country. They took over Germany and Austria, then Czechoslovakia, then Poland, Belgium, France . . . They tried to take over the whole world."

I needed to finish my thought but felt I had already lost him. I blurted out, "The Nazis were not the German people. They tried to force me to be a part of their youth program, to brainwash me. We were trying to escape them too . . ." The life went out of my voice as my words trailed off. I felt intensely guilty, without fully knowing why.

David appeared lost in another world. The wait for him to speak again was agonizing. Finally, he broke his own silence by repeating his original question.

"Do you *really* know all that happened, Rosel?" This time, he didn't wait for me to answer. "I am not sure you do."

David pulled up his sleeve, revealing a set of prominent, blue-tinged numbers. B11921 . . . I gasped before I could finish reading them. It appeared he had been branded, like cattle.

"The German devils cut these numbers into me, until I was bleeding. Then they rubbed ink into my wounds. It filled with pus and burned for days. I had a fever from it."

I struggled for breath, fixated on those numbers. Inside, a torrent of emotions swirled. David's voice hardened as he gained momentum.

"When the German soldiers invaded Poland, they marched all the way to Lwow, pushing the Russian Red Army back into the Ukraine. When they came into the city, we came out of our homes and cheered, like it was some sort of victory parade." David gave a humorless laugh. "Imagine that, we thought they were coming to liberate us from the Russians! That was in the summer of 1941; I was just ten years old."

Another flash of memory jolted me. *That military parade that marched down the avenue below our apartment. Mutti said they were heading toward*

Poland. They stormed all the way through to Lwow? Oh mein Gott, mein Gott! I had wanted to give them flowers . . .

Before I could finish my thought, David pressed on. "The Germans rounded us up like cattle. We soon realized their wicked intentions. Those who protested were shot on the spot. They forced us to march down to the synagogue, our place of worship. They took newborns and infants from our mothers' arms and killed them. Rosel, they shot children in front of their parents and their siblings, at our house of worship."

He roughly swiped his sleeve across his eyes. "They pushed and dragged the rest of us inside and bolted the doors. They poured gasoline all over our temple and lit it on fire. They wanted us to burn alive. Rosel, it was . . . it was . . ." David fought to get the words out. "Some of us, my family included, managed to escape by breaking a window in the back. We could hear people screaming as we fled into the woods."

Stunned by the unimaginable horror, I felt as if there was no air left for me to breathe.

"With the help of some of the Poles, we managed to hide in several little villages for the next two years, but the German soldiers eventually found us . . . in the village of Piaski . . . There is so much more, Rosel. When they discovered us, they took our elders, carting them off to God knows where. My grandmother and grand—" David choked up, unable to finish.

"David, please, you don't need to go on." Feeling unable to tolerate any more, I wasn't sure if I was protecting him or protecting myself.

He was still looking right at me, but David's eyes looked vacant, as if he was detached and adrift somewhere. It didn't appear as if he was actually seeing me as he continued. "We pleaded with the soldiers to keep our families together. 'They are of no use to us,' they said. They told us our grandparents were too old to work, that the babies were burdens—so they killed them." David grimaced while I froze. "They killed them! Then they loaded the rest of us in the back of trains, putting us in filthy livestock cars, where pigs had been. Those devils said they were taking us to a work camp."

I wanted to look away but couldn't. His eyes now dark pools of pain, it felt like they were drawing my own pain to the surface. I fought to stay in the moment with David.

"They took us to a place in Poland that they had captured. It took hours to get there in the open train car. We nearly froze to death. We finally came to a place they called Auschwitz, near Krakow. It looked like it was an old horse farm or something. They had set it up like some ghoulish prison."

I interrupted, desperate to find anything in my experience with which to draw empathy and compassion for him. "Yes, I know about the concentration camps. My mother told me about them—for prisoners of war. But why would they take your family there?" As soon as the words left my mouth, I wanted to take them back. *Had I been in some sort of denial, unable to see?* The Nazi atrocities had been going on around me for years.

David ended what was left of my naïveté. "No, Rosel, these were not concentration camps for prisoners of war. They were death camps, killing centers. The Germans built many of them. There was another camp right before we got to Auschwitz, called Birkenau."

The image of the Jewish boy at the *Hauptbahnhof* flickered again in my mind's eye. Unable to speak, I braced myself. I was about to meet my own demons face-to-face, in the daylight.

"When we first got there, children were separated from parents. If families protested, they just shot all of them on the spot. They then said they were inspecting us, for disease and for fitness, and they forced us to go into two lines."

My eyes still fixed on him, I could not find enough air to produce a single sound.

"The line my parents stood in . . . the ones they said were unfit, they killed immediately, in front of us. Put a gun to their heads like they were executing criminals. I had to watch my . . . my parents' brains splatter out as they dropped lifeless to the ground."

David, too, was struggling to breath, his voice now coming out in ragged gasps. He couldn't hold the poison back anymore. He sounded like he was gagging on it.

"A German soldier told the people in our line that we must work hard, or we would be next. 'Work sets you free,' he said. There was even a sign over the camp's entrance that said that. ARBEIT MACHT FREI. Of course, that was a lie too."

With all my heart, I wanted to help him, but there seemed nothing I could do or say.

"There is so much more, Rosel. Nearly every day in Auschwitz, we saw the German SS officers taking prisoners to a certain building. They said it was a factory. They told us our people were going off to work."

The sea air suddenly heavier, I was afraid to hear what might come next.

"This building . . . It had smokestacks, like a foundry would have. Many people were taken there. But they never came back. Do you hear me? They never came back."

David drew a deep breath as the pace of his speech slowed slightly. "They took some of us for what they said were medical tests. They injected experimental serums—poisons—into us. One of my cellmates said they were getting ready to practice chemical and germ warfare. We were their rats, their test cases. Just to see what would happen. What kind of doctor does that?"

I was overwhelmed with horror as awareness flooded through me. My legs began to tremble. I now knew how terribly naïve I had been, inundated with Nazi lies for years. The blares from the kiosks, the BDM leaders' pressure, having to keep my identity secret—these experiences were not comparable to what David had endured. I was shocked at how blind I had been.

David's face went slack as he pushed out more sickening truth amid my silence. "They murdered both my brothers in their depraved experiments. I don't know why I was spared. They are human demons, devils incarnate."

I shook myself out of my stunned silence. Finally able to push some words out, all I could say was a woefully naïve, "Thank God you survived."

"Thank God I survived?" David looked incredulous, as his voice rose. "I wish I had been killed too. You think I am grateful for still being alive? In this hell? Roaming the earth, a ghost with no family, no home?"

David lowered his head and turned away. I desperately tried to think of the right words, but none came. The silence was unbearable.

Finally, David turned back to me. "I am sorry for snapping at you, Rosel. It is not your fault."

I wanted to cry but couldn't. David looked like he needed to cry, but like me, somehow wasn't able to. I wanted to hug him, maybe even hold him, but I didn't feel I had the right.

"We were just animals to them, pests to be exterminated. They even called us vermin, contaminating and infecting their bloodlines. One drop of Jewish blood made you inhuman."

He turned his back on the sea and stood against the railing with his eyes closed for what felt like an eternity. I started to speak, but he held up his hand to stop me. He wasn't finished. There seemed an endless amount of toxin to purge.

"What I am about to tell you, Rosel, we had to figure out . . . us children, by ourselves, in the death camp . . . The people who were taken to what they called the factory . . . they killed them with poison gas, then burned their bodies in ovens they had built. Imagine, Rosel, they constructed ovens to get rid of people."

I felt my own poison emerging, putrid and vile as it reached my mouth. "We could smell it in the air. We'd even hear people screaming for some seconds, then silence. Oh dear God, that silence after the screaming stopped . . . and that smell. The smell that came from hell. I will never forget."

"David, please, oh please, no more . . ."

But he had to continue. He had one more demon to slay. Paradoxically, it was my demon too.

"The smell from their human ovens was the most evil smell you could ever imagine. I am unable to shake it. I can't even tolerate the smell of burning charcoal being used to cook a meal. It makes me vomit. I do not know if I will ever erase that smell from my mind."

It coursed through me all at once, a sickening stream of images, sounds, and smells. *Those German officers who took my friends Seth, Jakob, and Viktor from my class. My parents, talking about* Kristallnacht *in the still of the night. Gisela and Helga, the BDM wolves dressed as sheep trying to brainwash me with their lies.* Frau *Schmidt and* Frau *Richtenhoff:* Heil Hitler! "Pay attention, Rosel, like a proper child of the Reich!" *That sinister black, white, and red flag. The soldiers marching below our apartment, going off to invade Poland, like it was a celebration. My dear father, a victim of two global wars, forced to join the Volkssturm for that madman and his satanic army. The stench of the cattle cars. And above all, Dresden.*

"Yes, yes, oh God, yes, I do know, David! I do know what that smell is like. Dresden. I was in Dresden when it happened. The firebombing. It is the most sickening, vile smell imaginable. You are right—it came straight from hell."

Spinning around and leaning over the railing, I vomited into the sea. I retched until it was just dry heaves, nearly convulsing, trying to rid myself of years and years of poisons that had accumulated inside of me.

Finally, my knees gave out, and I slid to a heap on the ship's deck. Time passed, suspended and meaningless. When I could gain a sitting position, I peered up at David. He stood rigidly at my side, his face a mask, looking disconnected and adrift. I had seen that vacant expression far too many times, and now, I too felt numb.

"I am sorry, David, I don't know what came over me." I felt utterly ashamed as the words left my mouth. Any apology could not possibly cover what had just happened. And whatever I might feel could not be compared to his agony.

I stayed down, sitting on the deck feeling immobilized. I hadn't the strength to rise. I watched him for a while, finally breathing easier when color returned to his face and he seemed like he was coming back to himself.

After a while, he said gently, "I am sorry too. The evil just comes and takes hold."

I thought of my father. Everything was all too clear now. I spoke, barely over a whisper. "I have tried so hard to forget. But it never leaves. It never leaves me alone."

"I know. It is like poison we are trying to expel, but it just keeps coming. I don't think we will ever really get rid of it."

"I wanted so badly to forget, to leave this all behind me. And I hadn't even known the worst of it. David, I am so sorry."

"It seems impossible to just forget, yet that is what we all keep trying to do. Maybe we should *not* forget, so this horror can never happen again."

I tried to pull myself up by the railing but couldn't. My arms were too weak. David took both my hands and pulled me to my feet.

I held on to his hands like a lifeline, still weaving a bit as I looked directly into his eyes. "I am so ashamed. What I went through is not the same as you. I have no right to compare myself to you—my experiences to yours."

Summoning my last vestiges of courage, I tried to muster what little strength I could.

"So many people stood around and did nothing to stop this. When the German officers came for the Jewish children, we were told they were going on vacation. Your people were being carted away like sheep, to be slaughtered, murdered, and we were told that they were going on vacation! Yes, they are devils, unfit to walk the earth. Oh my God, it is unforgiveable."

David's face looked haunted, but he was there again, his eyes alive and connecting with mine. "Rosel . . . I know about Dresden."

Without thinking, I hugged him. Holding on, it might have been longer than I had ever held anyone in my entire life.

"We were just children, David. I was nine years old when all this started."

"I was eight. We didn't deserve any of this."

"Some day, we will tell the world what happened. I promise you that."

David hugged me back, tightly. No more words were needed.

I wanted to cry, for him and for me, for all of the children, for all of the innocence that was stolen. But tears would not come.

After a while, David cleared his throat and gently pushed himself away. Without another sound, he walked back to the port side of the ship.

As I watched him walk away, the line became clearer. A line that separated right from wrong, goodness from evil, heaven from hell. I had seen so many people straddling that line, afraid and unwilling to make a stand.

It was a choice. It had been a choice all along.

I was exhausted, lost in reflection for the rest of the afternoon. But more of the puzzle pieces fit now, and I could almost see the whole. I now knew that what I had experienced, what had happened to Papa, to my whole family, to Liesel and Kurt—it was not the worst of what had been wrought by the Third Reich. David's suffering was immeasurable—almost beyond my ability to comprehend.

Over the next two days, I saw David differently, as he played his miracle clarinet. I understood now what strength it took for his soaring, ethereal notes to eclipse their mournful foundations, as he raised his instrument skyward and lifted us all toward the heavens. I knew now where his song was taking me, and that I could go safely with him, to a safe and well illuminated place, where hope and goodness did exist.

David would smile at me a few more times, understandingly if not compassionately, but we would never speak again.

SATURDAY NIGHT, JULY 13, 1946

70 Miles South of Clark's Harbour, Nova Scotia, Canada

In my bunk, I tried to withdraw into my own world for a while. Night was approaching.

I heard muffled tears below me, from my bunkmate. It had become a nightly occurrence. I wondered what her story might be, what the war took from her. For a second, I thought I should poke my head down there and comfort her. But after hearing what David had suffered and endured, I wasn't sure I could take any more.

I kept replaying what David had told me, my mind returning to those horrible scenes despite my attempts to blot them out. I felt such pain for him, and yet, no tears would come. Not then and not now, even in the solitude of my bunk. *Am I defective? Am I doomed to become cold and callous, indifferent to pain, another ghost with lost and vacant eyes?* Perhaps I was no different than anyone else aboard this ship.

Trying to distract myself, I wanted to draw my sister and me standing in a field of wildflowers, my tried-and-true escape from the world and its ugliness. Using my blue and yellow pencils, a scene was trying to emerge from somewhere in the back of my mind. The words of my uncle Alfred popped into my head. *"Remember to use your colors, Rosel*chen. *For without color, there can be no joy in the world."* His words had once been used to teach and guide me, to inspire good feelings, and to help bring joy to others. But right now, all they served to do was to call attention to everything that I had lost and now felt incapable of expressing.

As I waited for the second curfew bell to chime, I wondered if my life would ever contain color again. There seemed to be no safe places left. All the walls protecting me had collapsed. On my second to the last night aboard the *Flasher*, it felt as if there were too many demons to hold back, far too many to try to fend off.

My bunkmate's crying persisted. Amplified by my own guilt, the pained sounds seemed to become louder, building to a maddening cacophony inside my head.

Maybe I should just accept defeat.

Just then a thought moved me to action. A wave of warm shivers traversed my spine, comforting and soothing. My angels were reminding me I was not alone, inspiring me to stand up to the evil that had infected us all. Reaching over to my suitcase, I pulled it close to unlatch it and take out my cherished prize. Still wrapped in parchment paper, I had wanted to save it to celebrate my arrival in America.

Climbing quietly down the ladder, I found my bunkmate curled up in her bed, her pillow darkened with tears.

"Here." I smiled and handed her the chocolate I had been saving, the large, remaining piece that Kurt had given to me the morning after the storm.

"You give this to me? I cannot."

"Yes, please. You take it. Please."

"*Děkuji.*"

I didn't understand what she had said, but I didn't need to. Touching her shoulder ever so gently, I smiled and headed back up the ladder.

The second bell chimed. *Two more nights to endure. When I get off this ship, when I get home to New York, maybe then the nightmares will stop.*

★ ★ ★

Callous and unforgiving, my dream world wasted no time tonight. Landing me sometime in March of 1945, it was freezing cold, and *Frau* Meier's apartment building was crowded with Dresden's homeless. Although there was no running water, no electricity, and no heat, it was one of the few buildings still inhabitable.

There were no rules anymore. Common courtesy and decency had now abandoned Dresden too. We had to be careful all the time, around everyone.

We were all on edge, waiting. The BBC told us that the Red Army of Soviet Russia was positioning itself around the outskirts of the city. We knew the Russians would not be on a charity mission but would instead be arriving to claim the spoils of war. We still prayed that it would be the Americans entering the city, bringing with them civility and hope. But with the Russian forces already situated, their chess pieces in place, that didn't seem very likely. They were not going to be an army of liberators.

The Russians, the Bolsheviks, were the most feared of the Allied forces. Bent on punishing and pillaging anything German, the Russians would be seeking revenge for Hitler's invasion of their country four years before. Our fears would be materialized. Men would be executed, women raped. Rumors were already circulating that teenaged German girls were being kidnapped and taken into Russian military units to be used as concubines. It was time for the Germans to pay for their crimes.

Faced with the certainty of Russian retaliation, the adults in my world decided to flee once again. *Herr* Günter, one of Frau Meier's neighbors, had offered to get us out of Dresden in his old utility truck. A plumber before the war, he had a bad leg from a shrapnel wound suffered in the Great War and had not been ordered into the People's Army. I surmised that the total destruction of Dresden was now protecting him and other previously excused men from being found and called for conscription. Somewhere in his fifties, Herr Günter had a strong, decisive presence, like my father had once had. Since he had never married, and had no family in the area, Frau Meier and her husband had sort of taken him under their wing.

Putting our fate in Herr Günter's hands, I was glad to see he at least appeared able to make decisions. Instructing Frau Meier to load up his truck with as many people who were willing to take the chance, he said his plan was to head for a small town several hours to the south. Zinnwald was near the old Czechoslovak border, isolated from the major cities and highways. From there, we would head for the remote villages up in the Saxony Mountains. Far from any military targets and well off the main lines, we could hide up in the foothills until this dreadful war was over.

Through the dirty-brown haze of my dreamscape, the memories found there seemed all-too real. I could barely breathe for the choking smell of gasoline inside the aging truck. Hidden beneath the grimy, oil-stained tarp were eight of us, ready to risk everything. Our straggling group included Frau Krobott and her two boys; Eleonore, Mutti, and me; and a young mother, Anna Schumacher, with her infant son, Emil. Frau Schumacher's husband, Wilfred, assisted Herr Günter from the passenger end of the front seat. Though only in his late twenties, Herr Schumacher had also been exempted from the German Army's draft, likely due to the patch over his left eye. Herr and Frau Schumacher had been students at a fine arts academy in Dresden.

The Schumachers felt they had no choice but to flee with us. Baby Emil had a nagging and persistent cough that had surfaced the week before and was not getting better. Fearing pneumonia, or even typhoid or tuberculosis, his parents wanted to get out of the city to find medical attention for him.

The Schumachers weren't strangers to me. I had offered to help babysit baby Emil a few times each week so his parents could get some sleep. Born some weeks before the firebombing, he was barely a month old, and the cutest baby I had ever seen. I already felt a bond with him, and proud that I could sometimes get him to settle when his parents couldn't.

I could hear the feeble, rattling cries of the tiny little boy being cradled by his mother in the back of the nearly dark truck bed. It had been too dangerous to take him to a hospital in Dresden. Hospitals there were understaffed, clogged with burn victims, their wards rife with communicable diseases. People were desperate. There was very little medicine left, and we were told that all supply lines had been destroyed by the bombings. Maybe in Zinnwald the Schumachers could find a doctor who had access to life-saving antibacterial sulfa medicines.

With very little fresh air circulating in the back of the truck, I found it hard to breath. We were told in no uncertain terms by Herr Günter that the truck's tarp had to remain fastened down to hide us should the Bolsheviks pull us over. There were small gaps along the tarp's edge that provided a little ventilation and allowed us children to peek out from time to time. The air inside stank of body odor mixed with nauseating gasoline fumes from the reserve fuel canisters. The cries of the younger children, including baby Emil and my little sister, needed frequent quieting by the adults. Emil's cries foretold how desperately sick and frail he was, as he wheezed and gasped to get enough air.

I fought off the emergence of uncomfortable feelings as our truck zigzagged erratically, finding its way along crude paths civilians and relief workers had carved through the rubble. We finally reached a section of the city that had been spared the bombing, and found one of the country roads leading south from Dresden. Peeking through the tarp, I could see vestiges of Dresden still smoldering behind us, a dirty and ominous haze of smoke and chemicals overhanging what was left of the city.

Feeling no relief at our departure, I was starting to question the adults' decisions inside my head, wondering what was going to go wrong this time. Would today be any different than many other days of the last few months, another seemingly impulsive and poorly planned excursion into a dangerous unknown? But what choice did we have? There was nothing to sustain us in Dresden. And the Russians were coming.

I chided myself, feeling guilty that I was ungrateful and turning on those making the decisions. The adults in my world had been doing the best they could to keep us safe and out of harm's way, my poor mother among them. But it was becoming harder and harder to trust the assurances of anyone around me, including Mutti. Being accustomed to my father's strong decision-making, Mutti seemed to have never developed her own ability to lead or at least had forgotten how to muster such strength during times we needed it most. She had become almost unbearably passive at times, deferring the most important decisions— the ones that would keep us alive—to other adults I didn't really know. For a while I had secretly entertained fantasies that Papa would magically reappear, ready and willing to take charge. But such hope had left me a few weeks ago, amid my near certainty that he was no longer alive.

Gasoline fumes drifted through the stagnant air under the tarp. I coughed to expel them, but there was no escape. My head throbbed as I huddled beside my sister. I closed my eyes as tightly as I could, my last defense against the anxiety rising within me.

Eleonore stirred. "Mutti, Rosel, I can't breathe. There's hardly any air in here. When are we going to be there?"

Mutti didn't answer. In truth, there was no reasonable answer to give. We didn't really know where "there" was going to be, anyway. Miserable, Eleonore started to fidget and whimper a bit. I worried it would soon spread to the other children.

I offered the only thing I could think of. "Eleonore, let's just close our eyes and pretend we are someplace else. That's what I am doing. Think happy thoughts."

"*Ja-ja*, my dear sister. I will try."

I thought I had settled her, but I had inadvertently made things worse.

"Rosel, I am thinking about Papa and how happy he is going to be when he sees us." Of all the thoughts she could bring to mind, she chose the one that sank a dagger into my heart.

"That's a good girl, Eleonore. I am proud of you. Just keep your eyes closed and pretend."

As we continued down the bumpy road, steering around potholes and occasional bomb craters, I could hear Herr Günter and Herr Schumacher conversing in the front seat. We had caught up with a German Army regiment in front of us. Tagging behind them were their pathetic and ragged Volkssturm reinforcements, along with a few civilian vehicles presumably driven by refugees, like us.

I could hear Herr Günter saying that the German Army was invincible, the strongest army ever assembled on earth. We would be safe following them. Bolstered by his continued belief in Nazi propaganda and German superiority, he decided to join the rear of the convoy for protection.

How can they still believe all those lies? Can't they understand that kind of blind acceptance was how we got to this point? All they had to do was open their eyes. Peering out from under the tarp, all I saw before me was a ragtag army running out of supplies and in full retreat. As I scanned the ranks, I hoped against hope that I would see my father's face among them.

Anyone who could still think for themselves could see it—the hopeless draft of teenaged boys and older men who had taken Papa had done nothing to strengthen the ranks of the German Army. The People's Army was a cruel joke, no more than a death sentence.

TAT-TAT! TAT-TAT! TAT-TAT-TAT! My thoughts stopped instantly. Staccato shots hurtled through the air, sounding dangerously close.

TAT-TAT, TAT-TAT! I peered through a gap in the tarp as Herr Günter abruptly pulled off the road as those around me gasped.

TAT-TAT, TAT-TAT! The machine-gun fire from diving fighter planes alternated with the drone of their engines. Up ahead, German soldiers and the civilians following them scattered and swerved in crazy, desperate chaos. I watched and listened in horror as a young German soldier, no more than sixteen, cried out for his mother. Severely wounded in the head, he was catching his own blood, using his helmet as a basin.

I turned to see my little sister looking out beside me. *Oh meine Gott!* I tried to shield Eleonore's eyes from the ghastly sight, but it was too late. Her eyes were huge and glassy, transfixed on the mortally wounded boy.

The sounds of machine-gun fire became louder. I could see the agile, single engine planes lowering in the sky ahead, then diving down in our direction.

TAT-TAT! TAT-TAT-TAT-TAT! The spray of bullets hit the ground, this time not far from our truck.

"Oh mein Gott! Ach du lieber Gott!" I covered Eleonore with my body to protect her from getting hit. My mother, silent but her face permeated with fear, extended her hand toward us, but we were just out of her reach.

The cries of the children, and of baby Emil, now accompanied the adult screams, a mocking reminder that we had left Breslau for safety.

TAT-TAT! TAT-TAT-TAT-TAT! More screams and now, a terrible smell drifted through the already putrid air under the tarp. Terrified at the sound of bullets tearing flying around us, Brandt had soiled himself.

Herr Günter gunned the truck's engine, sending the truck veering down a bumpy path, wrenching my sister out of my arms and across the truck bed. My sister screeched in fear. Mutti reached over and found my sister's arm, pulling her close, but I was still too far from her grasp.

TAT-TAT, TAT-TAT-TAT! The sounds seemed farther away this time as our truck barreled along the narrow trail. Soon I heard branches and scrub brush scratching the truck's sides and undercarriage.

The noise of machine-guns and airplane engines lessened, but I could still hear the attack going on in the distance. Had we escaped or at least gotten out of immediate harm's way? As I looked around, it seemed miraculous that none of the bullets had torn through the tarp. My angels had saved us, once more.

By the grace of God, we seemed safe for the moment. Herr Günter had taken us to a spot partially hidden by trees. Riding along a tractor path, we had come to an abrupt halt at the edge of some woods bordering a muddy farmer's field.

Peering through a larger gap I created in the tarp, I could see people diving under stalled trucks and wagons off in the distance, trying to escape the gunfire still coming from above. Smoke rose everywhere from the disabled convoy.

I heard the passenger door of the truck open and the sound of boots squelching in mud. Minutes later, Herr Schumacher returned, his voice frantic and out of breath, stammering frantically to Herr Günter.

"Günter . . . we must . . . we must get out of here! The convoy ahead, it has been disabled. The Bolsheviks are blocking the road and taking prisoners. Many are dead. They are inspecting all the vehicles and shooting people. We have no choice—we must turn back!"

Herr Günter appeared in an instant and lifted the front edge of the tarp, revealing to our eyes the long line of paralyzed vehicles on the road ahead. There was no time for him to mince words.

"*Achtung! Pass auf.* Listen now. The Red Army is blocking the main road south. Our enemies are dive-bombing the convoy from behind. Our soldiers are like sitting ducks."

Herr Günter continued, increasingly urgent. "We must turn back. The Russians are executing the men and seizing all vehicles. They will be looking for teenaged girls. They will discover us if we do not go back."

He paused for a split second to catch his breath. "It is imperative that we hurry. We must follow the farmers' tracks north. There is no time to discuss. Hilde, you must hide Rosel, now!" The tarp dropped back down. The driver's door slammed, and the truck shifted forcefully into gear.

Eleonore was feeling the danger now. "Mutti, I am scared—what is going on? We have to go back to Dresden? But I thought it wasn't safe there either."

Mutti finally spoke. "Shhh! We must all listen to Herr Günter. He is like the papa now. We must do as he says." Eleonore began to cry again, despite Mutti's attempt to calm her.

I put my arm around Eleonore, trying my best to soothe her.

"Eleonore *und alle Kinder*, listen. We must be quiet now. We are playing a game that is like hide-and-seek, and it is our turn to hide. We must be ever so quiet, *ja*? Shhhhh."

"*Ja-ja*, Rosel. Shhhhh . . ." Eleonore put her index finger to her mouth to show she understood.

"That is good, Eleonore. I will tell you when we do not need to hide anymore."

"*Ja*, Rosel, we too, we will also try." I had Willy's and Brandt's attention now too.

As we raced off, Mutti and Frau Krobott scrambled to secure as many blankets and coats as could be spared, making a pile in the rear corner of the truck bed.

Mutti spoke nervously. "Rosel, we must keep you safe and hidden if the Russians discover us. Get under these blankets." Using her fist, she propped open a small space between the layers of material. "Here, don't disturb this space, so you can get some air. If we are stopped on the road, do not move."

Frau Krobott tried to encourage me but used words that felt completely contradictory. "Do not worry and do not make a sound. Not one word. We will be right here beside you if we are stopped, and we will keep you safe."

TAT-TAT, TAT-TAT-TAT! Another round of attacks had begun off in the distance. The roar of attacking planes had resumed. A small group of German Army vehicles that had not been disabled had tried to break away from the main line. It was open season for the dive-bombers.

TAT-TAT, TAT-TAT-TAT-TAT!

★   ★   ★

I screamed, my dreamscape awash in red. I startled to consciousness and found myself curled up in the corner of my bed, my ragged pajamas soaked with cold sweat. This time I was not relieved I had awakened. It was clear there were no safe realms left.

Still dark in our sleeping quarters, I was unwilling to take my chances with returning to sleep. Awake and alone with the memories of my dream, I played out the final scenes, even though I already knew the ending.

Our harrowing escape from the Red Army of the Russians concluded in the place we had started, back at Frau Meier's apartment building, where, ironically, we resumed waiting for the Russians anyway. Under cover of darkness, Herr Günter had crisscrossed through farmers' unplanted fields all the way back to Dresden. With the headlights off and Herr Schumacher sitting on the hood of the truck directing him, the return trip had taken the entire night.

We arrived early in the morning, just as the sun was coming up. Without water, heat, or electricity, there was no way to care for baby Emil. With him now fighting for every breath, the Schumachers made the only decision they could make.

Baby Emil was taken to one of the makeshift hospitals in Dresden and admitted to a crowded triage unit with pneumonia. Two days later, Mr. and Mrs. Schumacher returned alone, their faces pale and emotionless. Emil had died of a lung infection, another of the countless innocents lost to a senseless war. Fighting through tears, his parents said he would have survived had there been even a little antibacterial medicine left.

Devastated, I felt partially responsible for his death. Although it made no sense, I thought I should have somehow been able save him.

SUNDAY JULY 14, 1946

250 Miles East of Boston, Massachusetts, United States

Following the faint nightlights, I made my way down the *Flasher*'s empty corridors, toward the rusty iron stairs to the upper deck. Unable to bear lying in my bunk anymore, fearful of falling back to sleep, I had gotten up and dressed before the sun came up.

I found a spot along the portside railing, proud of myself for venturing out all alone in the darkness. Tranquil and serene, the ship seemed different without any human activity, quietly rocking in time to the gentle ocean swells. Looking out over the vast ocean, I could not make distinctions; the water and the horizon had become one, the definition lost in the darkness.

Blowing in from the west, a warm breeze caressed my face, perhaps carrying the promise of my destiny from the unseen American shoreline. I let myself daydream for a while under the dazzling canopy of stars, lulled into a state of timelessness by the cadence of the sea. I remembered what Papa had told me once when I was a child, that when far out to sea, the stars at night felt so close you could almost touch them.

Was this where Liesel disappeared to, late at night? Perhaps she came here, where she could be alone with the heavens.

How on earth had I managed to become friends with her? It had only been a week since I stepped foot on the *Marine Flasher*. I'd never before had a true confidant and close companion, and I questioned whether my friendship with Liesel was even real. Had I simply been desperate for companionship, for any semblance of belonging? Were we only thrown together by the circumstances?

Coming up the stairs behind me were footsteps. Sure enough, it was Liesel. She approached wearing a soft smile and, without saying a word, wrapped her arms around me and held on tight.

After a minute, she took a step back. Holding both my hands, she spoke softly, just above a whisper. "I see that you found my secret place. I'm surprised that you are up so early."

"I couldn't think of anywhere else to go. I'm too wound up to go back to sleep." Despite earlier feeling content to be alone, I was relieved that she had found me.

"Just one more day, Rosel. One more day and then we'll be home."

"*Ja*. Our journeys will finally be coming to an end. I can hardly wait to get off this ship." I sighed and said, "I have such terrible dreams now."

Liesel let go of me and nodded. "Me too. It's hard for me to be alone. The nights are the worst. When I come up here, and the stars are out like this, I can almost see a window to heaven. I can feel my father's presence up here, like he is still close to me, as if he is still within my reach."

I wanted to ask her if this was where she came during all her unaccounted hours, but I left it alone. It didn't seem to matter anymore.

"I understand, Liesel. I do."

A tear rolled down her face, clinging to her chin before it fell. "I miss my dad. I was his little champion. We were inseparable. He wanted the world for Kurt and me."

A few more tears appeared, and I gently wiped them away for her. "I'm sorry about your father. I know he was a good man and a loving father." I wished I could cry too, to show her how much I cared about her, and to let her know I had felt that pain too.

I redirected the conversation to happier thoughts, befitting of our last full day aboard the *Flasher*. "It is so beautiful out here, at this hour. What a good feeling it must be to know you will be reuniting with your mother soon."

"It's been so long. I was just a little girl when we left. I can't wait to see her again." Attempting a smile, Liesel wiped her eyes with her palm.

The morning sun peeked over the horizon, casting a warm ray of light upon her softly defined face. For an instant I could see the sweet-cheeked girl she must have been.

"I hope she will still recognize me."

It dawned on me that perhaps she was just as needy as I was. "Liesel?"

"Yes, my friend?"

I looked directly at her and held her gaze. "We were just young children when all of this started."

"Yes, we were . . ."

"We did not ask for any of this. Do you hear me? Not any of this."

"No, we did not."

"And," I continued, my voice gradually strengthening, "we do not deserve to be punished for the things we could not control."

"No." She looked down at her feet. "I suppose not."

I felt the right words flow through me, a welcomed shiver running up my spine. "You did not deserve what happened to you. I did not deserve what happened to me. We all did what we had to in order to survive. I think that you and I, and all of the children, should be forgiven for the things we had to do to just to make it to the next day."

Liesel's eyes welled up again, and her voice almost sounded grateful. "Forgiven?"

"*Ja*, Liesel, forgiven."

I stepped forward to embrace her, feeling her fresh tears upon my cheek.

After a moment, she gently pushed away. "I want to show you something."

Reaching inside the neck of her dress, she pulled out a small envelope and carefully removed a small black-and-white photograph, worn and heavily creased, revealing a handsome, well-dressed couple standing behind a young boy and a little girl.

Liesel leaned over. "These are my parents. That's me, when I was five, and that's Kurt at about seven. The picture was taken in 1933, in Ocean City, New Jersey."

"May I?" I reached out to take the old photograph, being careful to only touch its edges. Her father was tall, like Kurt was now, with features similar to my own father's.

"His name was Johan. Born in Leipzig, in 1901. I sort of look like him, don't you think? I have his sandy hair and blue eyes. Kurt looks like him even more. And this is my mother, Celia."

I moved the photograph closer to see it more clearly. A beautiful dark-haired woman with olive skin and well-defined features, she did not look German to me. And then I noticed the pendant hanging from her neck.

Stunned by what I saw, it was a few seconds before I spoke again. "She's striking. That's a beautiful necklace she is wearing."

"Thank you, I think she is too. That necklace, it was my grand-mother's. Someday it will be mine."

I studied the photo for a moment longer. The necklace's pendant was a six-pointed star, with a curious symbol at the center that I recognized. I had seen that symbol years before, in some of the storefronts along the Hundsfelder Strasse, on my way home from school.

Her hand shaking slightly, Liesel pointed to the pendant. "That is called a *chai*. It means 'life.'" She cleared her throat and said, more quietly, "This photograph and the image of my mother's necklace is what got us aboard this rescue ship."

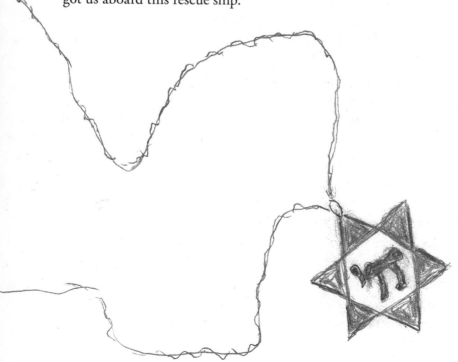

I looked up and found her watching me, and after a moment, I nodded. Content with the unspoken awareness, there wouldn't be need for any more words.

With the sun breaking into morning, sailors were coming up the stairs behind us, moving with purpose. They were cheerful and talkative this morning. One of them casually spoke to us as he passed by.

"Hello, ladies. I see you are up early, like us! Beautiful morning, isn't it?" A robust, dark-complected man, he had features I had only seen before in exaggerated form on Nazi propaganda posters.

Liesel greeted him warmly. "Hi, Ernesto. How are you this morning? We-are-al-most-there!" Liesel's singsong banter drew him closer.

"It won't be too much longer." He grinned and took a moment to stretch his back. "It's been a long term of duty for me this time around. Once we make harbor and refuel in New York, I will be heading home to my family."

Making harbor? Refueling? We are that close? It was hard for me to take in what I had just heard.

"I am happy for you, Ernesto. You must be excited!" Liesel's ability to connect with people was a joy to watch, and I envied her ease.

"Yes, I am. Did I tell you I received a letter from my wife last month, telling me that we have another child on the way? Perhaps my first son! I have two beautiful daughters already, you know. It's been so long since I've seen them. I have been at sea for more than four months."

"For your sake, I hope it's a boy!" Liesel put her hands on her heart.

"Thank you, Liesel. That's kind of you. Well, I've got to go make my rounds. Let's keep our faith in the future, for the sake of the children. In case I don't run into you again, good luck in America, both of you."

"Good luck to you too!" I exclaimed, trying to emulate Liesel's comfortable manner. To my surprise, the sailor smiled back at me, giving me a thumbs-up gesture before moving along on his way.

"Liesel, where is he from? I have never heard someone who speaks like that. He doesn't sound American."

"Oh yes, he is American. He is from Puerto Rico, an American territory. It is an island in the tropics, far to the south in the Caribbean Sea. There are a number of sailors on our ship from there."

"America is so big! I want to someday see all of it." I caught myself sounding excited and adventurous. Papa would have been proud.

Liesel smiled. "You will have plenty of time to do that, Rosel. You have your whole life ahead of you."

Just then, floating in through the air above us, came what sounded like the clatter of laughter, playful and happy.

Ca-caw! Ca-caw!

"Rosel, look!" Liesel clutched my hand, pointing overhead.

I wanted to hear the words come from my own mouth, needing to validate that what I was seeing was not just another illusion.

"Seabirds!" We both said it at the same time and laughed in delight.

They were soaring and diving with ease in the gentle, early morning wind. Two of them landed gracefully atop the ship's upper support cable.

Our welcoming committee, just as the sailors had said. Land was near! "I can't believe it, Liesel." A host of forgotten feelings fluttered in my head.

Turning our backs to the morning sun, we gazed out across the water, watching the gulls' life-affirming harmony above us. I followed the ocean's ripples all the way to the horizon, squinting, trying to will all that was just beyond it into view. The wait of an entire childhood was almost over.

SUNDAY NIGHT JULY 14, 1946

200 Miles East of Long Island, New York, United States

Although I couldn't fully trust it, the sea remained calm on my last night aboard the *Marine Flasher*. Fueled by excitement over our impending arrival, I tried my best to stay awake, my mind filling with the expected sights to come. I imagined that the outline of the emerald Lady Liberty might be first to appear through the shoreline haze, her welcoming torch held high for all to see. Coming next into view would be the breathtaking skyscrapers of New York City. I imagined I might hear the bustle of city streets when we got close enough, a triumphant crescendo of cars tooting their horns, celebrating the promise that was America. Papa had said that every day was cause for celebration in America, if you believed in yourself and worked hard enough.

I tried to immerse myself in those pleasant thoughts, but I couldn't hold on to them for very long. Missing from my mental images was my family; I was always alone. I wondered if I would someday be able to make good on my promise to bring my parents and sister back home to New York. The thought of going a decade without seeing them, like Liesel and Kurt had endured with their mother, was unbearable.

I also remained troubled by worries that the Wagners might not be at the harbor to meet me. What then? Would I be sent back to Germany?

Although I wanted to stay awake and avoid dreams altogether this last night, I was utterly weary from getting up so early. Unable to fight it off,

I found myself once again drifting through wispy clouds of consciousness, until I was fast asleep.

★   ★   ★

Tonight's dreams began differently from the rest. Instead of being thrust onto some unwelcoming and illusory stage, I remained magically up in the sky, looking down upon Earth. Zeroing in until I found my mother, sister, and myself far below, it seemed as if I was watching an old movie filmed from some otherworldly perch. Feeling safe way up high, far away from the scene unfolding below, I thought maybe tonight I would be spared the worst of it.

I could see the three of us walking along a winding country road, somewhere to the north of Leipzig. Mutti was holding Eleonore's hand, pulling her along, while I walked doggedly ahead. Bolstered by a warm breeze, the morning sun was breaking through patches of fog that had settled overnight. Spring's leaves had begun to open, and familiar flowers bloomed along the road's edge. In happier times, it would have looked serene and picturesque.

We were told we were in peacetime again. A month before, thousands of pieces of paper had dropped from the skies over Dresden, proclaiming the war in Europe had come to an end. In the face of certain defeat and the collapse of his Third Reich, the "great" Führer, orchestrator of the "glorious" *Aryan* empire, had committed suicide, along with his not-so-secret mistress. We were also told that Hitler's right-hand man and Nazi Party chief, Joseph Goebbels, had poisoned his six children before he and his wife had also killed themselves. Even after all the bizarre ideas the Nazi leaders had propagated, their end was almost too strange to believe.

The leaflets told us not to panic, that the occupying Allied forces would bring safety and oversee the rebuilding of the country. Although the words appeared reassuring, none of us really believed them. It was too easy for this to simply be more propaganda, more lies. For most people in northern and eastern Europe, the suffering had hardly abated. Many people found it impossible to accept that the war was truly over.

As my dream played on, memories flashed back, in unhappy and disjointed fragments. We had left *Frau* Meier and Frau Krobott back in Dresden weeks ago, along with Willy and Brandt, *Herr* and Frau Schumacher, and scores of others who had become our unlikely neighbors. I tried to keep from passing judgment on them, even though they clogged the halls and now the roads we were trudging. I scolded myself for thinking that way; as refugees ourselves, were we really any different?

The remains of Dresden were still hanging in the air weeks after the bombing, a noxious cloud of smoke and chemicals hanging over the city's blackened and decimated landscape, the ashes recoating everything after it rained. That god-awful smell still lingered in the air. Beaten down and defeated, those who chose to remain were resigned to waiting now. Unwilling to take any more risks, maybe for them it was good enough to just be alive.

Walking, walking, and more walking—the days seemed all the same. Our destination was Berlin, where Papa's sister Johanna lived, 120 miles to the north. Mutti's plan was simple enough, though undeniably hazardous. Take the trains when they were running, walk when they weren't, and stop each night in the refugee camps along the way. It would take us a few weeks, maybe longer, but who could argue with her? There was nothing for us in Dresden. The travel was arduous, especially with little Eleonore in tow. I took consolation in knowing that Mutti had at last stepped up and made a strong decision on her own, with the safety of us kids in mind.

Although surrounded by hundreds of other refugees at times, it still felt as if we were abjectly alone. The strangers rarely talked to one another, lent a hand, or offered anything that could be construed as helpful. Although it seemed people didn't care about anything anymore, even seeming to lack inhibition when nature called, I knew better. Most people were utterly spent, with nothing left to give. Many of them probably felt life was not worth living any longer. While it was a certainty that millions had been killed in the war, millions more had become the walking dead.

Behind us, the dreaded Russians—Soviets as they were now called— were pouring into Germany from the east, threatening parents and children alike, telling us we were their subjects now. We had hoped it would be the Americans coming to our rescue. But some kind of deal had been struck between the Americans, the Russians, and the British. It was already finalized. We were going to be part of the Soviet Union now. Another "glorious empire," I supposed, not knowing whether to laugh or cry. Sometime during the last few years, my thoughts had become sarcastic and cynical, my innocence and once-hopeful outlook crushed by war and shattered dreams. I wondered if I would ever be able to find myself again.

Mutti and I presumed Papa was dead, either killed in combat or starved somewhere along the eastern front. Mutti didn't want to talk about it at all, but the odds of his survival were impossibly small. It was remotely possible that Papa had made it to *Tante* Johanna's, as her home was designated as the family's emergency meeting place when the war broke out. But for Mutti and me, that seemed like some absurd dream now. Eleonore clung to the fantastical hope that he still lived, always envisioning him waiting for us somewhere up ahead. Sadly, I couldn't share in such childish beliefs. I had left those dreams behind, in the ruins of Dresden. It wasn't just Papa who had likely died, either. The dream of returning home to America seemed to have died along with him.

Locating Tante Johanna seemed just as unlikely as finding Papa alive. We had already seen Dresden and Leipzig reduced to rubble. If those cities had been leveled, certainly Hitler's stronghold of Berlin had been demolished too. We would be lucky to discover my aunt's apartment building standing, and even luckier to find her still alive and living inside it.

My feet ached from being squeezed into shoes that no longer fit me. I was the only one with ill-fitting shoes, my toes painfully curled up and crushed inside, my eczema running rampant. I couldn't tell which was worse, the pain of my feet or the incessant itching of my skin, as both occurred simultaneously. Mutti had let us stay four days at the Red Cross relief camp in Leipzig, so my feet could heal and we could rest up for the final push to Berlin. Dog-tired and filthy, we dragged along, not really knowing what lay immediately ahead. All we knew is that if we kept heading north, we would eventually reach Berlin.

I could remember a little bit about Tante Johanna and her home from my childhood visits. Her apartment was spacious, by our standards, with sunlit windows and grand rooms. She had been married once, to a much older man, who died before I was born. She and her husband had put all their energy into a food truck and catering business, selling grilled *Bratwurst* and *Knackwurst* over open buns topped with sauerkraut, mustard, and onions. She had managed to keep the business going by herself after her husband's death, drawing upon the boundless energy she seemed to have. I recalled her fondly as being robust and talkative, scurrying around, always juggling several tasks at once.

Still watching from the ethereal roost of my dream, I could make out where the road was expanding up ahead, marking the entrance to the huge city, or rather, what was left of it. Suddenly, I felt myself falling through surreal clouds, helpless and with nothing to grab hold of. And then I was back on the ground, a familiar actor playing out a familiar role.

Treading through the decimated streets, there seemed to be few sounds that would indicate life, or at least hope. The one exception was Eleonore's busy voice, oblivious to the carnage—excited, high-pitched, and unbearably full of a young child's optimism.

"Mutti and Rosel, I can't wait! It will be so good to see our family again. And I know Papa is going to be waiting for us at Tante Johanna's house."

As we entered the remains of my aunt's neighborhood, seemingly oblivious to her surroundings, my eight-year-old sister asked Mutti her usual barrage of questions that we had no answers for. Her words came out with the speed and force of a machine-gun.

"How long before we get there? Do you think we can have a feast when we arrive, you know, like a holiday supper? I don't want to eat out of a can anymore. Do you think she will let us take a bath, with hot water and soapy bubbles? And after we are done and all cleaned up, we can head back with Papa to our home in Breslau. Peter the Cat must be wondering where we are."

"*Ja-ja*, my *Liebchen*. I hope you are right." Mutti tried to put some enthusiasm in her voice, and I could guess what she was thinking. What harm could come by allowing Eleonore a few more minutes of hope?

Stepping carefully around piles of broken concrete and glass, we hiked over the debris that used to be homes. Berlin looked like much like Dresden, but without that sickening smell.

As we finally came to my aunt's home, Mutti and I were surprised to find that her residence was still standing. Part of a small cluster of structures that had been largely missed by the bombs, the apartment building looked neglected, its garden overrun with weeds. I saw, too, that the building's western corner had been partially blown out, and faded sheets were draped across the gaping hole. It looked like people might still be living in the apartments, however, since the entrance door was propped open with a brick.

"Hurry! Hurry, everyone! Papa is waiting inside. Maybe he is looking out the window right now, with a big smile on his face!" Without anyone challenging her, Eleonore remained steadfast in her anticipation of what certainly would be a miracle.

We stepped into the chilly lobby of a once-grand, multiunit building that now smelled faintly of mildew. Along the wall, the mailboxes had been pried open. Plaster fallen from the ceiling caked the floor, littering our path. But down the hall and to the right was apartment number six, just as I had remembered it.

Mutti's knock on the door was followed by an expected long wait. She glanced over at me before knocking again, this time with urgency. Sighing out loud, I made my unspoken point.

Turning to leave, we heard the click of a lock opening. *What? Someone is in there?*

Eleonore spun back around and rushed to the door. "Papa? Tante Johanna?"

The door creaked open, revealing my nearly unrecognizable aunt. "Hilde? Rosel? Little Eleonore! Come in, come in." Managing a faint smile, she made a vague gesture to welcome us inside.

Before she could say another word, Eleonore burst past her. "Papa! Papa! We are here!" Soon out of sight, I heard her charging through the apartment's five rooms.

Tante Johanna's face was pale, her cheeks sunken. Emaciated, she had aged two decades or more since the war began. Her apartment appeared ransacked, in saddening disarray except for a small sitting area that had been cleared in the living room. She invited us to sit down, seemingly oblivious to Eleonore's frantic search in the other rooms.

My aunt spoke feebly, with the all-to-familiar tone of defeat. "Where is Herman?"

Mutti lowered her eyes and just shook her head.

Moments later, I heard what I had expected. "Papa! My papa, no . . . where are you?" Eleonore's wail carried throughout the apartment, followed by the sound of her dropping to the floor. Hurrying to her side, I found her curled up in a corner, sobbing, in a room with only three walls.

★   ★   ★

We left Tante Johanna's after just one night. Mutti did not want to use up any more of my aunt's meager resources. Following a meal of thin soup, a handful of boiled potatoes, and some dried-out bread, we said our goodbyes. Vowing to meet again someday under better circumstances, we patted each other lightly on the back before heading out the door. It seemed as if we should cry, but only my sister could. Perhaps she was crying for all of us.

Outside, shivering in the chilly morning air, we resumed our endless march, this time to the north and east. Mutti wanted to make it to Dölitz, which I remembered as a quaint little village near the Polish border, in the rural province of Mecklenburg. We had vacationed there a couple of times when I was little. Our mother felt the remoteness and fond memories of Dölitz might bring us a little relief from the war and its aftermath and perhaps even a return to some sense of normality.

Tante Johanna had given Mutti a little money, just some coins, enough for the three of us to take one segment of a train ride. I wanted to use it right away because my feet ached so, but Mutti said no. Better to save it until later in our trek, in case we became immobilized by fatigue, illness, or bad weather.

Once again, it felt like we would be plodding along forever, our filthy changes of clothes flung over our shoulders, tied into knapsack-like buns by shirtsleeves. We now had a little wagon, more like a workman's dolly, that Mutti had fashioned out of plywood scraps placed over an old luggage carriage given to us by my aunt. We took turns pulling it along with an old piece of rope.

I grimaced when it was my turn to pull, embarrassed by our condition, although we were no worse off than anyone else in the sea of refugees all around us. Currently, our makeshift cart held a loaf of bread we had bought on the way out of town, the remains of Tante Johanna's soup, an old, banged-up pot, and Eleonore's doll, Baby Bridget, perched on a full canteen of water we had boiled the night before. To my weary mind, Bridget was lucky: she always wore a smile, never lost any weight, and, as far as I could tell, remained unfazed by pain and homelessness.

My feet ached so much that I didn't know how I could possibly walk another hundred miles in my painfully tight marching shoes. The soles were completely flattened by wear, unable to provide any support. Pretty soon my toes would begin to blister again. I told myself to block out the pain and just keep moving.

Day after day we plugged along, and my thoughts circled between numb and mindless boredom, tired daydreams of the past, and reflective moments where I tried to make sense of what had happened to our lives. Being surrounded by fellow refugees in the same condition as us brought no comfort, but rather a reminder of what we had all lost. The absence of our men—fathers, brothers, uncles—was the most obvious. No one seemed to have any money or real resources either, and the stench of not being able to keep clean wafted through the air. We were a people of nothing, walking without a spring of hope in our steps.

To pass the time, I thought about where our weary companions were heading. To find old homes that had been leveled or relatives who had been killed was the most probable answer. People were undoubtedly only ghostly shells of their former selves. I didn't want to know that we more than likely appeared the same.

We didn't see many soldiers, except when we crossed intersections. There we would see regiments with their vehicles identified with their red, hammer, and sickle flags. To me, they seemed just like the red German war flags, with a different emblem. The soldiers and their commanders seemed unaffected by the sight of us marching by. It was hard to believe that they wanted to help restore lives or even protect us, but on the other hand, they didn't seem to want to harm us.

We would only stop after a long day's walk—from sunup to sundown. We usually made our camp at refugee stations that were free and easily identified by Red Cross flags and signs. Displaced Persons Camps, they were called—sanitized and emotionless words for the homeless thousands or millions who were walking to God knows where.

I sometimes wondered if it might be better to sleep outside than to stay at the refugee camps, but Mutti insisted we needed to keep a roof over our heads at night. More like stark military barracks, the camps were always nearly full by dusk. Sometimes the unpretentious little buildings contained bunk beds with straw mattresses; other times they were furnished with nothing more than simple, portable cots. The beds were occasionally disgusting, smelling of urine and other, even more disgusting signs that people just didn't care anymore. Once inside the shelters, people didn't talk at all. No one appeared to have the energy or spirit to help anyone outside their own family, often becoming territorial about beds and space. My little family was no better than the rest, keeping tightly to ourselves.

More than once the three of us had to sleep in the same bed. It was miserable, lying in each other's filth, but at least we could stay warm from the still-chilly spring nights and hopefully gain a few hours sleep. Although the food at the camps was most often a meager soup, powdered milk, and canned beans, there was usually plenty of it. At least we could go to sleep with our bellies reasonably full. Rarely were there any bathroom facilities, though, forcing us into the woods or a nearby clump of bushes, where we passed many people doing the same. There was no privacy anywhere.

It was a miracle that we hadn't caught typhus, dysentery, or tuberculosis yet, even though such diseases had reached pandemic proportions throughout Germany. Mutti had told us not to go anywhere near people who were sweating or breathing hard or who had any kind of cough. We had not been lucky enough to avoid lice, however, given where we had to lay our heads each night. There was nothing we could do about it, at least at this point, so it was pointless to complain. Maybe when we reached Dölitz we would find some soap and mix it with the poisonous powder that killed them. It was strange, but within the towns, it sometimes seemed easier to find lice-killing chemicals than food.

We were occasionally warned by strangers to watch out for rogue bands of Russian soldiers, as the rumors about them abducting teenaged girls persisted. Otherwise silent and coldly aloof, many people would go out of their way to warn Mutti that I was of the age the soldiers targeted. My mother used a word for that, *die Schadenfreude*, which I came to understand meant to take delight in someone else's misery. Although scared and always wary, as we passed by many companies of soldiers, we failed to see anything like that happening. The Russian soldiers were standoffish, if anything, keeping their distance and looking callously disinterested in us. Yet those stories lived on. It reminded me of the tales I used to hear about the traveling Romani families back in Breslau. Those days seemed to belong to another world now.

We marched on, blindly following the throngs of refugees northeast, presumably toward Mecklenburg. The road sometimes hugged the train tracks, and we came into little towns with *Hauptbahnhofs* here and there.

Crammed inside my marching shoes for days, maybe a week now, my toes were blistered and had begun to bleed. I was envious of Mutti's and Eleonore's shoes fitting better, and they didn't have to contend with blistering eczema like I did. Why couldn't we use our train fare? Or stop for a day or two as we had done in Leipzig, to tend to our weary bodies? What would a couple of additional days matter? I found myself getting angry with my mother each time we passed a train station. Even one leg of a train route would provide some necessary relief right now and bolster our spirits. What were we saving it for?

The next day, I felt like I had reached my end. I told Mutti to just stop; I could go no further. My little sister soon came to my rescue, complaining that her feet ached too. Although I knew she was clever enough to try to manipulate our mother by joining forces with me, I was also grateful she could see what I was enduring.

But Mutti didn't want to hear it. She said we were too close to our destination now to stop. She probably thought that if we took a longer break now, we might give up altogether. Motioning for me to sit down on a tree stump, Mutti took her fingernail scissor and loosened the front stitching on both of my shoes, allowing my toes a little more room to breathe and stretch out into the open air. It was extremely embarrassing but actually helped a lot.

We rested no more than an hour, finishing off the stale bread and canned white beans we had taken with us from our last stop. With Eleonore now beginning to whine and complain, me with my beleaguered toes sticking out, and Mutti pulling Baby Bridget in our homemade wagon, we pressed on.

I worried that we were out of supplies. Although the refugee camps had been predictably frequent, every six to eight miles, it was impossible to feel secure when it came to food and water. More than once during the war we had to go a couple of days without eating anything except thin broth and wild carrots.

Increasingly, I was preoccupied as to why Mutti was reluctant to use the coins she had to better our condition. I didn't want to stoke my anger, figuring there were plenty of reasons why Mutti wanted to hang on to that money. We might need it for a necessary meal or to even buy some medicine if we became sick or my toes got infected. And I was secretly impressed by my mother's newfound strength and determination. Our old mother, the one who had raised us, had been frustratingly passive and indecisive, often overwhelmed and immobilized by anxiety. This new version of her was admirable. Was it because we didn't have any other adults around us to take charge? Or had Mutti gone through some kind of change, a metamorphosis of sorts, like some ordinary caterpillar that had turned into a regal butterfly?

As our endless trek continued, Mutti began taking out her battered, palm-sized Bible at night to read to us from the Old Testament before we drifted off to sleep. She said she hoped the ancient passages, psalms, and parables would inspire us to keep our heads up. Her favorite set of verses came from Ecclesiastes. She soon had read the first verses of chapter three so many times that I nearly had it memorized. *For everything there is a season, a time for every purpose under heaven. A time to be born and a time to die. A time to plant and a time to harvest. A time to kill, a time to heal, a time to break down, a time to build up. A time to weep and a time to laugh, a time to mourn and a time to dance . . .* I had forgotten the next few verses, except for the last lines, which seemed to sum up everything thus far in my life. *A time to love and a time to hate. A time for war and a time for peace.*

Far out in the middle of nowhere, inside a country so broken it might well be unmendable, I wondered if Mutti's quiet humility and faith had allowed her to endure when so many others more able than her had fallen. Mutti had held our family together through the very worst of times. Even with Papa presumed dead by everyone except Eleonore, Mutti had remained steadfast in her quest for us to survive.

It was getting dark on this particular day, one that was just like all the others that had gone before it on our march. Soon we would be looking for our camp for the evening, along with scores of other refugees. And we were out of food again.

Up ahead, our faith was going to be tested. Squinting to see what was happening, I could see just enough to conclude that we would face yet another unpredicted obstacle. We were either about to add many more miles to our journey or be forced to turn back toward Berlin. Scores of refugees had pooled up alongside the shore, unsure of their next move. The bridge that spanned the Oder River had been blown to bits.

The Oder River was not some creek or lapping little stream. It had a significant presence, with hidden power beneath its dark, sluggish surface. Many refugees had turned around, seeking an alternate way. Some had pushed on through the cold and murky water, looking unsteady and filled with trepidation as they carried their children above the waterline. Adding to my trepidation, I saw some of them lose their footing against the strong current.

With no food, open sores on my feet, our rickety wagon, and my little sister to worry about, I was certain Mutti was going to have us turn around. None of us knew how to swim very well.

But I was wrong. We were going to chance it, like I suspected Papa would have done.

Mutti told us to leave our shoes on, as we didn't know if the bottom of the river was slippery. Although the water seemed harmlessly slow from the shore, it pulled so hard even a few steps in that I thought it might sweep me off my feet. But my biggest worry was if we didn't hold on tight to her arms, Eleonore would certainly be carried away.

After surveying the situation, Mutti and I decided that it would be safest if we carried Eleonore, but after a couple of attempts, we were forced to abandon that idea. Eleonore was heavier than she used to be, while Mutti and I each weighed barely a hundred pounds, owing to the war. We were already exhausted, and if we fell while crossing, well, I could easily picture the worst. With a look of defeat, Mutti said we'd have to turn back.

My spunky sister wouldn't have it, though, despite never having been in water more than a few inches deep before. "I can do it, Mutti; let me cross with Rosel. You carry Baby Bridget. Come on, Mutti, come on Rosel—we can do it!"

I could see Mutti hesitating, struggling with thoughts of placing Eleonore completely in my hands and fretting as to how to carry our makeshift wagon across the threatening river. We had no time to debate. With the sun sinking low and everything ahead fading into shadows, it was now or never. Mutti decided to abandon our wagon, taking Eleonore's doll in one hand and our family canteen in the other as we entered the cold and dark Oder River.

The first few steps went fine, in water up to our knees, and I thought that maybe we had worried for nothing. But seconds later the current made itself known, soon becoming scary and intimidating. We appeared to be stepping into a trench of some sort, the water reaching our waists and, for a moment, our chests, forcing me to pull Eleonore through the current when her feet no longer touched the bottom.

I gripped Eleonore's hand tight. Scared, I looked down at my sister's face and was surprised to find her eyes bright and optimistic. "We can do it, *meine hübsche* Rosel."

Fortunately, the deepest part of the river was only a few steps wide. Soon we were moving into the shallows again and then climbing up the embankment on the other side. We had made it across successfully, but soaking wet and shivering, what would we do now? Darkness was nearly upon us, and the refugee camp might be miles away.

Anxious and hungry, and my raw feet now sloshing around inside my shoes, I checked for leeches that might be clinging to my legs. None, thank heavens. After I checked Eleonore for the little bloodsucking monsters, evening encroached upon us, and it was clear that we wouldn't be able to go much further before dark. Would we have to sleep outside in wet clothing, without food or shelter, in the chilly night air?

It seemed to Mutti and me that it would be best to stay with the flock. Resuming our trek, blindly following other refugees who had dared to cross, I assumed that we would camp whenever and wherever our pack of strangers decided. But as we reached the road that continued on the other side of the Oder, Mutti flung her arm out and steered us toward a barley field and a solitary light. She said we would go there instead, that it might be a farm.

We trudged through the fledgling grain for a half hour before it was fully dark. But for the single light that Mutti had spotted, we might have lost our bearings. We could see a cluster of lights further away, maybe a mile or two beyond. As we got closer to our beacon, I could see the dim outline of a farmer's barn. Mutti said we would spend the night here.

After opening the creaking barn door that was tall enough for a giant to pass through, I was surprised to find it hospitable inside. There was ample hay for us to lie down in and no farm animals to contend with. Most importantly, it was completely dry. If we left the door ajar, the light from the outdoor bulb could illuminate just enough of the space for us to see our way around.

We fashioned a little sleeping area out of square bales of hay, knowing that without blankets we would have to huddle together to keep warm. With our knapsacks still wet across our backs, our only change of clothes now damp, we would do what we had to. While Mutti and I fashioned beds and pillows out of hay, Eleonore set off to explore our surroundings, careful to remain within sight.

"Mutti, would you like some coffee and a snack?"

I rolled my eyes at Eleonore's question; she was much too old to play house anymore. With all of us hungry and already worried for tomorrow, she had picked a poor time for her imaginative play.

"I think there will be plenty for all of us."

I watched as my sister reemerged from the shadows and start to set a makeshift table atop a bale of hay.

What?

Across the dimly lit barn, Eleonore was indeed laying out a "meal." Placing a canister of some kind in the middle of her little table, she arranged metal tins at place settings for each of us.

"Rosel, would you like milk and sugar in your coffee?"

Mutti and I rushed over to my sister to find her unpacking a large, already opened box stamped COMPLIMENTS OF THE UNITED STATES OF AMERICA. I knew what it was, as I had seen many such packages back in

Leipzig. Hundreds of them, in fact, had been stacked against the walls of the city refugee camp.

I read the front of the canister Eleonore had placed at the center of her table. *Sanka, instant coffee!* It had come complete with cans of condensed milk and packets of sugar. The tins at our places were Spam, that delightful American rations meal that was already cooked and tasted like fried ham. Even a box of crackers, still unopened, so we could make little sandwiches.

We had received a godsend. Had some other refugees seeking lodging in here accidentally left it behind?

Relishing Eleonore's treasure, we ate our fill. We had to drink our coffee cold, mixed with the canned milk, but with a little sugar, we imagined it as a fine dessert from some fancy restaurant. How lucky we were to have found this, with enough tins left over to take as insurance for tomorrow.

Before we settled down for the night, Mutti shared another one of her favorite sets of Bible verses. It was too dark to read, but she had committed this particular chapter to memory. It was the parable of the Good Samaritan, about a Samaritan man who came across a destitute Jewish traveler lying along the road after being attacked, robbed, and left for dead. Although Samaritans and Jews were taught to hate each other, the Samaritan rose above society's prejudices and cared for the traveler anyway.

With that message still fresh in our heads, we slept pretty well that night, the three of us huddled together, our noses mostly accustomed to one another's smells by now. Upon awakening the next morning, we found our socks and shoes almost dry. Following a breakfast of Spam and more sugar-sweet coffee, we prepared to set off again, our spirits lightened and bodies refreshed.

Stepping out from the barn, we were greeted by a warm breeze, telling us that a better day might be in store. Our American relief package had done more than fill our stomachs. To me, it was a sign sent by kindhearted angels just for us. Maybe America was still out there, alive and well, ready to help us.

As we found our way back to the road and rejoined the motley flock heading north and east, I couldn't stop thinking of the tins of food and milk we had left behind. Mutti refused to let us take them, despite Eleonore's and my protests. She said we had all we needed and to leave the relief box to help another family who might also seek refuge in the barn. When I had argued that we should take the remaining tins for security, Mutti had gently rebuked me. "Remember your parables, Rosel."

Back on the main road, Mutti said we had to be getting close to our destination. She showed me her Bible with all of its dog-eared pages. I thought she had marked important passages, but my mother had actually folded the pages over to keep track of the days. By her count, we had been walking for eleven days since leaving Tante Johanna's apartment in Berlin and over thirty days since leaving Dresden.

After a morning of plodding along, we came to the next little town, where we found a modest *Hauptbahnhof*, complete with a running train parked there. With the three of us already exhausted and my toes blistered, cracked, and bleeding, Mutti showed the conductor the handful of change given to her by Tante Johanna. Our mother had come through. The last miserable leg of our journey would be in the comfort of a passenger train.

The conductor shook his head at Mutti's handful of coins. I was ready to argue our way on to the train, but then he smiled, pointing to the nearly empty passenger car behind him. He wouldn't take the last of our money. We asked if this was the train going to Dölitz. He nodded, chuckling a bit.

We soon found out why. Dölitz was the very next stop, less than ten minutes away! When it was all done and said, we had walked the entire way, from Dresden to Berlin to Dölitz, a distance of over 250 miles.

We arrived in Dölitz hungry, dirty, and disheveled, by now our predictable and familiar condition. Too small to be of any significance, the village hadn't been bombed during the war. There were a few Russian soldiers here and there, as well as a temporary Soviet administration headquarters, but otherwise the little town was surprisingly intact. When we couldn't walk any farther, we found refuge in a neglected but once stately mansion not far from the one-block main street. It appeared abandoned by its owners, and it didn't seem like we needed anyone's permission. Many other refugees were squatting there too.

Later, after unpacking what little we had, we registered with the local Soviet administration. The Russians made it clear they didn't like us, some of them even telling us they would be repopulating the area someday and removing any Germans who lived there. We were issued ration cards, one for each of us, for soap, food, and basic medicines that we would later find weren't always available. Like always, Mutti reminded us to be grateful for what we had.

Although we lacked Papa's skills and mechanical aptitude, we were able to create a makeshift home in the rear of the rundown mansion. The servants' quarters offered several small kitchens and a semiprivate entrance that led to an expansive room, where people had carved out "apartments" using whatever they could find for partitions. If we didn't look beyond the crude room dividers, we could maintain some sense of privacy from the other families encamped on the other side of the "walls." Like us, they kept to themselves. Most of the time, we pretended they weren't there.

Although we had a functional kitchen sink, there weren't any working bathrooms in the servants' quarters. Rather ingeniously, Mutti constructed an outhouse of sorts, with partitioning made of plywood scraps for privacy and a hole dug into the ground to accommodate a bucket. We fashioned a crude toilet seat out of a metal seat frame taken from the charred remains of an abandoned military truck. Strange as it was, it was the best we could do, and it worked just fine. We made our outhouse available to everyone in our little colony; it was certainly better and safer than making the long trek to the woods multiple times each day.

We passed our neighbors from time to time going out to our improvised toilet, occasionally forcing smiles but never really saying anything to each other. Every three days it was my turn to clean out the bucket and dispose of its contents in the woods. *Scheusslich!* What a horrible chore that was.

Even with our new accommodations, it was difficult for us to keep clean. We could use the running water in the kitchen to wash our hands and food but had to boil it first in order to drink it. Deadly typhus and tuberculosis were running rampant throughout occupied Germany. Some of the other residents in our building were coughing fitfully, so we had to be extremely careful. Once in a while, Mutti would heat enough water in a big pot she salvaged, so we could wash ourselves down with a sponge. That was embarrassing, given the lack of privacy, so it didn't happen very often.

We could make do with our ration cards, barely, and with the old pots and dinnerware found in our kitchen cabinets. There was very little work to be found, no schools that were open, and no promises that anything would really get better. As summer slowly blended into fall, Mutti found part-time work for me after listening to a farmer and his wife complain about their harvest in the rations line. Lacking enough help to reap their crops, they worried that their yield, which they depended on for survival, would rot in the fields. They couldn't afford to pay me, but thanks to Mutti's negotiations, they would give me free meals for the hours I worked. That turned out better than anyone imagined; not only did I get ample suppers, but they often sent potatoes, cabbage, and squash home with me. I stuffed myself as much as possible while working there, and Mutti was able to use my ration card to squirrel away canned goods for the long winter to come. Our colony of refugees was not exactly charitable, but at least they didn't steal. Mutti counted our goods and made a telltale scratch on the cans; nothing ever seemed to come up missing.

Although we finally had a roof over our heads, the thought of another severe winter like the last one terrified me. We were far from being self-sufficient. If we ran out of food or fuel, if the Russians decided to end their welfare out of spite, I didn't think there would be much chance for our survival.

I awoke for a minute, aboard the *Flasher*, uncomfortable and rolling onto my side in bed. *Oh please, God, just let me sleep in peace. Please, just once, for my last night on this ship.* To summon good feelings, I again imagined our arrival in port and tried to picture the Statue of Liberty. Unable to find that image in my head, I soon fell back into the clutches of my nighttime world.

My dream pushed me back to Dölitz, where it was nearly winter now, at the end of 1945. We were still living in the old mansion-turned-squatters'-apartments, getting by as best we could. It didn't make much sense to me, being stuck there without any long-term plans. Were we waiting for something or just going to scrape by indefinitely? For Mutti, going home to America had been forgotten or at least suspended. We never brought it up anymore. With Papa gone, no one was left to reinforce my memories, I could no longer call to mind any images of New York, which saddened me almost as much as Papa missing from our home. Although I couldn't cry about it, I was beginning to finally grieve the magnitude of our loss.

Although just four in the afternoon, it was already getting dark, as December marched relentlessly toward the winter solstice. Having turned fifteen two months before, I had taken on the role of an adult, acting as a necessary partner in helping Mutti run our household. It didn't feel like much of an honor.

A half hour before, we had finished our *Sonntag Abendbrot*, or Sunday supper—a rare sufficient meal of canned beef, boiled potatoes, and dark rye bread baked in one of the servant quarter's ovens that we all shared. We even had a little butter to spread on the bread. Standing next to Mutti by the kitchen sink, I helped her dry the dinner dishes while Eleonore played across the room. While pretending to feed Baby Bridget, she was telling her cherished little doll what snow looked like.

Mutti had come into her own as an unexpectedly strong head of our household. Practical, kind, and ever fortified by her Bible, Mutti had a routine that was different than the rules and expectations my father had once put forth. Her sole focus seemed to be on making it through to the next day. Sensible and reasonable, she had long ago given up on looking too far into the future. I wondered if, in the postwar world, we should all follow her pragmatic, less-complicated ways.

After finishing the dishes, I turned my attention to folding the laundry that had been hung above the kitchen windowsill to dry. My sister stood by our only other window, in what we jokingly called our living room, gazing out into the courtyard and walkway that led to the mansion's servant entrance. Eleonore was singing a Silesian folk song to her doll, a lullaby Mutti had sung to us when we were little. "Dear little one, don't you cry . . ."

As nightfall encroached and our space darkened, Eleonore called out to me from her spot by the window.

"Rosel, it's so creepy looking outside. I know there's no such thing, but the shadows from the light posts look like monsters!"

Indeed, the dim lights were casting eerie shadows along the narrow, cobblestone walkway. Suddenly, Eleonore shrieked.

"Mutti! Rosel! There's something out there. It's coming this way. I really think it's a monster!"

Expecting that this was yet another one of Eleonore's childhood fears, I tried my best to calm her. "Eleonore, it's just a branch that is moving. The wind is quite strong tonight, and it's blowing the tree limbs all about. It only looks like someone is out there."

"No. Something's moving, Rosel, and coming toward us! It is a monster!"

I was hardly impressed. "Eleonore, please. You are old enough to not believe in such made up things."

"Rosel it's coming . . . it's coming for us!"

Now our mother joined in from across the room. "Eleonore, listen to your sister, *ja*? I think your mind is playing tricks on you."

I reminded myself that Eleonore was behaving like so many other little kids, believing in monsters. But deep inside, I knew better. We all knew better. Monsters did exist. We had seen many of them during the war, and they always came in human form.

"The monster, it's almost here! Rosel, Mutti, don't open the door!"

A sudden, loud rap on the door caused Eleonore to scream and me to jump.

Another set of sharp knocks jolted us again, followed by a man's anxious voice.

"Hilde? Hilde? Are you in there? Rosel? Eleonore? I was told you were here." Though feeble, the voice was unmistakable.

"Rosel, Eleonore, it's Papa, your papa! *Mein Gott, mein Gott!*" Mutti lunged at the door, unlatching it as fast as she could.

The door swung open, and we couldn't believe our eyes. Mutti could barely contain her emotions. "Girls, your papa . . . he's here! I cannot believe it. Am I dreaming? Dearest Herman, you are alive! *Mein Schatz*, you are alive!"

"Papa!" I ran to his side and gave him a tremendous hug, holding tight.

He ran a rough hand over my hair and said, "How is my American girl?"

I looked up at my father, stunned speechless. The silence lasted but an instant before Eleonore was chiming in excitedly, "Papa, Papa!" Clutching his pant legs, she was not about to let him go.

With Eleonore and me holding tight, Papa reached out for Mutti, pulling her in with a sweep of his arm. "*Meine Familie*, how I have prayed for this moment. I never lost hope. My angels and faith in God saw me through."

After a long embrace, Papa let go of Mutti and reached into his front pocket of his fraying worn-out pants. With his hands shaking terribly, he pulled out a tiny piece of wrinkled brown paper that had been folded over many times. Our eyes grew wide as he carefully opened it, finally revealing the diamond birthstone that Mutti had given to him to keep him safe, some ten months before. How he had managed to safeguard it in a time of war was beyond me.

Next, Papa pulled out the now-battered photograph of Eleonore, Mutti, and me that he had once placed under the insole of his shoe. Although thoroughly creased and faded, it was still recognizable. "*Meine liebste Familie*." His gaunt face grew paler, and his body began trembling. "You were always with me, never far from my heart."

I felt a powerful shiver run down the length of my body and back up again.

"*Meine liebste Hilde, meine zwei Töchter*." A soft and loving smile spread across his face, though his eyes were red and pained. "I would never have survived without thinking of you all. You were always on my mind."

Mutti pulled out a wooden packing crate that we used as one of our chairs at our humble dinner table. Papa didn't seem to even notice our makeshift furniture. "Come, Herman, you must be starving. We made beef stew for dinner. There is still some left."

Papa sat down heavily. He did not need to say a word to convey the terrible toll the war had taken on him. It was impossible not to notice how frail he had become. The day he left for the Volkssturm he perhaps weighed a healthy 175 pounds. Now he would be lucky to weigh 120. Emaciated, looking far older than his forty-three years, our father had become a living stick figure.

"I have not had one of your good meals in so very long, Hilde." Papa looked like he was about to weep, but tears escaped him. "*Danke. Vielen Dank.*" His trembling continued, at times looking uncontrollable.

I tried to tell myself that Papa needed to eat and rest, to slowly regain strength and heal, that I should leave my questions for later. It was obvious, though, that that would take days, weeks, maybe even months. I could not bring myself to listen to that advice, even if it came from my own heart. His return to us was astonishing, surely fostered and guided by his angels. I hadn't needed to carry our cross to protect him, after all.

I couldn't help myself. I sat down beside him, filled with so many questions, feeling an urgent need to know all of it. "How did you find us? How did you get back, Papa? Where were you? Did you escape from capture?" The questions came easily to me, like a young journalist intent on getting the story regardless of consequences.

Mutti glared at me, undoubtedly disturbed by the insensitivity even I was aware of but chose to ignore. But Papa indulged my prying, as he tried to steady his hand so he could use a spoon. Eleonore sat close by, fidgeting atop her crate-chair and biting her lip—but not taking her eyes off Papa.

"It is a long story, Rosel. I don't really want to remember it, but I have accepted that it will probably always stay with me . . . I . . . I was captured and taken to a prison camp they called a *gulag*. It was almost all the way to China, in a place called Kazakhstan."

"Rosel, please," Mutti scolded. "Papa must eat now. This is too much to expect of him." Mutti was being sensible and protective, making clear that this was not the time for my questions.

Papa interrupted her, kindly. "It's all right, Hilde. Let Rosel speak. She wants to know. I will have to tell it all eventually, I might as well start right now and get it over with."

231

Papa was battered and sickly, but he was still in there; his essence had survived, if little else.

"You know, it felt as if we were going nowhere, that we would be walking for all eternity." He sighed deeply. "Maybe until we all dropped dead. Days and weeks of endless marching, no matter the conditions. Many did die along the way. Even some of the young boys didn't make it."

Our dimly lit room grew quiet, the only noise now the scuffling of Eleonore's shoes on the floor. "We started out strong, but it soon became freezing cold. Some got sick. The boys called out for their mothers at night. Some of the grown men cried like infants."

Papa paused for a moment before putting a spoonful of stew into his mouth. His hands shook so badly that he could barely manage getting the badly tarnished, oversized spoon to his mouth. *Das ist gut. Danke,* Hilde.

Papa's gaze retuned to me, "They fed us only once a day, in the morning. Like swine being slopped from a trough. It was sickening and often spoiled. The Russians wanted us to suffer. They told us so."

"Oh, Herman. *Das ist so grausam*; it is inhuman. You poor dear." Standing behind him and a little to the side, Mutti put her hand on his shoulder and he patted it absently before continuing.

"I cannot really blame them, Hilde. They told us what the German Army did to them, years before."

"What did they do?" I couldn't restrain myself, and as I leaned forward, Mutti gave me another sharp look.

Papa glanced over at Eleonore, perhaps uncertain if she should hear what would be coming next. After a moment, he said, "The German Army burned their homes, killed their men by firing squads, and violated their wives. Dear God," he rasped out, "all this in front of their children. Then the German soldiers took their food and left the survivors to starve."

Papa looked very far away again, even distant. There must have been more inside of him that he could not contain.

"Before we were captured . . ." Papa bowed his head. "I . . . *ach du lieber Gott* . . . I had to kill a man." He set his spoon down and rubbed his eyes with shaking hands.

"I saw his face. On the ground, dead, with his eyes open. I shot him." He shook his head, as if still in disbelief. "He wasn't even a man yet, really. His face had never seen a razor. He was just a boy."

Papa's face was a grimace of pain as he looked up at my mother's face. "Oh God, how can I ever be forgiven? Just a boy. *Mein Gott*, Hilde, a boy! I will never be able to forget his face as long as I shall live. He keeps looking at me inside my dreams."

Eleonore had given a little gasp, and I noticed that although she had stopped fidgeting, her eyes were huge in her face. My own face felt strangely tight, and Mutti's stew sat uneasily in my stomach.

Mutti rubbed the back of her hand on Papa's pale cheek and murmured his name. Unable to fully comprehend my father's horror, I, too, tried to comfort him as best I could. "It's okay, Papa. It was wartime. You had no choice. You are safe now."

But Papa didn't respond to any attempts to provide relief. He was back to staring vacantly into his bowl of stew. His shaking had left him unable to hold his spoon any longer, and he had given up trying to eat.

Mutti began rubbing his shoulders. "It's just the war, Herman, just the war. You are home now, safe, with your beautiful girls. That's enough for tonight. You can stop now."

Papa was determined to continue, despite the toll it was taking. "War. Such a vile, devilish thing. Worthless. Disgusting. People say being a German soldier is honorable. Nonsense! It turns people into animals. No, even worse. It turns them into monsters, into demons."

"So, Papa, how did you get home to us?" Eleonore interrupted with childish impatience, perhaps anxious to get to the happy ending of Papa's scary story.

"My sweet little Eleonore . . . When the war ended, I was put on a train heading to the Russian-occupied zone southeast of Dresden, near the Czech border. I walked and hitchhiked back from there."

"Near Zinnwald?" I remembered our destination when we tried to flee Dresden.

Papa's eyebrows rose. "How did you know that, Rosel?"

"We will tell you our story soon, I promise. But you made it all the way back from there? By yourself, Papa?" It was beyond belief. How could anyone in Papa's condition walk for so many hundreds of miles?

"*Ja*. By the grace of the divine, I made it to my sister's home, walking and sometimes hitchhiking. It seemed like it would take all eternity to get back." He turned to Eleonore to finish explaining. "But I made it, to your Tante Johanna's, in Berlin . . ." His voice trailed off but was a bit steadier when he resumed. "I was very sick when I arrived at her door. She took care of me until I grew stronger. Along with her neighbors, I helped fix her wall. Finally, I was well enough to travel again, to come here."

Papa's trembling subsided a little, and he went on. "Tante Johanna said that the three of you had come by some months before, last May, looking for me. You don't know how much that boosted my spirits." His voice sounded relieved, thankful, when he added, "You never lost faith in me."

I looked down at our grimy, improvised table, unwilling to let him see the truth in my eyes. Only Eleonore had maintained faith for his survival. But I kept that part to myself, feeling guilty but grateful that I had been wrong. To cover my discomfort, I persisted with my questions. It all seemed so incredible, so fantastic, and I needed to know.

"How did you find out that we were here?"

"Tante Johanna told me you might all be here, managing as best you could, somewhere in Mecklenburg. I guessed Dölitz because we used to come here for holidays, way back to when you were a little girl, Rosel. Thank God this is such a small village."

Eleonore interrupted in a burst of excitement. "Papa, everyone thought you were dead, but not me! I knew you would come back. *Mein Vater*, my papa." Eleonore jumped up and clutched his neck.

"Eleonore!" Mutti snapped at her for revealing a truth Mutti and I had hoped to keep secret.

"Ah . . . *kleine* Eleonore, you are so expressive. I shall soon be calling you my little American too. We will all be returning home to America someday. Yes, we will, indeed."

Stunned, it was the first time I had heard "back to America" in eight years. I echoed his pledge fervently. "Back to America, Papa!" It was music to my ears.

Eleonore, her face still buried in his neck, sought the assurance of our papa's own words. "Will you promise, Papa? Please, do you promise to bring us all there?"

Before Papa could answer, I blurted out. "I promise you, my dear family. You will all be Americans, just like me. We will all be together in New York again, someday, and soon. I will see to that."

Papa smiled at me, and I knew why immediately. For the first time, I had openly embraced the role that he had been preparing me for for years. Now it made more sense why he had held such lofty goals for me as a child. Now I understood why he had been so demanding, why he had pushed me so hard during my childhood. If Papa wasn't able to get us back home, he must have wanted me to. Perhaps he had sensed something. Maybe there had been a purpose behind it, all along.

"*Ja-ja*, enough now." Mutti's voice was thick and brusque. "It's past time to let Papa finish eating, and then he must rest. We can talk more, later." With another twinge of guilt, I understood that Mutti was trying her best to wrestle the conversation back to something less stressful. We needed to take care of Papa now. Everything else could wait.

Unceremoniously vaulted back aboard the *Marine Flasher*, my eyes fluttered for a moment as I stirred in my bunk. No longer dreaming but not yet fully awake, a host of childhood images of my father swirled through my mind—some warm and friendly, some harsh and sad—until they finally settled, in a place of peace.

I heard my own voice as the words left my mouth. "I forgive you, Papa."

MONDAY MORNING, JULY 15, 1946

23 Miles East of New York Harbor

"Rosel! Come on, wake up. Wake up! You are sleeping so soundly."

"What?" I was having a hard time awakening. I felt myself drifting off again, but the voice persisted.

"It's time! Come now—time to get up and get dressed." I felt someone shaking my leg and thought I smelled flowers.

I rubbed the sleep from my eyes, still not quite sure what realm I was in.

"Let's go. Hurry, my friend!" Finally, I sat up to find Liesel clinging to the top of my bunk ladder.

"Come on, Rosel. Get up, quickly now. We are approaching the harbor!"

I felt foggy and was having difficulty rousing.

"Rosel, get going. Do I have to drop you from your perch to awaken you?" Liesel laughed mischievously. "I couldn't wake you earlier; you slept all the way through breakfast. Hurry. We are almost home!"

I cleared my throat, my voice scratchy. "What time is it, Liesel? Morning?" Barely awake, I wasn't quite hearing what she was telling me.

"Yes, yes, it's later than you think. Let's get going to the bathrooms to get cleaned up. I will fix your hair."

"*Ja-ja.*" Still groggy, I had not yet grasped the magnitude of the moment.

"The sailors say we will be landing in New York in an hour. An hour, Rosel! I can't believe it."

"What? We are here?" My heartbeat quickened, and my mental fog cleared.

"Yes, and we must be ready. Come on—take my hand. We've got to hurry. We'll be arriving in no time at all."

I grabbed my dress hanging next to me, making sure my money was still safely hidden inside the hem of my dress. After climbing down my bunk ladder, Liesel was soon pulling me out the door of the sleeping quarters, hurrying us down the corridor toward the women's bathrooms.

We had to dodge the rush of people passing by us in the noisy corridor. People were scurrying about, suitcases in tow, all making their way to the rusty stairs that led to the upper deck. I had never seen the passengers aboard the *Marine Flasher* move like that before. Many were talking excitedly, some even smiling. Were these even the same people who had boarded back in Bremerhaven?

"Hurry up now. I will wait out here for you. No time for dawdling or daydreaming. We don't want to miss a thing up top." Reminding me of my mother, Liesel pulled the door open for me.

"*Ja-ja*, Liesel. I'll be back in just a minute or two." I laughed when she playfully pushed me inside.

I was so late that I had the bathroom all to myself. While Liesel waited in the hallway, the sense of urgency settled over me. As I turned the shower lever, an unusually warm stream greeted me. As the water cascaded over my head, I felt alive for the first time in what seemed like forever. The warm water seemed luxurious, almost heavenly. Getting myself as clean as I could without any soap, I hastily dried myself with one of the ship's towels.

I chuckled out loud as I joked to myself. "Now, which dress to wear for such a glorious occasion? Hmmm . . . how about this nice blue one?"

I stepped into my blue dress and the shoes I now saw as ugly and stood before the mirror, trying to grasp what was happening. In another hour, my cross-Atlantic journey would be over, my dream fulfilled, my life permanently altered for the better. Worries about the Wagners tried to creep into my thoughts, but I wouldn't let them.

I ran my fingers through my curly hair, having forgotten my toiletry bag back at my bunk amid my haste. Excited, I probably wouldn't have taken the time to try to tame my snarled hair anyway. I hurried through brushing my teeth, thankful I had been stingy with the little clump of baking soda I still had left.

Thinking I would probably be the very last to use the lavatory, I turned off the lights, aware that I was closing a chapter in my life. Bursting into the corridor with a spring in my step, I sensed the enormity of what I had been through to get here beginning to dawn on me.

I found Liesel eagerly waiting for me on a nearby bench in the interior corridor. Next to her was a small array of cosmetics laid out on her kerchief, including a lipstick canister, a makeup compact, comb and brush, and a small mirror—all of which had apparently come out of the purse that sat beside her.

With a sweeping motion of her left hand, Liesel gestured for me to take a seat next to her, like some hairdresser at a fancy salon getting ready for her next customer. "Today is going to be such an important day, Rosel. And you must look the part."

I smiled hesitantly, not quite sure what she had in mind.

"You are not a girl anymore, Rosel, and you must look the young woman you are."

Feeling overwhelmed and then a little embarrassed, I said in a rush, "Liesel, you are so nice to do this, but I do not know . . . Makeup is a bit much, you know, for someone like me."

"Oh, nonsense! You are a confident young American woman about to make her way in New York City." Liesel smiled and chuckled mischievously. "Now, please sit down, Miss Rosel."

Working her comb through my thick and tangled hair, Liesel complimented me unexpectedly. "Such beautiful hair. I wish I had your pretty curls."

I giggled, my whole body shaking from Liesel's frenetic combing. "Ow . . . ouch! Liesel, not so hard, you are worse than my mother!"

Liesel replied with an exaggerated German accent, like one of my old teachers. "Now, sit still, Rosel, you are making this harder than it has to be."

We both laughed, loud, boisterous laughs from deep in our hearts. We had made it, beating what once seemed like insurmountable odds.

Our laughter gained momentum, and soon we had trouble catching our breath. We couldn't squelch our good humor, nor did we want to. For the first time since I was a little girl, I could let go.

Some minutes later, my stomach aching from laughter, Liesel finished combing out my unruly hair. She then pulled it back and fashioned my ponytail into a bun, like some debutante. "There you are, my friend. All done. My, don't you look beautiful."

I squirmed excitedly as Liesel held up her compact mirror for me to look at myself. Astonished, I only had one thought. *Who is this person I am looking at?*

Sensing my approval, Liesel nodded in satisfaction. But she wasn't done. "Now for some color. Not too much for someone your age. Just a touch."

Liesel pursed her lips. "This is how you put on lipstick, Rosel. Pay attention, because next time you will be doing this yourself."

Liesel drew a pink line of color across her lips and smacked them together. I copied her demonstration, intentionally exaggerating her motions.

"Not so hard, Rosel—you will hurt yourself!"

We started giggling again.

"And now, the final touches." Liesel pulled out a small brush from her purse.

"Liesel, no, really. I mean, thank you, but please . . . I don't think I am comfortable with eye . . . "

"No, no, Rosel. This is rouge. It will give your face a bit of color, just a hint." She dabbed her brush.

"Your eyes do not need any makeup. They are so beautiful. I would love to have your turquoise-blue eyes."

I didn't really need any of the rosy powder on my face. I could already feel myself blushing. No one had ever complimented me like that before.

As Liesel applied her finishing touches, a familiar shiver ran up and down my spine, reminding me that I was not alone. I never had been alone. My angels were right here with me, guiding me, bringing a feeling of sanctity and hope, telling me I was on the right path.

Liesel took my hand and pulled me up, grinning. "Ready?"

"Ready." I grinned back and grabbed her hand as we rushed down the corridor, toward the stairs that led to the upper deck. When we arrived at the stairs, Liesel tugged on my arm, laughing again but stopping me in my tracks.

"Where are you going?"

"Up top, of course, to see the harbor draw near."

"We will, silly, but we must first get our things. Let's get your old suitcase packed for the last time."

I must have looked baffled.

"You will not be in that bed or in those dreary sleeping quarters ever again." Liesel kept talking, but I wasn't listening anymore. Her words were barely registering within my mind.

I just stood there, feeling stunned.

"Rosel?"

Liesel gently shook me with both her hands, her voice sounding a little concerned now. "Rosel. Look at me . . . We must be ready to get off this ship."

"Liesel, is this really happening?"

"Yes. Rosel, this really is happening. We did it! We are back home."

"It feels like a dream."

"I know. It seemed so far away once. But here we are, about to step off the ship into our future. Our future in America. We made it, Rosel. Believe it! We are so lucky."

Liesel steered us back to the sleeping quarters. Beyond the whiff of her perfume, I could smell how musty and dank it was back in there. Walking over toward my bunk while Liesel went to get her already-packed suitcases, I knew there was little about the room that I cared to remember.

Beside my bunk ladder stood another survivor, her face aged prematurely by war and sadness, her long black hair streaked with gray—my bunkmate. I had never seen her in such light before, as a complete person, and she was smiling at me. I noticed that her skin was tanned, a little more than my mother's, and she had emerald-green eyes.

"We get off the ship now, yes?" Her voice was soft but purposeful, as if she had something to say to me.

"Yes, we get off now. We are arriving in New York." I felt ashamed for not befriending her. She was hardly threatening.

I now understood that all the other reticent souls aboard the *Flasher* were real people too, with real feelings, real lives, and painful stories like mine. I had not given them much of a chance. They had not given me much of a chance.

"I'm sorry . . . my English, not so good. I speak Czech, you know." She said her name was Reina and that she was from Prague.

"Nice to meet you. I am Rosemarie. Rosel for short."

"You have kind eyes. You must be American."

"Thank you. I am." I tried to answer calmly, but I thought my head would burst. *What? Someone sees me as American? How did she know that? With this accent and these clothes?* I felt a shiver traverse my spine.

"No, no. I wish to thank *you*. Your people freed my country."

Completely unprepared for what she had said, my mouth fell open a bit before I snapped back into the moment.

"You will go on to have a blessed life . . . Rosel. I give you something of mine to remember me and this special time." She held out her palm, opening it to reveal a beautiful amethyst crystal on a silver chain.

"You take this. Please. It has been in my family, and now it comes to you. It will keep you safe."

My eyes wide, I didn't know what to say. It was so beautiful. I had seen such crystal amulets before, in Breslau, as a young girl. Many Romani people wore them.

Without giving me time to respond, she said, "I go now," picked up her battered suitcase, and turned toward the sleeping quarters door. In moments she was swept up by bustling crowd hurrying through the corridor.

Infused with good feelings, it took less than a minute to throw my meager belongings into my suitcase. There was nothing of value to put in there anyway, except my sketchpad and now the amethyst crystal.

I went over to help Liesel, who was cheerfully humming as she packed her belongings. I recognized the melody as "Wiegenlied," a Brahms lullaby my mother used to sing to me.

"That's such a pretty song, Liesel."

"My father used to sing that to me as a little girl. At bedtime."

I wanted to tell her that my mother did too, but I stopped myself. It was best left to her as a cherished memory between her and her father.

Liesel's suitcases, though well-traveled, were huge compared to mine. I was surprised that none of her things had been stolen during our voyage. I watched her press her clothes down to make room for one last dress and felt a twinge of jealousy. *Oh, what I would give to have even one outfit like hers. And just one pair of her stylish, well-made shoes.* As she latched the case, I thought, *Someday I will have clothes like that too.*

With suitcases in hand, we banged and bumped our way back down the crowded hallway, past the mess hall, and up the stairs for the last time. On the observation deck, I heard the familiar notes of the clarinet wafting through the air. As they emerged from their blue foundations, I could hear David's heartening song burst through the salty air, drawing me in and lifting me skyward.

He stood along the port side, and I saw that his audience had grown, encompassing people of all ages and many nationalities. Eyes closed, David elevated his clarinet as if aiming for the heavens.

I thought of taking out my sketchbook to record the sight but then decided not to. No sketch could ever capture it nor take the place of directly experiencing this moment.

Without a second thought for its safety, I dropped my suitcase next to Liesel's on the deck. Surrendering for the first time, I allowed her to pull me forward. We paused at the group's perimeter, where I had been content to merely watch before, noticing that today people were clapping and dancing as a group for the first time. Encouraged by the heavenly music, perhaps inspired by the majestic skyline before us, the passengers of the SS *Marine Flasher* had come back to life.

Here was the celebration I had hoped for ten days before. I supposed it had been reserved for now, at the very end of the long and tumultuous journey we had all shared. I suspected that for most of us, America had been just an idea—a fantastic dream—when we boarded. I smiled at the thought, newly aware that I was no different from any of the others. I had felt the same way too, all along.

"Come on, Rosel!" Liesel gleefully pulled me into the circle of celebration. I caught myself, for an instant worried that I might get in trouble with some hidden authority, and then laughed out loud as my eyes met Liesel's. Her fearless delight was contagious, and I began to join her dance. *Oh, what a feeling, to be liberated at last!*

Moved by Liesel's smiles and David's melody, I reveled in the outpouring of emotion. Recognizing the feeling of joy within me, I realized it hadn't been lost after all. In time with the music, allowing my arms and legs to express the powerful sense of freedom arising within, I felt the unfettered happiness of the headstrong little girl I used to be.

"Liesel, Rosel, we made it!" Kurt had joined our merry dance, a broad grin on his expressive face, head and shoulders above everyone else's. "To America!" he shouted, raising his hand in a mock toast.

"To America, Kurt!" I shouted back, giving him an exaggerated thumbs-up sign.

I looked over at David, his eyes still closed, both hands moving on his instrument as his melody soared upward. As he raised his clarinet toward the heavens, I was startled by what I saw beyond him. To my left, dwarfing our ship, was the colossal emerald statue of the woman I hadn't seen in over a decade. Holding her torch, welcoming all who had made passage, she had kept her promise. America had remembered me.

David's melody continued its heavenly ascent, taking all who were willing, as the *Marine Flasher* proudly steamed into New York Harbor. The seabirds sang in the sky above as we danced below. Out ahead, shining in the distance, was the childhood image I'd had so much difficulty remembering in my childhood. Welcoming me home, now in vivid detail, were the tallest, most awe-inspiring buildings imaginable.

My eyes caught Liesel's. And in that moment, all was right with the world, and everything good seemed possible again.

FRIDAY EVENING JULY 19, 1946

Borough of Queens, New York City

Although there were still some hours of daylight left, it didn't feel like it. The only light came from an old lamp with a weak bulb in it, casting an eerie, yellow-brown glow across the basement floor. As I looked across the room, with its haunting array of old furniture covered with dingy sheets, the scene felt like one of my nightmares back aboard the *Marine Flasher*. I was completely awake, however, suffocating in the only space the Wagners had offered me.

Sitting up in my narrow and uncomfortable cot, I propped myself against the wall in a room that was already threatening to become my prison. Next to me, on a nightstand I had made out of an overturned cardboard box, was the letter I had jotted to my family nearly two weeks before, aboard the *Marine Flasher*. It felt as if the words had been written in another world, in another lifetime.

I was planning on mailing it in a few days, perhaps on Monday. Not having sealed my letter yet, I wondered if I should add another few lines to update my family. Maybe a note about how I was doing with my surrogate family.

Dear Papa and Mutti, the Wagners are such despicable people! I burst into laughter, unconcerned whether Mr. and Mrs. Wagner heard me upstairs. I could never write that, even though it was the first thing that came to mind. I wouldn't want to worry my parents.

My Dearest Family,

As I write this note aboard the SS Marine Flasher, *my journey to America and a new life has begun. When you read this, you will know that I have arrived home, for I will be mailing my letter from New York. Oh how I long for that day!*

More to come soon, but for now, know that I am safe, encouraged, and determined to make a new way for myself in America. One day, you will join me there. Try to stay hopeful, as I know that day is coming.

Please do not worry; my angels are here with me. My love to all of you.

Herzlich,
Rosel

PS: Mutti, you will be happy to know my old marching shoes are now at the bottom of the English Channel!

Letting out a long, resigned sigh, I turned off my solitary lamp for the evening. Even though it was early, there was nothing else to do. I wasn't welcome upstairs unless I was invited, except if I had to use the bathroom or get a drink of water.

I lay awake for a while but soon drifted into another restless dream, back through a collage of flashing images that summed up the past week. Finally, the chain of images slowed, replaying the day of my arrival. My grand welcome to America had lost its luster minutes after I stepped off the *Marine Flasher.*

★   ★   ★

The Wagners had not shown up at New York Harbor when we docked. I had hoped they would be there, of course, but was not exactly surprised when they were not. As I stepped from the ship's departure ramp, amid throngs of celebrating people, it seemed as if everyone had a place to go. I watched David join a long line that was marked Jewish Aid Society. He waved when he saw me, his once exotic features now more common in the line where he was standing. At first I worried that he might be detained, but then I reminded myself that I was in New York. The war was over. More than likely there was a Jewish home already picked out for him.

David's face finally looked at peace. Giving him a return smile and an emphatic thumbs-up, I said a prayer for the angels to watch over him.

As I searched for two strangers who might be my aunt and uncle, I watched Liesel and Kurt's joyful celebration with their mother. They looked elated to see one another, and I overheard Kurt commenting on how much taller he was than his mother now. Liesel signaled to me to join them but then marched right over to take my hand and pull me into their family circle. She introduced me enthusiastically as her "wonderful friend" from the *Flasher*, and I blushed as her mother hugged me tightly. Seeing that I was still alone, they said they would wait with me until the Wagners arrived. I felt safe for the moment.

After some time, it became clear that the Wagners were not going to show up. Liesel offered for me to come home with them to New Jersey. My heart lifted, but it was not to be. An American immigration officer who had noticed earlier that I was alone and anxiously looking around, escorted me to the unaccompanied minors' line. Liesel scrawled her mother's address on a piece of paper and ran it over to me at the back of the line. Her last words before leaving were "So, my good friend, I will see you again, *ja*? New Jersey is not that far away from New York City, you know." We embraced, and when she began to tear up, she broke away.

Sad and worried—maybe even abandoned—I felt my fears magnify as I waited and waited in the slow-moving line. After minutes that felt like hours, I reached the immigration officer inside the customs building.

The officer seemed kind enough but was pointedly direct. "I'm sorry Miss Lengsfeld, but without a parent or guardian, we will have to refer you to the New York Children's Bureau."

He pointed to a little room to his rear, where I joined a handful of children who had traveled without parents or guardians aboard the *Flasher*. Anxious, wondering what would come next, I had been marked as a refugee all over again.

After a couple of hours' wait, we were introduced to a kind and very determined social worker assigned to help us. A slender young woman with a pleasant smile and beautiful auburn hair, she explained that her job was to help place non-Jewish refugee children in the homes of American relatives. Giving us each a firm handshake along with a gentle smile, she told us to call her Miss Roberta.

After taking down names, ages, and passport information, Miss Roberta walked us to temporary lodgings she had secured at a nearby hotel. As we walked, I noticed the confident, purposeful spring in her step, as well as her stylish, glossy-white shoes. She had seven charges, counting me, ranging in age from eight to fifteen. The other children all came in sibling pairs, a painful reminder of having left my own sister behind. We straggled along like a band of urchins, and I couldn't help but worry that if the Wagners were not found, I would be sent back to Germany.

Walking into the lobby of the stately hotel, my fear and apprehension were momentarily overtaken by its luxury. It was so clean and fresh smelling, with brilliant crystal lighting in the lobby. *They are putting us up here for the night?* I had been expecting someplace that looked more like a refugee camp.

Taking my first elevator ride, I found it to be a mixture of fun and apprehension—I had never been in such a tall building before. Up and up we went, the younger children giggling when the elevator's speed tingled their stomachs. Reaching the tenth floor, my heart raced as Miss Roberta opened the hotel room door, revealing several large rooms that were part of a connected suite that overlooked the bustling New York City avenues below. Through one of the large windows, Miss Roberta pointed to an imposing building down the street, one nonetheless dominated by the skyscrapers around it. She informed us that she would be walking us there each morning until our relatives were located. Although the day's commotion had rattled me, I tried to allow myself to relax in her presence. She had a calm and confident air about her. Maybe things would still work out if I remained by her side.

Miss Roberta had arranged for the hotel kitchen to send meals up to us. Soon a knock on the door signaled dinner's arrival. A friendly young man in a white uniform wheeled in an elegant cart draped with fresh linen. Each plate was covered with a shiny chrome lid. Raising one of the lids, the man grinned and said, "Voilà!" revealing a juicy hamburger with french fries on the side. The kids squealed with delight.

After we gobbled down our quintessential American meal, Miss Roberta wheeled the cart back outside the door. When she told us she was going home for the night, my heart fell to the pit of my stomach. I had thought she would be with us night and day until our homes were located. She said that with me being the oldest, I was to be in charge during the overnights. We were to stay put and not leave our room. Smiling at me, she handed me her card and told us she would be back at nine the next morning. The door closed behind her, leaving me with six squirrely children I did not know.

Once again, being seen as one of the adults didn't seem to be much of an honor. Fortunately, all the kids spoke English. I instructed them to take turns getting cleaned up in the bathroom, assigning each older child to help their younger brother or sister. I tried to keep them occupied with made-up games and storytelling while they were getting ready for bed. That was difficult because of their wide spread of ages and my tendency to revert back to German. Recalling my peers who rebuffed me for being too bossy back in Germany, I thought, at least these children seemed to like me.

I stayed up for a while with my sketchbook, sitting by the window and taking in the sights of the city. Sketching the outlines of the well-lit and majestic buildings all around us, I found myself once again becoming mesmerized by the city's musical street noise. Pounding out a lively rhythm, the frenetic traffic buzzed late into the night. It appeared that New York never slept. I so badly wanted to be part of that energy.

As I drew, I tried to reassure myself. I had made it this far—why would my angels arrange for me to be sent back? That couldn't be right. My angels were the ones who had made my destiny possible.

With each passing day, our motley collection of children waiting inside the Children's Bureau building grew smaller. The hours sitting in the building's lobby seemed endless. No one was allowed to leave, even at lunch; our boxed meals were delivered and eaten in the tiresome reception area. Miss Roberta brought in some children's games, and I had my sketchpad, but none of that really helped pass the time.

By Wednesday, there were just three of us left. Jeffrey and Lizzie had an aunt and uncle who were driving all the way from Wisconsin to get them; they were due to arrive tomorrow. I was already preparing myself for being alone again, the only one without a home, the only one still a refugee.

Sure enough, on day four, Jeffrey and Lizzie's aunt and uncle arrived from Milwaukee. I watched their aunt and uncle run to them in the waiting area, hugging them and handing each of them a present. I wanted to cry as they happily walked off together, but no tears would come.

Waiting, waiting, and more waiting. All Miss Roberta had to go on was the Wagners' post office box number in Queens. Mutti had written it down from memory and wasn't sure that the address she had given me was correct. Hour after hour, the day crept along, and by three o'clock, I had given up hope. Another day and an entire week had passed. All that remained now was for Miss Roberta to deliver the bad news that the Wagners could not be located. I pictured myself sadly boarding the *Flasher* for my return to Germany.

However, at four thirty, Miss Roberta entered the lobby, after an afternoon of detective work in the city. Trailing her was a middle-aged couple well-dressed in shades of black and gray. She had found the Wagners. They were older than I expected and very reserved. With a file in hand, Miss Roberta spotted me across the expansive room and waved to me with a smile. She motioned for them to follow her over to me, but they didn't seem to share her enthusiasm.

I told myself not to be pessimistic. Maybe they were just shy and intimidated by the formality of it all, like I was.

As my aunt and uncle approached, the hopefulness that remained within me evaporated. I could feel their reluctance to take me in just by scanning their faces.

Miss Roberta spoke first. "Rosemarie, I have good news for you. This is Mr. and Mrs. Wagner."

"Hello, Uncle Klaus." I smiled and offered Mr. Wagner my hand. I looked him in the eye and squeezed firmly, like Papa had taught me.

My uncle was a complete stranger to me. He did not say a word. Returning a weak, lifeless handshake, the kind I had always been warned about, his eyes skirted my face.

My first impression of my aunt Verna was that she looked a little like Mutti, though even shorter than her. I towered over her petite frame. At least my aunt spoke to me, albeit in a subdued tone. "It's nice to see you again, Rosel. You are nearly grown up. It's been such a long time."

Holding my arms out, I had to encourage her to embrace me, but my efforts were only met with an awkward pat on my back and a quick release. Her body was tense, and her eyes kept flicking back to her husband, as if she was seeking permission to interact with me. Was she afraid of him?

An awkward silence ensued. Mr. Wagner looked at his watch, tapping it demonstratively as if to say we were taking too long.

Miss Roberta gave a smile that to me appeared anything but happy. "Rosemarie, would you mind waiting here just a few more minutes? I need to take your aunt and uncle back to my desk to complete the paperwork."

I nodded. I wasn't even sure I wanted this to work out anymore.

The scene at Miss Roberta's desk across the room was hardly reassuring. She was almost arguing with my uncle, her arms gesturing in frustration as Mr. Wagner repeatedly shook his head. When Miss Roberta returned with papers signed and in hand, she looked perturbed, if not outright angry.

"So, Rosemarie, you will be leaving now with Mr. and Mrs. Wagner, for their home in Queens. I will be out to see you once a month, to check on how you are doing. The Wagners have agreed to enroll you in their local public high school, which doesn't start for a couple months yet."

The Wagners had stayed seated at her desk and were not even looking at me. "Yes, Miss Roberta. Thank you for helping me." The words came out flat because they weren't true. I really wanted to shout, *Please don't leave me with these people!*

I left the Children's Bureau office feeling cheated and uneasy. The Wagners barely acknowledged me as we walked to their car. Speaking German to each other, they made no effort to include me, and I trailed behind, feeling like an invisible child once again.

The Wagners' drab black car was not the fancy, colorful American vehicle I had once pictured in my mind's eye. To me, it looked more like one of those funeral cars. When Mr. Wagner opened the trunk to store my suitcase, I saw the big burlap bag he had laid out on the floor of the luggage compartment. He placed my suitcase inside it and tied off the top. *What on earth? Does he think I am carrying a plague or some other scourge?*

I sat alone in the back seat, biting on my lower lip to keep from saying something I would regret later. My aunt and uncle continued speaking German in the front seat. It sounded harsh and discordant from the onset, with Mr. Wagner talking to his wife as if she were a servant. Although he didn't even know me, he was already complaining about how their lives were going to have to change to accommodate me. He didn't care if I was listening and could understand his every word. I was a burden already, and I felt sure he wanted me to know it.

Driving through the crowded, noisy thoroughfares of New York City, I was further overwhelmed by the sights streaming by. The city streets stretched as far as my eyes could see in every direction. The buildings were massive. We soon climbed a towering bridge that made my stomach tickle. As I gaped at the swirling water below, I felt scared, insignificant in size and importance.

Two hours later we arrived at the Wagners' house in what a sign said was the Bayside section of Queens. Driving through an endless sea of concrete, stopping and starting in the relentless traffic, we had never left city pavement.

Parking his car in the street, Mr. Wagner opened the trunk for me, but that was all. Approaching the house, carrying my suitcase inside what seemed like a garbage bag, I was struck by the enormity of their residence. I had never seen such an expensive-looking house before. I wondered why they needed so much space, especially for a couple with no children.

Lagging behind, still feeling invisible, I bumped my way through the front door. There was no color anywhere about their house. No cheery decorations, no bright wallpaper or paint, not even some pretty flowers in a vase. They couldn't have cut any flowers from their yard anyway. Unlike the more modest houses on either side of them, there were not even welcoming flower gardens in the Wagners' front yard.

I paused inside the expansive entrance. It looked like the floor was made of gray marble, the ceilings raised like I had seen at the American Embassy. We walked down a long hallway, passing what appeared to be the main bedroom, which Mrs. Wagner entered, leaving me stranded with Mr. Wagner. More than uncomfortable with him already, I felt almost unsafe in his presence.

We then came to a smaller bedroom with an open door. I peeked inside the attractive slate-blue room, thinking we had reached my room. It looked like it had been freshly laid out for me, with a vanity and mirror, a set of makeup brushes, even some perfume and pretty soap atop some towels and linen. *Mrs. Wagner must have arranged all this for me. Maybe this isn't going to be so bad.*

As I took a step into the room, Mr. Wagner shook his head, steering me with his arm away from the bedroom's entrance. Pointing ahead, I saw a set of stairs at the end of the hall, leading downstairs. My heart sank.

Mr. Wagner told me to follow him, down the creaking stairs into a dark and musty-smelling basement. Feeling like I was in trouble, it reminded me of the time Papa had marched me down to the incinerator with my Huggy.

My sense of awe over the enormity of their house was replaced by the shock of seeing the squalid space reserved for me. Pointing to a rickety old cot against the wall, Mr. Wagner switched on a single lamp that only faintly lit half of the room, throwing unsettling shadows across the rest. *Depressing* wouldn't even begin to capture the feeling of the space.

"You will stay and sleep here. We will give you a list of chores each day. You will be respectful and do as you're told. We will call you when it is time for meals." Mr. Wagner turned and marched back up the stairs, firmly closing the door at the top. He had yet to smile or to call me by my name.

None of this made any sense. There was plenty of room on the main floor of their house. That blue bedroom could have been mine. I didn't understand. Why would they keep me hidden away in a dark basement, choking in this musty air? I had come ready to be of help and contribute to their household, to laugh and get acquainted with my relatives, and maybe even engage in some political discussions with my uncle, as I had with Papa. Instead, I was being locked away out of sight, a virtual prisoner in this abysmal basement.

Unpacking my much-mended, soiled belongings, I laid them out on my cot, wondering where I should store them. My aunt and uncle clearly had not prepared for me. There was no dresser anywhere, nor a chair or nightstand.

I looked around for something I could use for a bedside stand and perhaps some storage space for my few belongings. Against the far wall was what looked like an array of old furniture, covered in sheets, but I dared not touch them, already anticipating that Mr. Wagner would be upset if I disturbed anything.

I heard the basement door open again.

"Come up to the top of the stairs, please. *Komm schnell.* Right now, hurry up. I have something for you." Mr. Wagner's stiff voice again intimidated me, and for a moment I stood shocked and immobilized.

"*Schnell.* Hurry up now. No dawdling—I'm waiting."

"*Ja-ja*, I'm coming Mr. Wagner." Hastening up the basement steps, I saw the backlit silhouette of my uncle at the top. He was holding another burlap bag that appeared nearly full.

"We noticed that your clothes contain a horrid smell. *Scheusslich!* Mrs. Wagner has taken some time to collect some things for you from the attic. Go ahead and put these on. Then put all your old clothes and that awful blue dress back in this bag and bring it up to me."

I assumed that my aunt would wash my old clothes, but I quickly learned that would not be the case.

"Make sure you tie off the top of the bag when you are finished. I am going to put them in the trash tomorrow. *Mach schnell.*

"Mr. Wagner?" I already sensed that he didn't want me calling him Uncle Klaus. "These are all I have."

"They are filthy and embarrassing. There is no way to clean them. Now do as I say, and not another word."

I took the bag and headed back into my dungeon, an unwanted dog given scraps that I was supposed to be grateful for.

As I placed the sack of hand-me-downs on my folding bed, I shuddered as I took out its contents. Old underwear, an ugly black pants suit, stockings that were badly stretched and wouldn't cling. Beneath them were a few drab brown and black blouses, an oversized patchwork coat, and some hideous shoes way too big for me. It was hard to believe that Mrs. Wagner had saved these things, much less thought they were suitable to give to someone.

As I placed my old clothes from Germany into the bag, each one brought back a memory: utility shoes that I had worn on the *Flasher*, cotton nightclothes that had been patched and stitched so many times in the refugee camps, a fraying undershirt and two sets of underpants—all reminded me of how we had lost nearly everything. Finally, after removing my passport and the hidden bills still sewn inside the hem, I placed my blue dress in the bag too.

That dress had been through so much with me. I had expected this moment but had envisioned replacing my tired garments with fashionable new clothes from a fancy New York department store. The "new" clothes I had been given were merely someone else's old rags.

"Rosemarie! *Schnell!* I asked you not to dawdle."

Pushing my dress down and tying off the bag as instructed, I trudged back up the rickety stairs.

"*Danke.* I hope you appreciate what we are doing for you."

"*Bitte, Herr* Wagner." It was hard to say it politely, the sarcastic thoughts burning inside me, so I quickly turned and headed back downstairs. I heard Mr. Wagner close the door without even as much as a "You're welcome."

★   ★   ★

I grimaced as I awoke from my nightmare, the first since I stepped off the *Marine Flasher*. I told myself not to dwell on it. Who wouldn't have nightmares staying in the home of this wretched couple, being forced to sleep down here in this gloomy basement?

As far as I could tell without any windows, it was still the middle of the night. Sitting up on my wobbly cot, alone in my cell, I already knew the Wagners' house would never be home. These people couldn't possibly be part of my destiny. I turned on the lamp, thinking I needed a glass of water before returning to bed. I saw the slip of paper that held Liesel's address on the overturned box that had become my nightstand. I thought of what she would do in my predicament.

That was easy to imagine. *Rosel, you do not have to put up with any of this!* She would tell me I needed to find a way to get away from them and back to the pulsating American world outside, the one that had been promised me.

I tiptoed upstairs to use the bathroom and get a glass of water. But I had been told to stay out of the kitchen after dinner. I couldn't be chastised for using the bathroom, though, could I?

Careful to remain quiet as a mouse, I headed down the hall for the bathroom. The clock on the wall said it was only 11:30, much earlier than I had thought. Fortunately, judging by the snores coming from their bedroom, Mr. and Mrs. Wagner were already asleep. Gently closing the bathroom door, I took a long, refreshing drink from the faucet. It had been years since it had been safe to do that in Germany.

Satisfied with my fill of cool water, I quietly opened the bathroom door, poised to sneak back down the hall. Closing the door ever so gently behind me, I heard something.

What is that? It sounds like a woman's voice, softly giggling. And it's coming from the guest bedroom. Now a man's voice, also laughing quietly. I hurried my way back down the hall, making as little sound as possible. I reached the basement stairs just before the door to the blue bedroom opened. Out of sight on the top step, I took a quick peek back down the hall, only to see Mr. Wagner leaving the room. *What on earth? Who stays in that room? And what was Mr. Wagner doing in there so late at night?*

Warily heading down the stairs, trying to avoid the creaky spots, I thanked God that Mr. Wagner had not seen me.

MONDAY MORNING, JULY 22, 1946

Borough of Manhattan, New York City

As I walked the short distance to the bus stop, the sultry New York sun could not put a damper on the wonderful mood stirring within me. Nothing was going to keep me from my mission today. Not Mr. Wagner's sour mood this morning nor the ugly, ill-fitting, hand-me-down green dress I was wearing, given to me by Mrs. Wagner. And certainly not that strange scene two nights ago, when I had come upstairs for a drink of water.

I had learned the following morning that the Wagners had a boarder who stayed in the blue bedroom. Her name was Maria. I had been coolly introduced at breakfast. Mrs. Wagner told me that Maria helped do the books for their business, a painting company that was apparently booming with all the construction going on in New York City. Somewhere in her twenties, Maria was intriguing but had kept mostly to herself so far. I would keep quiet too if I had such a secret to protect. I had seen the way they looked at each other when Mrs. Wagner wasn't around.

Whatever Maria's relationship with Mr. Wagner, I didn't much care. That was their problem, if they even saw it as that. All I was concerned about now was how to get out of that awful house.

Today I set out to teach myself the bus routes. I had a destination in mind, in Manhattan. As I walked to the bus stop a block from the Wagners' house, I marveled at all the colorful and inviting flower gardens in front of my neighbor's homes. Some had American flags proudly hanging out front. I could hear the all-enveloping, robust sounds of that unique big band music coming from an open window somewhere nearby.

Away from the Wagners for the day, I was already relishing my independence. I had told them I would be back by three, in plenty of time to do my chores before dinner. Handing the driver a nickel, I took a seat behind the driver, remembering for a second that I used to do that back in Germany for safety. I relished the sights along the way, as the bus meandered its way onto Manhattan Island. America was loud, colorful, fast, and upbeat. The Wagners seemed like such an anomaly among the happy bustle.

I got a whiff of exhaust fumes as I stepped off the bus and onto the busy city sidewalk. Surveying my surroundings as the city bus pulled away, taking in a breath of sultry summer air, I could already feel the magnificent energy of the city. People scurried everywhere, each looking like they were on a mission, in their colorful outfits and well-cut business suits. The door of a nearby diner opened, and out wafted the smell of breakfast sausage. Out in the street, the beeping of taxi horns told people to watch out. The sights, smells, and sounds created a hectic atmosphere for sure, but the city still danced to an American rhythm. I was glad to be back.

Following the directions given me by the bus driver, I headed east, toward the main post office on Manhattan's lower east side. Soon absorbed into the throng of busy pedestrians, I felt a part of things, and finally free.

Although I hadn't told the Wagners yet and wasn't sure how I would do so, I had already made my decision to leave them. I would not be dissuaded. I had not survived a catastrophic war and nearly two years as a refugee to be stuck with an aunt and uncle who did not feel remotely like my family. They clearly didn't want me around. Mr. Wagner would certainly be happy for me to leave, although I wondered if he even knew what happiness was.

Focused and resolute, I walked down the sidewalk that paralleled the busy avenue. I felt like skipping along to the beat of the city traffic. The effervescent American culture was such a far cry from war-torn Germany. I had left behind a country of grays, stark and foreboding, with harsh rules and a faint pulse. A country where people didn't look at you and no longer smiled, where faith and joy had been crushed. I was now in a land of sunburst colors, an optimistic place full of hope and dreams, a nation with a loud drumbeat for a heart. In Germany I could barely breathe. In America I wondered if I could breathe fast enough.

People were expressive here, so self-assured and determined, that they seemed almost aggressive, but in such a good way. They appeared to know what they wanted from life and how to go after it. And many Americans seemed generous, ready to extend a helping hand. *These people just love being alive*, I mused. *Well, all except my aunt and uncle.*

The Wagners served to remind me of the way things had been back in Germany. They spoke formal German in their home, read German-language newspapers and magazines, and cooked only German food. I was expected to speak only when spoken to. Mr. Wagner rarely spoke spontaneously, other than barking commands to me, like I was a dog or his servant. Mrs. Wagner—I could hardly believe she was Mutti's sister— wasn't a whole lot better. She acted like a subservient maid and never stood up for herself or for me. At least she called me by my name, though.

I thought of the envelope I held in my hand, addressed to my family back in Germany. I didn't want to tell them of my decision to leave the Wagners just yet. I would wait until I had found another family to live with or at least a job to support myself. I pictured myself living with some kind, nurturing family, like the Naborczyks, the Polish family who lived next door to the Wagners. Mrs. Naborczyk had welcomed me with a tray of wonderful oatmeal-and-chocolate cookies the day after I arrived. She had also asked me if she could call on me from time to time, to babysit her two young kids.

Reaching the intersection, I stopped and waited for the light to change, my mind still wandering. Why couldn't the Wagners have been like the Naborczyks? I wondered why my aunt and uncle needed to be the way they were. They too had come to America seeking a better way of life, though it had been well before the rise of Adolf Hitler and his menacing Third Reich. But they had not adapted to America or embraced the American vitality. Maybe their identity was too engrained, and they couldn't shake it. Or maybe they didn't want to.

A taxi driver beeped his horn several times, short, friendly toots to remind me to cross the street. I startled briefly before waving to the driver as I stepped into the crosswalk. He nodded back and smiled.

Ahead, the impressive U.S. postal building stood proudly, vibrant and humming with activity. It seemed to embody all of my expectations of America. Surrounded by a well-manicured flower garden, at ten in the morning, the post office was already full of life.

An older man entering the building smiled as he held the door for me. "Good morning, miss."

"Good morning. Thank you, sir." I was finding it increasingly easier to smile and talk with people I didn't even know.

"You're welcome." It struck me how surprisingly easy it was just to be nice to people.

Inside, I joined a crowded line of talkative people. *Good morning, Esther. Nice day, isn't it? . . . Hey, Tony, the Yankees won again last night! You going to catch a game this week? . . . Oh, say, Jimmy, are you going back to the office after this? Can you tell the receptionist . . .* The Americans I'd encountered seemed happy even going to work. Papa was right; every day in America was cause for celebration. I wondered for a moment why the Wagners did not embrace this vibrant culture. Why did they choose to immigrate here in the first place?

Moving slowly up the line, I spotted a bulletin board to my left crammed full of notices affixed with little pins. How trusting Americans were, to put their personal needs and wants on view in a public space. Curious, I paused for a moment, surveying the array of ads and messages. Dog walking for hire, music lessons, furniture for sale, moving help wanted, typing services—the postings went on and on, reflecting a diversity of needs and wants that seemed uniquely American. One handwritten note grabbed my attention, squeezed into a little spot near the bottom of the board.

Wanted: Live-in au pair for delightful little boy and his soon-to-be infant sister or brother. Warm, friendly, welcoming family. Flexible hours with time off. Please inquire only in writing to the address below.

With my heart thumping excitedly, I took a pencil from my hand-me-down purse and wrote down the details on the back of my bus route guide. I noticed that the address was in Connecticut, and I wondered why they had chosen to place their advertisement here, in Manhattan.

Looking up, I saw that the line had moved on without me. The folks behind me had waited patiently while I had written down the address.

When I reached the front of the line, a gentlemanly postal clerk with kind, hazel eyes under handsome brown eyebrows greeted me from behind the counter. "Lovely day out today, isn't it? How can I help you?"

"Yes, it is, such a beautiful day!" I replied. The clerk's energy was infectious. "Just one overseas stamp today, please."

"Certainly. Where is your letter going, miss?"

"To my family, back in Europe." Tentative for a moment, I did not want to acknowledge that they lived in Germany. It wasn't going to matter, though. My accent was a dead giveaway.

I handed him my letter. After inspecting the address, he looked over a page of new postage stamps. "I'm so glad the war is over. Now we can all get back to building this great country of ours."

His words struck me. *He said "ours." I am included! He sees me as a fellow American.*

"Yes, I believe we will," I exclaimed, happy to finally use the word *we* in the same context.

The clerk continued to peruse the collection of stamps, running a thick finger from row to row. Without looking up, he kept the conversation going. "Where are you originally from, if you don't mind me asking? You sound maybe Polish? I am Polish; well, my mom is. My dad is Italian."

My amazement continued. Back in Germany, cultures rarely mixed, and when they did, one certainly did not announce it. During Hitler's reign, having even one Jewish or Polish grandparent could get you detained and even sent to the camps.

"I am an American. I was born here."

"But you have a Polish accent, yes?" I could tell he was curious and meaning no harm.

"Well, my parents are from Silesia, in eastern Germany. We got trapped there, when Hitler closed the borders. But I was born here, in the city, some years before the war." I was surprised at how open I felt I could be with someone who was a complete stranger two minutes ago.

"You sound just like my mother, from western Poland, near the city of Poznan. Maybe you know it by its German name, Posen . . . it's in Silesia."

I nodded. I recognized the name of Posen. It was not far from Breslau.

"You look like you might be Polish too. Let's see, that will be five cents . . ."

I was daydreaming. The clerk's comments about me looking to be of Polish heritage had completely thrown me. It was kind of funny after worrying so much about appearing German.

"Five cents, please." He waited patiently, seeing that I had momentarily lapsed and was somewhere else.

"Oh, I am sorry, excuse me."

"It's quite all right. Not a problem at all, miss. I can only imagine what it's like to be in your shoes, without your family. You must have a lot on your mind."

I gave the clerk a nickel and watched him put an interesting stamp on my letter. It was a picture of Franklin D. Roosevelt, with the caption "Freedom of Speech and Religion, from Want and Fear." It shouted freedom, it shouted protection, and it shouted America. The clerk then wrote below my family's address in big, bold letters, "American-Occupied West Berlin," which he underlined before stamping it.

I grinned when I saw the words *West Berlin*. Three months before we had visited the consulate, my family had found their way out of Soviet-controlled East Germany, now part of the Soviet Union. We had been authorized to live with my aunt Johanna in the American-controlled side of Berlin. My family was fortunate—we had my aunt Johanna's home to go to on the American side.

Remaining polite, but probably wanting to get the line moving again, the postal clerk cleared his throat to regain my attention. "Your letter should arrive in about three weeks. I hope you will be able to get your family over here. Our country has plenty of work these days for people immigrating. Good luck to you! I hope you have a good day."

"Thank you, sir." As I walked away from the service counter, I immediately wished that I'd replied more enthusiastically, but I was still lost in my thoughts. I glanced at the notice on the bulletin board again, making sure I had the address right. Double-checking, I realized that I had initially skimmed over the words. *That position is for an au pair, not a babysitter.* I heard Liesel's voice inside my head and knew that she wouldn't think twice before telling me, "It's yours for the taking, Rosel. Go after it!"

Back outside, my thoughts wandered again as I made my way back to the bus stop. *I looked and sounded Polish to the postal clerk. And he would know, because his mother is Polish. And Posen, that does sound familiar. But how could that be in Poland?* I made a mental note to find the answer the next time I went to read the newspapers at the city library.

A clock on an ornate lamppost reminded me of my promise to the Wagners. Three o'clock wasn't far enough away. My good mood slipped away; it was almost time to return to my cell.

I resented going back. I tried to summon a measure of self-confidence, telling myself that I was in charge of my own destiny. *I just need to make it to my sixteenth birthday, so I can be legally emancipated. I can then leave that awful house, forever.* Well, provided I had a new home and a job and could convince Miss Roberta that I would remain in school. I exhaled hard; that was a lot to accomplish in just a couple months.

In no hurry to catch the bus for Queens, I walked past the bus stop, drawn by what I could see just a few steps down the long city block. It was the start of Manhattan's business district, with rows of impressive stores and their attractive display windows.

Reaching inside my ugly brown purse, I felt a surge of happy relief when I found the small wad of American money now folded inside my passport. *Still right here, safely tucked away.* I paused for a few seconds, realizing my mother's quiet, unassuming wisdom, and the journey those bills had taken alongside us. Knowing that money would be worthless during the war— even seen by the Nazis as contraband—Mutti had bravely and secretly protected our leftover American money from our trip over, totaling eighteen dollars. She must have never lost faith that we would someday return home. Those bills had endured what we had endured. They had survived what we had survived. Always by my side aboard the *Flasher*, they were now home too.

I passed by the freshly cleaned windows and brightly decorated displays. I stopped at a clothing store that had an array of new shoes in the window. *Oh my word, there they are, those shiny, round-toed black shoes Liesel was wearing aboard the* Flasher!

Ever since I had seen her dressed in them, I had longed for those shoes. And now, here they were, waiting for me on the other side of the store window.

They are so beautiful. Shall I go inside? Oh, my dear angels, I pray I can afford them. As excited as I was, I didn't want to get my hopes up. They were probably going to be too expensive.

As I entered the store, heart pounding, my eyes were eagerly met by those of a dark-haired, impeccably dressed man who looked to be about the same age as Papa. Maybe he was the store's owner?

"Excuse me, sir, those shoes in the window, the shiny black ones with the buckles? Do you carry my size?"

"Oh, you mean the Mary Janes? They're very popular, stylish without being too bold. We just got a shipment in. I am certain we have your size. Would you like to try a pair on?"

"Yes, please. May I?" Too late, I caught my naïve question and wished it back, but the salesman kindly brushed it off.

"Why, of course, dear, that is why we are here, to serve you! I am David. David Silverman, owner of Silverman Shoes and Fashions. And you? You are . . . ?"

My mind flashed back to David and his clarinet, and it took me a second to respond.

"My name is Rosel . . . I mean Rosemarie. Rosemarie Lengsfeld."

I braced myself, waiting for comments on my accent or my German-sounding last name. But none came.

"Pleased to meet you." Mr. Silverman smiled again, warmly. "These are our most popular shoes for young women."

Kindly gesturing to a nearby leather-cushioned bench, he continued. "Please. Allow me to get your measurements."

"Oh, sir? I guess I should ask first. How much are they?" My heart was throbbing in my chest.

"Well, they are not cheap. They are very well made, in Missouri. Well-made and very durable. They will last you years, unless of course you decide to grow some more." Mr. Silverman's warm smile was as captivating as those shoes.

I cautioned myself before any more excitement could take root. I was almost certain they were going to cost too much. *"They are not cheap,"* he'd said. I readied my excuse that I would have to come back another time, which might well mean never.

"Let's see here, they just came in, so I am not quite sure . . . " He checked the inventory list.

"Ah. Here it is. They are $7.95, and that includes the tax."

Thank heavens, I have plenty, more than enough! But is it worth spending my precious money on them? I don't even have a regular job yet.

"That's just fine." The words came out calmly, but I wanted to scream with delight at the thought of my first luxury in America.

"So, if you have the time, let me get your measurements real quick. Don't worry—this will take just a minute." Mr. Silverman motioned for me to sit down upon the well-polished bench.

"That's fine. I am in no hurry." It felt good to say that breezy sentence out loud. *Why should I care if I am late? The Wagners are not part of my destiny. They will be grumpy whether I am back on time or not. I would much rather stay here in Manhattan for the rest of the day.*

I was relieved to take off those unsightly brown shoes given to me by Mrs. Wagner. They were so big they looked like clown shoes.

Kneeling in front of me, the shop lights shining on his fashionably cut hair, Mr. Silverman placed my foot inside something that looked like an adjustable wooden ruler. I had never seen such a clever contraption before.

"Uh-huh, let's see now . . . six, maybe six and a half, yes? Let's go with six and a half, in case you grow a bit more." I thought of my old marching shoes, with the tips unstitched so I could still wear them.

He measured my other foot. "Uh-huh, yes that appears right. Six and a half."

"Sir, that can't be right, that's so small . . ."

"No . . . that's right. And it's a common size, so I am certain we have those shoes in stock. I will be right back."

Six and a half? That isn't correct. Then it dawned on me. *Silly me, I am not in Europe anymore! Those are American measurements.*

I thought I would burst with joy when Mr. Silverman came back with the shoebox and opened it at my feet. I couldn't take my eyes off those shoes. So elegant and just for me? I could not believe it. I read the Mary Jane label on the outside of the box to stamp it into my memory.

My new shoes! My American shoes! Oh, how I wish my family were here to see this. I reached down to put them on, but they were already in Mr. Silverman's hands.

"Allow me, miss." He gently placed my left foot in its shoe, then the right, using a small metal gadget I had never seen before. And I had never felt shoes so comfortable. Like royalty, I imagined.

He stood and extended a hand to help me up. "Here, walk around a bit. There are floor mirrors about the store so you can see how they look. They sure are sharp-looking on you. Very stylish, and good walking shoes. How do they feel?"

"They feel so . . ." As I walked a few steps forward, I searched for just the right word, finding it in German and then translating it back into English. "Luxurious."

"I am glad. Shall I ring them up for you?"

"Yes, please." I opened my purse, pulled out my ten-dollar bill, and handed it to him without hesitation. I would be getting about two dollars back. I calculated how much I would have left, adding in the remaining one-dollar bills still inside my passport.

"Please, Miss Rosemarie, feel free to walk around a bit; you don't have to take them off just yet."

As he took my money and the shoebox back to the cash register, I watched another employee dressing a mannequin in the display window. *Wow, that dress is beautiful!* A bright-yellow gingham with cute little blue-and-white blossoms, the fabric reminded me of the Edelweiss flowers I had seen when I was little, on a family trip high up in the Alps.

The employee pulled the dress taut on the mannequin and then stepped back to check her work. "Isn't this gorgeous? It would look so pretty on you, with your new shoes. And it's a good price for such a nice dress, $8.99."

I stepped up to the display and let the smooth, beautiful material run through my fingers. I thought of Liesel. The dress was too bold and too fancy for me, but it sure would look good on her.

Arriving at my side with the Mary Jane box, Mr. Silverman motioned for me to sit back down. "Here, allow me to help you. I will put your new shoes back in the box for you to take home."

"No, thank you." I didn't need to spend any time thinking about it; those big old shoes from Mrs. Wagner belonged in the trash.

"I think I will just keep these on and wear them home."

"Ah . . . good choice! I would do the same with such gorgeous new shoes. Very well."

I had almost blurted out an additional thought, that the Wagners would be mad if I came back without the shoes they had given me. But then I remembered my uncle putting my clothes from Germany out in the trashcan.

"Mr. Silverman, you can just throw the old ones out. I won't be wearing them again."

"Happy to do so for you. Anything else for you today?" I wondered if he had seen me eyeing that dress in the window.

"I think that's it, at least for today. Thank you."

"Very well. We will see you again next time."

I thought about it for a second but shook my head as I approached the door. *If only that dress was blue. But yellow? That color is very striking. Beautiful, yes, but just too bold for someone like me.*

As I opened the door to exit, I stopped, surprising myself. Looking back over my shoulder, my eyes sought Mr. Silverman's.

"Oh, sir, Mr. Silverman?"

He looked up, his eyes twinkling. "Please, call me David. Yes?"

"I'll take that dress too."

*You may not control all the events that happen to you,
but you can decide not to be reduced by them.*

—MAYA ANGELOU

SUNDAY, APRIL 25, 2021

East Lansing, Michigan

I stand behind my old but reliable friend, my painting easel, excited and ready to affix my canvas and chose the colors that will compose my palette. A warm, sweetly scented breeze drifts through my open patio doors, whispering that another winter has gone by. Like sand falling through an hourglass, where has all the time gone?

My journey through my past is over now, its memories inked upon pages that will endure long after I am gone. As *American Shoes* reaches completion, I have been tasked with writing this epilogue, a reflection upon my life and all that has transpired within it.

Initially unsure about what to write, I recalled the many detailed and inspiring comments from our advance readers. Most of them wrote that they wanted to know what happened to me once I stepped off the *Marine Flasher* and resumed my life in America. How had my life unfolded? What blessings did I receive? How had my life experiences forged and shaped my life? And finally, perhaps most importantly, what had the writing of my story taught me, leading to the life lessons that I now want to share?

It was abundantly clear from their comments that the majority of our early readers were hoping for a happy ending to my life story, one in which everything worked out, America's promise was fulfilled, and all the dark tones that had been my childhood palette in war-torn Germany had been overcome. One reader had come right out and said it, that she was hoping for a happy American fairy tale, if you will. But such endings rarely if ever occur in real life, unless you are at Disneyland or absorbed in some uplifting movie. Although my life in America has contained a multitude of blessings, it has been far from an idyllic fairy tale. Allow me to try to explain.

As most people saw and may still see it, I made it in America, by all discernible standards. Working my way through my teenage years as an au pair for two wonderful families, the Salters and then the Starretts, I managed to finish high school, raise a family with three children, and attain two university degrees, all of which led to a successful career as an early childhood educator and teacher.

My parents and sister finally joined me, in 1951, some five years after I arrived in New York on my own. Mr. David and Mrs. Eileen Starrett surprised me one morning by offering to sponsor my family, even offering my family an apartment and Papa a job at Mr. Starrett's typewriter manufacturing company in Hartford, Connecticut. I can still remember that day clearly—there I was, a proud young American woman, jumping up and down like an excited schoolgirl, so I could see over the heads of the people in front of me, watching their ship came into New York Harbor. Oh, what a grand and joy-filled day that was!

A couple years later, Papa, Mutti, and Eleonore were granted American citizenship, their American dreams finally materialized after so much hardship. Though Papa never fully recovered from the trauma of war, his essence did slowly resurface over the years while building a life in the United States. This would have not been possible if not for my mother and my sister sacrificing so much of their personal lives to help bring my father back to the present. They made it possible for him to begin to enjoy life again—all while I was away at school.

In 1953, I married a medical student studying to be a physician—a young man named Walter from Brooklyn. He was like me, an American born to immigrant parents. We attended the University of Iowa together, where Walter received his medical degree and I my bachelor's degree in childhood education.

We started married life dreadfully poor, but after earning our degrees and starting our careers, we eventually tasted material wealth—living in a beautiful Southern California home, later a picturesque home overlooking Lake Michigan, and now the lovely condominium in which I reside. I have lived what I can easily call a privileged lifestyle, so much so that I occasionally feel guilty.

At ninety-one years of age, I can look back and feel grateful. My three children have all become successful adults with families of their own, each reflecting a different quality I can proudly claim as emanating from their upbringing. My son has my creative and artistic leanings, my older daughter my interest in childhood education, and my younger daughter my passionate and determined spirit. Although their lives have been met with bumps and bruises that come with any life, I am so very proud of them.

I count six grandchildren, four of whom live nearby. I am blessed to have been a part of nurturing their childhoods, having taught four of them inside my Montessori classrooms. Oh, how wonderful it was to see their bright and inquisitive smiles brighten my world each day, and for so many years. They are all grown up now and have brought me the additional joy of three great-grandchildren, who light my world with their smiles alone.

I have traveled the globe and explored so many of the world's rich cultures and heritages—even a few times with my children. My adventures are remembered in the scores of oils and watercolors that grace my condominium walls. For alongside my career, I became an accomplished artist, like my uncle Alfred, my works still housed in galleries and office buildings across Michigan.

Yes, I have received so many blessings in America. Like I used to say during my youth, "On my good days, I felt I could do it all." Looking at my life story and what I had accomplished and received, how could I complain? It seemed as if I indeed did it all.

People who know me believe that I have managed to put the past behind, trusting that I long ago overcame that most wicked time in our world's history now, some seventy-five years behind me. Because so many years have passed, most assume that I have come to terms with the pain of the war and its ghosts and the hurt that consumed most of my childhood.

But as I write my epilogue, it is not that simple. Nor is it easy to simply focus on my blessings. The ugly truth is that even after all my good fortunes in America, I have to some extent remained mired in the darkness that was Nazi Germany, its menacing and unyielding grip shackling me long after that evil regime was destroyed. Year after year, decade after decade, the damage of war and its hate continued to weigh me down, causing me to question if I would ever be able to free myself. Facing the horrible memories and truths of war, I have constantly struggled with the fear that I would emotionally or spiritually disintegrate if I tried to push any of it out.

It seemed necessary for nearly the entirety of my adult life to wall off the memories and lock them up inside some dark, well-protected chamber in the back of my mind. By my eighty-fifth year, I had all but resigned myself that my memories should remain closed off forever, banished to the past, never to be revisited, never to return. That seemed the best thing to do, regardless of the emotional cost. Most times, it seemed like the only thing I could do.

The telltale symptoms that came with my repression followed me, like some disease I could never fully shake. The unstable and forlorn moods, the sleepless nights, the sudden jumps and startles to unexpected sounds, the pervasive anxiety that something dreadful was always about to happen. Unwanted bristling in response to invitations for a warm hug or simple emotional closeness served to remind me of my still open wound preventing me from feeling whole.

Worst of all, I had not cried a single tear since the last year of the war, the day my poor father was marched off to a war he wanted no part of. I put on a brave face, maybe a blank face, and detached myself.

No one really saw the warnings, because I hadn't ever told anyone about my childhood in much detail or with any sense of importance or urgency. Oh, sure, I gave many people snippets of my life during the war when they asked, usually shared to test the waters of whomever I was with or to back them off from more questions and discussions I didn't want to have. "Those were tough years, but I learned a lot," I would say. Or, "I don't remember very much of it. I was just a little girl," and promptly changed the subject. When people noticed my avoidance and cornered me, I would slam the door shut with a joke that was never funny: "I used up all my tears during the war."

It slowly became apparent to me, as the years rolled along, that my protective strategy to banish my past came with a great cost. For in my efforts to cast out the pain of my childhood, I inadvertently locked up all my other feelings too. Joy, happiness, serenity, and spontaneity were also, to a great extent, walled off along with my pain. Locking up the demons of war was tantamount to making a deal with the devil.

It wasn't as if I didn't try to make peace with my ghosts. I went to counseling and read many books about it. In my early fifties, when working on my master's degree, I sought psychotherapy after experiencing surges of debilitating anxiety while completing my studies. An older therapist gave me a diagnosis of war-induced posttraumatic stress disorder, a categorical, descriptive explanation where all my puzzle pieces finally seemed to fit. Yet that label, along with its cold diagnostic number, only served to make me feel more stigmatized, reinforcing my feeling that I was defective or had even done something wrong. How could a single, damning diagnostic number reduce me to a set of uncomplimentary characteristics that summarized the whole of who I was?

After nearly nine decades upon this earth, I had all but convinced myself that I would never heal. The war robbed me of my most fundamental humanity, the ability to grieve, and to properly mourn. Now it seemed too late. I would have to carry my suffocating burden until the end.

All I ever wanted was to finally cry, be comforted, and for once, be at peace.

By the grace of the divine, *American Shoes* came along. I remember that snowy winter's day six years ago, when Garrett burst into my living room to tell me we were going to write a book together. I was happy and excited about it at first, thinking it would take a few months and provide a chance for my only son to better understand me. I thought our writing time together would be fun, an hour or two each day, naïvely ferreting out the happier times of my life. At the end of a few months, our writings would culminate in a fifty-page, pocket-sized memoir that we would print and bind on our own and only distribute to friends and our family.

My, oh my, was I wrong. Garrett soon had other ideas, bigger and grander than I ever imagined. Intrigued, I followed along, not knowing where it all might lead.

It wasn't evident at first, because we started our interviews during brighter days—the few happy years of my early childhood. But as my story unfolded, my biographical journey soon became a riveting nightmare, a roller-coaster ride through all that I had banished inside my mind. It seemed as if I had to wade through endless darkness without ever seeing any light to guide me. I told Garrett more than once that I didn't want to go on. But I was already too deep into it to turn back. The doors barricading my past had been unlocked and opened, the painful memories streaming out.

If it wasn't excruciating enough for me to face my past, I had taken my son, positioned as my storyteller, down into the depths of my despair with me. Garrett had virtually become me as our book developed, after his fiancée, Lindsay, rather brilliantly converted my story to a first-person narrative. As I unearthed more and more memories, Garrett soon seemed to be living inside my mind, virtually adopting my persona at will. He became so good at it that when I reviewed the manuscript drafts, I often couldn't tell where my actual words left off and his began.

Garrett's portrayal of my wartime story went well beyond documenting the events of my childhood. In his determination to walk in my shoes, he experienced bouts of depression, sleepless nights, and anxiety attacks that seemed to come out of nowhere. Months later, he confided that he had been experiencing a recurring, terrifying nightmare of being trapped in the Dresden bombing raids alongside me. He said that being inside *American Shoes* had conjured up the same fear and sense of dread that one of his favorite books and movies, *War of the Worlds*, had evoked in him as a boy. Inside that story, an unknown and cataclysmic terror was approaching, sight unseen, from just beyond the horizon. Forewarned by the alien invaders' dreadfully unnerving sound, there was no time or way for Earth's innocent people to escape.

I could certainly relate, replacing the aliens with Nazis and exchanging the movie's haunting sound effects for air raid sirens. For me, *The War of the Worlds* had actually happened.

The way I saw it, Garrett had entered hell—my hell—in order to understand me better, in order to capture the feel and essence of what I had lived through. When I told him that, attempting to acknowledge my appreciation for his compassion, he responded with a most unexpected reply. He said he had entered hell to try to pull me out.

Though I thought I would collapse under the weight of it all, my son would not allow me any real retreat. "We can't turn back now, Mom. Come on—there's light ahead, just around the corner. We can make it." With his encouragement, I pushed forward. Maybe he saw something that I didn't.

I wasn't sure at first, but slowly, quietly, unevenly, I began to feel a change coming from deep inside of me.

I could remember the day I began to heal. It was around this same time last year, in the early spring. Reading one of Garrett's countless drafts to help him with the never-ending rewrites, I documented the moment, with a quick pencil note, in the margins of my recollections of the Dresden bombings: "Garrett, writing about the war isn't bothering me so much anymore. It doesn't seem so personal. I think I am healing. Maybe I have made it through?"

When Garrett came by later that day to retrieve my edits, I showed him my note, without fully recognizing its significance. Then something amazing happened, something that I was not prepared for. For the first time in over seventy-five years, I cried.

It wasn't much at first. I could feel my eyes well up, perhaps barely even noticeable to anyone but me. But then my voice cracked, and my bottom lip quivered. Fighting it off, I put on my brave face, as I had so many times before.

Although I tried to play it down, Garrett noticed. He put his arm around me, and soon tears rolled down my face. My tears. "I am so happy for you, Mom. This is the first time in my life I have seen you cry. Yeah, I agree, I think you may have made it through."

Overwhelmed, I remember that I couldn't respond. Instead, my angels sent me a welcoming shiver up and down my spine, reminding me that they had never left me, telling me I was on the right path.

★　★　★

With my easel now ready to begin my next painting, I look out upon the delightful day going on outside my open patio door. I realize inspiration is all around me. As the season changes once more, the greens of summer are being replaced with the crimson and gold hues of fall. I hear my neighbors' children happily playing hide-and-seek amid the falling leaves out back. A bright-red cardinal lands upon my bird feeder. The sunshine streams across my coffee table, finding an old childhood photograph of me that my granddaughter enlarged and enhanced with pastel watercolors. I can tell myself to be grateful—and finally feel it.

Today I see my blessings in new light. The ghosts of my past are easier to accept now. Though not entirely disposed, most of the shame, anger, anxiety, and festering guilt that came with the war years is dissipating. Finally unshackled, I am able to look ahead, in peace, toward the future and all that it may bring.

My time on this earth has given me an abundance of experiences, good and bad, joyful and sorrowful, and everything in between. My life has been such an amazing journey, a most incredible ride, one that I must accept as uniquely mine.

Many different people have asked me, in so many different ways, the same question. How did I become a compassionate, empathic person, after all the war had wrought upon me? When I now tell people what I went through during the war, they often pause and are visibly affected. Some want to hear the story; others grimace and want to change the subject immediately. Some see the dilemma and ask existential questions such as "What is the best way to deal with the memories? Accept them and bring them into the light? Or try to squelch them, locking them away in impenetrable boxes that should never be opened?"

For me, the answer is now clear. The ghosts cannot survive if they are brought into the light.

Mutti used to tell me that everything happens for a reason in this life. Quoting her own version of Ecclesiastes, she often told me, *"Everything happens in due season, under heaven above."* I didn't entirely understand this in my younger years, but I think I do now.

What I can tell you is that every one of my experiences, traumatic, happy, sad, or indifferent, came back, sometimes in disguised form, to help guide me at a later point in my life. So many of my childhood experiences have allowed me to weather the obstacles that life would later throw at me. In retrospect, one might say that my most difficult struggles were the most important, as they became the lessons that shaped me for the better, and into who I am now.

When asked about the cruelty of war, I respond today by talking about forgiveness. The Hindu tenet of Namaste teaches us to always look for the good, to cultivate the light within all of us. I have learned that acceptance and forgiveness open the door to the light. That heavenly door will never be opened by the forces of bigotry, intolerance, and hate.

Mutti, Papa, and Eleonore have all passed on now, their life courses reaching their inevitable conclusions, bringing them into the realm of peace, their seasons with me over but their vivid and loving memories remaining within my heart. So many cherished friends have passed on too, their precious words and friendships pressed within the pages of my life. Some days I reflect that I might be the last one standing.

I often wonder what happened to the real-life David and even Liesel, Kurt, and Reina and all the other nameless souls aboard the *Flasher* whom my son and I turned into characters during the writing of *American Shoes*. I asked Garrett to try to find them on the internet once, looking at records of the ship's log to try to trigger some memories about names and identities. But no enlightening details emerged. I have come to realize my fellow passengers aboard the *Flasher* may have been there to help teach and guide me for just that one ten-day stretch of my life, that one season, as Mutti would have said. I have those souls forever imprinted within me, and I remain grateful to them to this day.

As my life winds down, I will tell you that I believe in God and the power of the Universe, karma, and a divine all-permeating love that is capable of transcending time, events, and souls. I will tell you that there is no one path to enlightenment. I have adopted religious tenets from many different faiths into my own brand of spirituality. They are blended to the point where I can no longer tell them apart.

I have no regrets now. For my journey has finally brought me here, to a place of peace, a place I had longed to reach my entire life. I hope I can now help guide all of you there as well, as our readers.

As I apply an undercoat of rich hues to cover the white space of my canvas, I wonder if I have saved my best for last. I still drive and attend art workshops, tai chi lessons, and self-improvement classes. My life is busy—too busy, according to my concerned children, who think I should be sitting at home relaxing every day. But for me, that would be the equivalent of simply waiting for my life to end. There is so much to live for, so many things to do and to still accomplish. Although I can feel the effects of Father Time, I continue to feel and act much younger than I actually am. Perhaps I am receiving all those lost years back, at a time when for me it matters most.

It is a fact that evil exists, as does human ugliness, greed, prejudice, sorrow, and pain. Nature still has her ways of humbling us, reminding us that we are not in control, telling us to respect her. People continue to fight, many for freedom and some for unimportant things that we can't take with us when we move on from this earth.

Nevertheless, it is a fact that light exists. And so does happiness. And so does peace. If I am here to impart one thing about life, about my life, it is that love is greater than hate, that good always trumps evil in the end, and that our lives do have divine purpose and meaning. The reasons for our existence may not always be apparent—we may have to fish for them—but they are there for the taking, for us to reap and use as our guide.

As I apply the brushstrokes that will bring my canvas to life, I find myself returning to the questions I had before my story was told. Did I bring some good for others, and for the world? Was my choice of colors and brushstrokes enough to inspire hope and compassion? Did I manifest my dreams and aspirations for peace, freedom, and equality? And perhaps most of all, did I leave enough of my canvas blank, trusting that there was still room for me to welcome in the future and the enlightenment yet to come?

As my journey through the past has finally come to its end, I will let my readers answer those lofty questions. For the answers lie within my life story, as you walk with me, inside my American shoes.

POSTSCRIPT

At the relentless urging of my son, I reluctantly agreed to have my DNA tested through Ancestry.com, as well as the *National Geographic*'s ongoing Genographic Study. Since I was raised to believe I was of nearly pure German heritage, Garrett said the results of my DNA test might be interesting. It could surprise me, he said. Perhaps he knew something already, as he had his own DNA tested some months before.

Garrett called me one quiet afternoon, keyed up and animated, as usual. He was going to come right over. Soon he was at my door, holding a printout taken from his computer.

"Mom, you won't believe it!"

Respecting my son's frenetic excitement, I didn't even bother to sit down. Standing in the hallway, I read that I am of more eastern European biological heritage than ethnic German.

Although I was raised culturally to be German, and brought up within at the time German political borders, my biological heritage appears to be as much Polish and Slavic as anything else. Perhaps this explains why I have sometimes been mistaken, especially in Europe, for being Polish or Russian or Finnish—or some other ethnicity aside from German.

Garrett also pointed out the small percentage of southern Eurasian DNA I also apparently carry. I guessed that might reflect our distant relatives that lived near the Black Sea, the ones Mutti talked about a long time ago. Perhaps we did have some Romani blood in us after all.

To my son, the findings cast an unexpected twist upon my life story, another chapter to be written for *American Shoes*. But I didn't see it that way. Baffled, Garrett asked why I didn't match his excitement. I did my best to explain.

"I appreciate your excitement, Garrett, but this report seems to be more for your journey, not mine."

Garrett looked at me rather incredulously. "Mom, I don't think you understand what I'm saying. This changes everything."

I didn't want to hurt his feelings. He had put a lot of work and time into exploring our DNA ancestry. But I didn't want to lie or mislead him, either.

"It doesn't matter that much to me, Garrett. Am I surprised? Yes. But it doesn't change anything for me."

"Mom, what are you talking about? This changes our thoughts of who we are, where we are from, our very identities."

"No, it doesn't. Not at all."

"That makes no sense, Mom." Garrett's perpetually youthful naïveté was still showing.

"You think my sense of identity is going to be altered by this new information. I get it. But you're wrong."

"It's all right here, Mom. How can you deny it?"

"My dear son. I am, and always have been, an American."

AMERICAN SHOES: AN IMPETUS FOR DISCUSSION

By Garrett L. Turke

On Fridays, my mom and I visit a small family farm where we buy fresh, free-range eggs that taste like no others. A beautiful, twenty-minute drive out into the countryside, it is one of the few things we have been able to do in the COVID-19 era that feels vaguely normal.

When we arrive, we are immediately surrounded by scores of roosters, hens, and turkeys. Unafraid, they sometimes follow us, the scene reminiscent of a children's petting zoo. Casim is usually the one who comes outside with our order. Warm and striking looking, he is of half-German and half-Palestinian heritage and very much looks like U2's front man, Bono. Originally from Israel, he sometimes speaks to my mom in German.

The eggs he brings us are all different colors: brown, white, tan, sometimes blue, and occasionally green. When I first met him, he reassured me that they all taste wonderful, despite their varied and unexpectedly colorful appearances. We have learned that by blending them together, they make the best scrambled egg dishes imaginable.

Casim, who is a distinguished mathematics professor at a large university, runs the family farm with his wife, Janet. She is of West African heritage, originally from Ghana. The couple has two sons, Tawfiq, who is in college, and Yusuf, still in high school. The sons are visibly African American, Black by American standards reflecting old, inequity-laden statutes that made each of us a color to determine our value.

After reading an early version of *American Shoes*, Casim opened up about his own family history, particularly reminiscing about his grandmother, Gertraude Eichorn, a German woman who survived World War II. He carries a small picture of her in his wallet, his eyes watering when he removes it, signifying how close he has kept her to his heart. Casim once told us that his grandmother was the only one who accepted his "mixed family," her openness an anomaly within both sides of a family torn by prejudice.

Casim said that his grandmother made a point to regularly talk to him about her experiences in Nazi Germany, saying of the period, *"Das war eine sehr böse Zeit,"* or "That was a very evil time." She had wanted to write a book about her experience but passed away with this dream unfulfilled. Casim said that she would have been touched by my mother's story and would have wanted to contribute something to our book.

Mom calls Casim each week before we go out, to ensure they have enough eggs for both of our households. On one of our egg runs earlier this year, he informed my mother that he wouldn't be coming out to visit with us this particular time. We would find our order on his back deck, ironically inside a cooler to keep them from freezing.

Driving along on an icy winter's day, my mom said Casim had sounded different over the phone this morning: flat, distracted, and lacking in his usual enthusiasm. The date sticks in my head, January 8, 2021, two days after the U.S. capitol riot.

I left Mom in the car upon our arrival, knowing that Casim wouldn't be coming out, absentmindedly turning off the ignition before walking up to the snow-covered patio deck. As I retrieved our eggs, the back door of the house opened. Out came the family's teenaged son, Yusuf, wearing a mask. He began talking, increasingly emotional, our frozen breaths escaping our masks, momentarily lingering in the frigid air above each of our heads.

"I just finished reading your book. My mom and dad made me read it. What happened is crazy, isn't it?"

"It certainly was." Thinking he was talking about the book, I wasn't prepared for what came next.

"My family is pretty shaken. All my friends are talking about it online. They keep saying, 'How could this happen, in America?'"

Surprised by his forthrightness, I was momentarily caught off guard. Yusuf seemed almost desperate to talk to me.

"Do you know what that mob would have done to someone who looks like me?"

Feeling the weight of his question and its obvious answer, I could only find one word. "Yes."

"I sometimes couldn't tell which country you were talking about, my mind kept switching back and forth between Nazi Germany and the U.S. Capitol."

Yusuf's intensity and piercing brown eyes had already reached into my soul. I had seen those similarities myself. My mother had even wondered if it was her divine purpose to help warn that history might be repeating itself, in America.

"All of my friends are shocked. They've been asking me why I didn't seem surprised."

"What did you tell them, Yusuf?"

"That this has been building for a long time in our country. If we are not careful, what happened in Germany could happen here. I told them the answers are right here, in this book I am reading. Your book, *American Shoes*."

Thirty minutes later, both of us now shivering, Yusuf and I were still talking. Time had evaporated. I belatedly realized that my ninety-year-old mother was back in the car with the engine off, the air temperature hovering around ten degrees. I had to wrap things up.

"Well, my mom must be wondering what's keeping me. I really appreciate our talk. I can see why your parents are so proud of you. See you next time."

As I turned to walk back to the car, Yusuf stopped me. "Oh, sir?"

I looked back over my shoulder. It had been a long time since someone had called me sir. "Please, call me Garrett; my sir days are over."

"I was wondering if someday it might be possible for you and your mom to come talk to my class?"

"We would love to do that, once this awful pandemic is over."

"Can I ask you one more thing?"

"Sure." Our eyes locked for a moment.

"Do you think we are going to be all right? I mean, our country?"

My mother used to tell me, like her father had done before, that freedom is not a goal that once reached warrants relaxing. Freedom is an ongoing struggle, a living and fluid entity that requires tending, nurturance, and frequent shots of revitalization. For as we have seen in *American Shoes*, well-organized societies, even democratic ones, are inherently fragile. They can rather easily succumb to division and polarity and, in the process, fall apart.

They say that the writing of history belongs to the winners. I wonder if my mother's story would ever have been told had the Nazis won. I have learned that just slight changes to the telling of history can change the perception of what actually happened, with consequences that are far-reaching.

Each of us needs to be tenders of our shared American dream, to keep that torch lit, to guide us toward freedom's light despite our differences, checkered history, and internal conflicts. We cannot simply be reduced to Right or Left, North or South, Rich or Poor, Red or Blue, Black, Brown, or White. We must all work together to be the keepers of freedom and our cherished American light.

DISCUSSION QUESTIONS

The Story

1. What do you think it was like growing up in the World War II era? How do you think you and your family would have been affected by the Nazis' messages of hate and intolerance of free speech? Do you think you or your family would have been targeted as one of "the threats"?

2. Prejudice takes many forms. People can be targeted based on appearance, language or accent, country of origin, or heritage, among many others. What are the different types of prejudice you found in *American Shoes*? Were there any examples you could particularly relate to?

3. A metaphor is a literary tool in which an object, idea, or situation symbolically represents and conveys something else, typically a larger concept, an important point, or generality. Metaphors are heavily used in *American Shoes*, ranging from David's song, the descriptive details of the *Marine Flasher*, the imagery within the dream sequences, and even the color of eggs in the story immediately before these discussion questions.

What were some of the metaphors that you found impactful in *American Shoes*? Why? How were these metaphors used to convey or represent a larger concept, feeling, or idea?

4. Were the Nazis inherently evil, or did they become that way? How did their hatred begin to build upon itself? Do you think we all have the potential for malevolence?

5. What are your thoughts about common, everyday people who sided with the Nazis out of fear? Are they to be excused, or should they be held accountable as contributing to war, mass destruction, and genocide?

6. There are many instances within the story that describe gender roles typical of the *American Shoes* era. How were women seen and valued during that period in history? Do you think we as a society have made progress in this area? Why or why not?

7. Media can be a powerful social manipulator. How did Hitler and the Nazi government use media to influence and then control the German people? Do you see any similarities of such media influence in modern society?

8. Color is intentionally and carefully used in *American Shoes* to set emotional tone, foster intensity, or foretell events or memories. Can you find or recall instances where the use of color was a powerful component of a scene or passage?

9. Were the passengers aboard the *Marine Flasher* insensitive to each other or simply numb, beaten down by war, death, and homelessness? Why did they not express any collective relief or emotion until the ship sailed into New York Harbor? In your opinion, what finally caused the passengers to come together with a sense of shared experience and camaraderie?

10. Do you see any similarities between Germany in the 1930s and '40s and the current political and social state of affairs in the United States and elsewhere in the world?

The Characters

11. Who is/are your favorite character(s) in the story? How did a particular character inspire or otherwise impact you?

12. What do you think attracted Rosel and Liesel to each other? Do you think their relationship was genuine or driven by mutual neediness and circumstance?

13. What is the allure of David? What attracted you to him? What do you think his clarinet and his music symbolized to Rosel? What did his music represent to the passengers aboard the *Flasher*? What did his music symbolize to you?

14. Liesel was born in Germany but acts stereotypically American. Rosel was born an American but struggles with her German attributes and often resists German culture. How did this come to be? How much does culture and environment play a role in forming a person's character?

15. How can Liesel's implied questionable conduct be reconciled with the admirable parts of her character? How did this dynamic affect your perception of her?

16. What were some risky, or leap-of-faith, decisions Rosel had to make in order to fulfill her dreams and her mission to return to America? How did these choices help her grow as a person? Did she sacrifice some of her childhood innocence in order to mature?

17. What do you think kept Rosel from succumbing to hate, despair, and bitterness? How did her belief in angels help guide, protect, and insulate her during her life journey?

18. Rosel's father, Herman, is described as a very complex person within the story, with both reprehensible and noble qualities. Was it hard for you to reconcile this? Do such complexities exist within each of us?

19. How did Mutti's character change during the story? What did she bring to *American Shoes* that other characters did not?

20. How did Eleonore's character evolve during the story? Was there a pivotal moment for you when Eleonore came of age?

21. How did Kurt's character contribute to the story? What do you think he meant by *"It's just the war?"*

22. What do you think is the significance of Reina, a relatively minor character whose identity is not revealed until the end of the story? Why is she important to the story?

23. Was the *Marine Flasher* a character to you? How so?

The Message

24. What would you do in the face of war? Would you take a stand to confront evil? Or would you keep a low profile to protect yourself, your friends, and your family? What choices would you make with your life on the line? What would you risk, and what would you sacrifice—to save yourself, to save loved ones, to save people you don't even know?

25. Was the Jewish experience during World War II comparable to that of other groups who suffered in the war? Is Jewish pain and suffering different from the war trauma other groups experienced? Why?

26. Should traumas of the past be remembered or forgotten? Is it emotionally healthier to remember, to re-experience and work through trauma, or to suppress it, to "lock it away in mental boxes" and never speak of it again?

27. Are we as a society repeating the transgressions of our ancestors and our past? Are we predisposed to making the same mistakes if we are not conscious of lessons drawn from our history?

28. Do you think history is valued as an important subject in our schools? Or has it been marginalized and devalued in favor of "hard" sciences? Do you think the presentation of history is sometimes altered, intentionally or unintentionally, to appease political correctness or to promote a belief? What are the consequences of distorting history to fit a particular agenda?

29. There is a well-known saying by ancient Chinese philosopher Lao Tzu, which is often used in Buddhist and Tao teachings: "We shape the clay pot, but it is the emptiness within that will hold whatever we desire." What does this saying mean to you?

Metaphorically, what did Rosel choose to fill her clay pot with? What will you choose to fill your clay pot with?

SPECIAL ACKNOWLEDGMENTS

We are forever grateful and indeed indebted to fellow writer and *American Shoes* team member Lindsay Marie Scott, without whose insight and bold, gutsy suggestions this book would not have come to pass. When you took that early, unpolished draft of our manuscript and surprised us by turning it into first-person narrative, you breathed life and intimacy into our story and forever changed its destiny. Thank you for being able to envision what *American Shoes* could be at its best and taking the journey with us. The success of *American Shoes* could not have been reached without you.

Another special acknowledgment goes out to Lindsay's father, Jim Brumgard, who, along with (Garrett's) Uncle Carl, served as our resident historians and initial fact-checkers. Your knowledge and respect for history were critically important in the evolution of this book. We are indebted to both of you; your painstaking research helped paint an accurate and affecting historical backdrop for our story.

ACKNOWLEDGMENTS FROM ROSEMARIE

There are so many people I need to thank for their support and contribution, not only to the development of this book but for guiding me to become my best possible self once I returned to America. For every person I am able acknowledge here, there are many more whose names I will never know or, sadly, have forgotten. You have all helped shape my life for the better, guiding and investing in that unpolished young woman after she stepped off the *Marine Flasher*.

To Papa, Mutti, and Eleonore, I will never forget the day in 1951 when you returned home to me in New York. Though you have all gone now to join the eternal, not a day goes by when I do not think of you, sometimes separately, sometimes together as our family. I can sometimes feel your presence, wondering if you have joined my angels, helping to guide me and inspire me during my last years on this earth. You are in my heart and always will be.

I would like to thank the families who helped root me after I returned to America. I was still a young girl in many ways when you took me in, providing me with a home where I felt valued and could contribute, where I felt safe and, most importantly, part of a nurturing family. Mr. Stefan and Mrs. Mildred Salter, and their children, Steffie and Peter, I am so grateful for the opportunity to care for your family, when in fact you were also caring for me. Mrs. Eileen and Mr. David Starrett, you provided me with my second au pair home, allowing me to help care for your beautiful little girl, Carla. I will never forget that day when Mr. Starrett offered to sponsor my family to come to America. And he didn't stop there, offering Papa a job and even helping to set up an apartment for my family while I continued with my schooling.

By the grace of God, I remain in touch with two of my childhood charges, Carla Starrett-Biggs and Stefanie (Salter) Keyte, though that sounds strange with the two of you approaching your eighties and me now at ninety. It has been a joy not only to have been part of your lives growing up but to still feel part of your families to this day.

I would also like to thank two of my best friends in high school, Billie Jane Ellson, and Judy Kredel-Brown. Billie Jane, thank you for convincing your family to take me in after the Salters no longer needed my services as their au pair. You gave me a place to call home, without worry, until I could find my second au pair family. I am eternally grateful for your family's act of kindness, as I had nowhere else to go. I also learned a lot from your family's Jewish culture and practices, and I am grateful to have been included as part of your household. *L'chaim!*

I remain in touch with my other old best friend, Judy, who helped me become adjusted in America, especially during that difficult first year after returning to America by myself. I was amazed to have again found you in the 1990s, relocated in Michigan as a professor of sociology at nearby Oakland University. Garrett and I enjoyed our lunch with you at the cider mill a couple of years ago and would love to visit you again soon, after the pandemic is behind us.

I am blessed to have had so many diverse friendships over the course of my life's journey. My remarkable array of friends has helped me get through so many difficult life events, circumstances, and transitions. Ruth, Silvia, Jan, Sueann, Delphine, Paul, Bette, Sue, Shirley, and Ilse, each of you have helped me negotiate and reconcile so many life experiences, all shaping the ongoing evolution of my self. Thank you, my friends; in different places and at different times, you have each helped forge my future and change my life for the better.

For one reason or another, many of my friends along the way have been Jewish. Garrett often jokes that he was raised a Jewish kid in Los Angeles, because of the strong influence of many Jewish friends and families around us when he was growing up. As a child, he probably went to more bar mitzvahs and Chanukah celebrations than secular birthday parties and Christmas events. Garrett's two adult children have Jewish heritage and continue to honor some of the age-old Hebrew traditions. I am thankful they have been raised in America where this has been not only possible but also nurtured and embraced.

To all my family, by blood and by marriage, those who have gone before and those whose lives have yet to unfold, I have so much love and gratitude. I give you my heart. For my children, Garrett, Tiffanie, and Sierra; my grandchildren, Aaron, Shani, Miah, Lindsey, and Brityn; and the youngest ones, my great-grandchildren, Ezra, Rosey, and Amina, our family's next generation. I hope my life lessons continue to light your way, even long after I am gone. And lastly, for my "adopted adult children," Lindsay Marie, Adam, Stacy, and all of their extended families. I love all of you dearly, perhaps more than you may know.

For Walt, I am grateful for the time we had together, the lessons we both learned, and for the children, grandchildren, and great-grandchildren we brought into this world as part of our lineage. I feel blessed to have been by your side when you journeyed on from this life, showing us your window to heaven, reminding us that we are in the presence of angels and never need feel alone.

For my sister's family: Carl, Ingrid and Walter, Caroline and Tom, David, Charlie, and Emilie. I hope we can still find time to celebrate our lives and our history, once this dreadful virus passes. I am grateful to have had you along for my journey as well.

I want my last words to be just for my little sister, who sadly passed away before *American Shoes* could be published. I feel blessed to have been able to share the opening chapters with you over the phone. Dearest Eleonore, you have been with me through so much, more than I will ever be able to fully express to you. You were an instrumental part of shaping my life. When I go to Lake Michigan and watch the big waves roll in, I often gaze at the seemingly endless horizon, reminiscing about the two of us as children. Walking along the shoreline, I still stop to pick the wildflowers growing at the edge of the dunes, recalling those precious days when we were little. You are in my heart and always will be.

ACKNOWLEDGMENTS FROM GARRETT

To our Beyond Words Publishing team, Michele, Richard, Chelsea, Brennah, Lindsay, Linda, Emmalisa, Bailey, and Sylvia, it is still hard to believe how we found you, at a point where publishing *American Shoes* seemed like it would become a lost dream. You saw promise in us when the horizon looked obscured, taking us in and fostering our dream to validate my mother's story and purpose. By investing your hope, vision, wisdom, and faith into our writings, *American Shoes* has truly become *our* book. As we see it, you are all angels on earth, not only helping to bring my mother's story to the world but helping us to stay grounded and immersed in light. We are deeply honored to be a part of your literary family.

Our heartfelt gratitude and appreciation also goes out to Gail M. Kearns, founder of To Press & Beyond, out in my old home of Southern California. You too saw promise in us, long before anyone else did, and steered us along with your guidance, faith, and wisdom. Thank you for believing in our *American Shoes* dream and, more importantly, in its message. We are enormously grateful.

To Marie Kar of Redframe Creative, who has assisted me with graphic design and visuals throughout my journey to becoming a "legit" author, not to mention her help with the cover of *American Shoes*. Your faith in my reinvention of myself as an author was unwavering. I am so thankful that you continued to push me along when the odds against me seemed nearly impossible.

To Mary Meierfrankenfeld, thank you for your incredibly thorough and invested editing of *American Shoes*, especially with regard to German language passages. You went well beyond the call of duty without blinking an eye. *Herzlichen Dank!*

To Jim Wahl; George Kitson; Jordan Horan; Jackson Kaguri; Antriece Hart; Del, Caleb, and Elijah Hart; Carla Guggenheim; David Hopkinson; Paula Davis; Bryian "Bo" Bobo; Kris Bobo; Brian Bush; and Gerard Mauzé, thank you for investing in *American Shoes* as our very first advance, or beta, readers. I am honored to have you as the foundation of our *American Shoes'* tribe.

To Danielle Clarke, Rachel Haas, Bethany Sexton, and the Words and Wine Book Club of Lansing, Michigan, thank you for choosing to read my second book, *There's a Window to Heaven*, and then volunteering to read an early manuscript draft of *American Shoes*. Your collective enthusiasm and heartfelt suggestions for *American Shoes* gave us hope that someday we would draw the attention of a major publisher for our story. I am indebted to each of you.

To John Campbell, "The Production Wizard," for your extraordinary empathy for my mother and all your expertise as a record and studio producer at Studio C. Thank you from the bottom of my heart! You made the audio interviews of my mother and me enjoyable and also captured the essence and power of my mother's spirit and purpose. Shine on, you crazy diamond!

To Kathryn Osterndorff, for saving the day with your last-minute photo search for our *American Shoes* promo videos. Clutch!

And finally, I give my heart to my dear mother, Rosemarie, for her patience with me as I diligently, obsessively, and neurotically worked on *American Shoes*, every day and every week, month after month, year after year, trying to get it perfect, on and on for what I am sure seemed like an eternity. Mom, your courage and fortitude in staring down the ghosts of your past inspired and refueled me, as we meticulously uncovered memories that many people would not be able to bear. I know I burned you out many times, but you hung in there with me. Thank you for picking up the flag and carrying it for me, for getting in my face when I needed it, and for simply pushing me forward when I felt too tired to go on. I love you so very much.

GLOSSARY OF WORDS, TERMS, AND HISTORICAL EVENTS

Basic Rules about the German Language

★ Nouns are always capitalized in German, regardless of their position in a sentence or phrase.

★ Adding *chen* to the end of a noun makes the word a tiny version of itself and is usually added to make the word an endearment. For example, Rosel*chen* means "[my] little Rosel," and *Liebchen* means "little dear one," or "sweetheart."

★ There are masculine and feminine versions of many words, depending on the subject noun and context. Usually the feminine version of a word is created by adding an *e* to the end of the word, e.g., *mein*, the German word for "my," becomes *meine* in its feminine form.

★ Adding an *er* to the back of a word indicates "belonging to"; for example, "Berlin's train station" in German would be *Berliner Hauptbahnhof.*

★ The unique German letter ß is called an eszett, and is pronounced *ss*. For simplicity, this letter is always spelled out as *ss* in *American Shoes.*

★ Umlauts signal the German-language reader to change the pronunciation of three major vowels. They are two small dots placed over the *a*, *o*, and *u*: *ä*, *ö*, and *ü*.

Glossary of Words and Terms

Aber beeil dich.—German phrase for "But hurry up"; also *Beeile dich*, meaning "Hurry up."

Ach du lieber Gott!—German phrase of exclamation, a variation of "Oh my dear God!"

Achtung!—German for "Pay attention!"

Alle Kinder gehören uns.—German phrase meaning "All children belong to us." It was used as a Nazi propaganda slogan and a not-so-subtle warning that children's attendance in the Hitler Youth had become compulsory.

Arbeit macht frei.—German phrase for "Work sets you free." These words were placed on a sign over the entrance to the Auschwitz death camp, now preserved as part of the Auschwitz-Birkenau Memorial.

Aryan—Hitler's term for blond, blue-eyed Germanic people with classically "Nordic" features. Hitler used these features for promoting ethnic purity and what he called the "German master race." Paradoxically, Hitler himself did not have these features. Additionally, the word *Aryan* is of Sanskrit origin, meaning "noble," and has historically applied to darker-complexioned, Indo-Iranian people of the Middle East and India.

Auschwitz—Or **Auschwitz-Birkenau** to include the nearby camp of Birkenau. Auschwitz was one of six "extermination camps" built by the Nazis, although there were thousands of smaller so-called deportation centers or work camps built across Germany and Nazi-occupied Europe. Many of the camps were specialized for types of slave labor or used as holding centers before victims were funneled to the execution centers. Jews were the largest group imprisoned at these camps, though Poles, Romani, political prisoners, those with criminal records, the physically disabled, Jehovah's Witnesses, homosexuals, and the mentally ill were also targeted, imprisoned, and murdered. In total, over six million Jews and over five million others were murdered. Auschwitz is believed to be the largest of these sites, and it included deported Jews and other targeted minorities from many regions of German-occupied Europe, including as far away as Scandinavia, Russia, and Greece.

About 1.3 million people, the majority of them Jews, were sent to Auschwitz located just outside Krakow, Poland, between 1941 and 1945. Over 1.1 million of them were murdered by gas or execution or killed by intentional neglect (disease, cold, sadistic "medical experiments," and starvation). Two years after the war ended, Auschwitz was made the site of a huge international memorial, today administrated by Poland.

bitte—German for "please."

Blitzkrieg—German word meaning "flash war" or "lightning war." Used by Adolf Hitler and the Nazis to describe an attack so rapid and overpowering that the enemy would have no time to mobilize any defense.

Bolshevik—A word of Russian origin referring to the majority faction within the Russian Socialist Democratic Party, which was renamed the Communist Party after they took power in 1917. It was used by the Germans during the war years as a common and usually derogatory reference to the Russians, with implications that they were invading revolutionaries.

Bratwurst—A type of German pork sausage.

braune Butter—German for "brown butter," butter that has been browned in a skillet, often used as topping for *Spaetzle*.

Braunschweiger—German word for a type of pork liver sausage, eaten as a spread on dense bread.

Bund Deutscher Mädel (BDM)—League of German Girls, refers to the female branch of the Hitler Youth within the Nazi Party. A paramilitary organization, the BDM proper was for ages fourteen through eighteen, although there was an introductory organization for younger girls, the Jungmädelbund, spanning ages ten through thirteen. In addition to promoting Nazi propaganda, German nationalism, and "ethnic purity," the BDM also sought to develop homemaking skills, artisan craftsmanship, and athletic prowess. Initially voluntary, the BDM became compulsory for all ethnic German girls in 1936.

Germans refusing Nazi Party affiliation, Jews, Romani, Poles, and other minorities were not only banned but also targeted for verbal abuse and attack by the BDM and the Hitlerjugend. Thorough background checks were made prior to each member's initiation. As little as one-eighth Jewish or Romani heritage was sufficient to be excluded, publicly identified, and targeted.

Butterbrot—German term for buttered bread or roll; *mit Marmelade* means "with jam."

chai—Hebrew word, symbolized as 'חַי , meaning "the living," but commonly translated as "life." It is pronounced with a soft *h* sound as in *Hanukah* (*Chanukah*), close to the English pronunciation of "hi!"

Clayallee—A major avenue in Berlin, Germany.

danke—German word for "thank you."

danke schön—German phrase for "thank you very much."

Das ist so grausam.—German phrase for "That is so cruel."

Das ist wunderbar!—German phrase for "This is wonderful!"

Das war eine sehr böse Zeit.—German phrase meaning "That was a very evil time."

děkuji—Czech word for "thank you."

Die Juden gehen auf Ferien.—German sentence meaning "The Jews go on vacation."

Dirndl—A traditional German, specifically Bavarian, type of popular or "peasant" dress, originally consisting of a bodice, blouse, full skirt, and apron. This dress was stylized as popular fashion attire in 1900s Europe and eventually the United States.

eine Festung—German for "a fortress," typically a military fortification.

entschuldigung—German for "excuse me" or "pardon me."

escalope de veau—French for "veal cutlet," typically pounded, breaded, and fried.

Es tut mir leid.—German phrase for "I am sorry."

Familie—German word for "family."

Fatherland—Traditional German term for Germany or German homelands.

Festung—German word for "military fortress."

Frau—German word for "Mrs." or "madame," typically a title for married or older women.

Fräulein—German word for "miss" or a younger unmarried woman, used as a title when addressing an adult and sometimes an older child.

Führer—German word for "leader." *Der Führer*, or "the Leader," was Adolf Hitler's preferred title as the dictator of Nazi Germany.

Gänseblümchen—German word for the small, common wild daisy.

Gestapo—German word for the Nazi secret police. The Gestapo was a feared branch of the Third Reich designed to find and arrest threats to the Hitler regime. The Gestapo was notorious for its sinister and sadistic practices, especially toward Jews. After the war, numerous surviving members of the Gestapo were rigorously sought by the free world, to be charged and tried for war crimes and "acts against humanity."

(the) Great War—Original term for World War I or the First World War, involving most of Europe, the Ottoman Empire, and later the United States, lasting from 1914 to late 1918. One of the deadliest wars in world history, the Great War took over twenty million lives and involved the introduction of aerial, armored vehicle, and chemical warfare.

gulag—Russian term for prisoner of war camp.

guten Morgen—German phrase for "Good morning."

Hallo—German word for "hello."

Hauptbahnhof—German word for "central train station." Most large cities in Germany have their own *Hauptbahnhof.*

heil—German word for "Hail!" or "Hail my leader!" Almost always used emphatically as a salute.

Herr—German title and term of respect for men, roughly the equivalent of "Mr." but also sometimes used for other masculine titles, such as "Master" or "Lord."

herzlich—German for "warmly," or "from the heart."

Hitlerjugend—Literally "Hitler Youth" in German, the Hitlerjugend was the male counterpart of the BDM for ages fourteen through eighteen. Its primary role was to groom German boys for eventual induction into the German Army by instilling German pride, "racial superiority," and acclimation to a paramilitary hierarchy. Like the BDM, the Hitlerjugend also contained a younger component for boys ages ten through thirteen and sought to exclude all individuals not purely German.

Hundsfelder Strasse—A large boulevard in Breslau, in German literally meaning "Dogfield Street."

Ich bin Liesel, und du?—German phrase for "I am Liesel, and you?"

Ich komme.—German phrase for "I'm coming."

Ich werde schon.—German phrase for "I will be [ready] shortly."

ja—German for "yes"; "*ja-ja*" means "okay," "surely," or an emphatic "yes."

Jungmädelbund—Literally, "Young Maidens' Association" in English. Refers to a branch of the Hitler Youth reserved for girls between the ages of ten and fourteen, a prerequisite step toward becoming a member of its parent organization, the Bund Deutscher Mädel, or BDM. Like all branches of the Hitler Youth, its role was to indoctrinate children and teens into the beliefs and values promoted by the Nazi regime.

Kachelofen—A charcoal-fueled tiled oven and stove, which was additionally used as a small furnace to heat rooms during winter.

kilo—A common abbreviation for kilogram, a unit of weight used in Europe. One kilogram is equal to about 2.2 pounds.

Kino—German word for "cinema" or "movie house."

kleine—German word for "little" or "small" often a term of endearment with reference to a child, as in "*kleine* Eleonore," or "little Eleonore."

Klösse—German for a type of dumpling, typically but not always made of potatoes.

Knackwurst—A type of German sausage made from pork and veal, similar to *Bratwurst* but plumper.

Komm schnell!—German phrase for "Come quick!"

Kristallnacht—German term, literally "Crystal Night," but also commonly referred to as "the Night of Broken Glass." *Kristallnacht* was a night of unabashed hatred toward Jews, Jewish businesses, and synagogues, occurring on November 9 to 10, 1938. Widely believed to have been encouraged by the Third Reich and local police, *Kristallnacht* saw the destruction of thousands of Jewish businesses and shops as well as synagogues throughout Germany, Austria, and German-speaking Czechoslovakia. Hundreds of Jews were killed in the rioting, and additionally, thirty thousand Jewish men were rounded up and arrested. Hitler later blamed *Kristallnacht* on the Jews themselves, ordering Jewish business owners to pay exorbitant fines for "atonement" and damages to city properties. The Third Reich then confiscated these monies.

Liverwurst—A kind of German sausage spread made from pork or calf liver.

Lyceum—Word of Latin origin that refers to secondary school or an entrance exam used to determine secondary school placement.

Mach schnell!—German phrase for "Make it quick!" or "Make haste!"

mein or *meine*—German word for "my," with both masculine and feminine versions depending on context and subject.

meine Familie—German for "my family."

mein Gott—German phrase for "[oh] my God."

meine hübsche [Rosel]—German phrase for "my beautiful [Rosel]."

meine liebe [Rosel]—German phrase for "my dear [Rosel]."

mein Lieber—German phrase for "my love."

mein Liebchen—German word for "my love," or "sweetheart," usually with reference to a child.

meine liebste [Hilde]—German phrase for "my dearest [Hilde]."

meine liebste Familie—German phrase for "my dear family."

meine Mädchen—German phrase for "my girls"; *meine zwei Mädchen* means "my two girls."

mein Schatz—German word for "my treasure," usually used as a term of endearment.

mein Vater—German for "my father."

meine zwei Töchter—German phrase for "my two daughters."

Mutti—German word for "mother" or "mom," usually informal.

Nazi—A common term, actually an abbreviation, for Nationalsozialist, or National Socialist German Workers Party. The Nazi Party, which seized power under Adolf Hitler in 1933, existed from 1920 through the collapse of Germany's Third Reich in 1945.

nein—German word for "no."

nicht jetzt, nicht hier—German phrase meaning "not now, not here."

nicht mehr—German phrase for "no more."

Oma—German word for "grandmother"; *Omie* would be less formal and more endearing, like "grandma" or "granny."

Pass auf.—German phrase for "Pay attention, watch out."

Piaski—A Polish town, also spelled Piasky, about 120 miles northeast of Lviv, Ukraine. Piaski was one of several villages Jews from Lviv (Polish: Lwow) fled to after the Nazi invasion of eastern Poland and the Soviet Union. On March 17, 1943, German soldiers discovered about 2,300 Jews hiding in Piaski. Of these, 1,500 were immediately executed; the surviving others were rounded up and placed on trains for the Auschwitz death camp. These people were the only Lviv Jews taken to Auschwitz; tens of thousands more had already been taken to the Janowska detainment camp and the Belzec death camp outside Lviv.

pogrom—An Anglicized Russian term that refers to an organized massacre of a particular ethnic group, most commonly used to describe the mass "ethnic cleansing" murders in eastern Europe and Russia during the late nineteenth and early twentieth centuries. The term was particularly used to refer to the systematic murder of Jews.

Pośpiesz się!—Emphatic Polish phrase for "Don't be long!"

proszę—Polish word for "please."

Pumpernickel—A type of dense, dark bread made mostly from rye flour.

quatre-quart—A type of traditional French pound cake.

Ranzen—German word for a leather satchel used by German school-children to carry their books and writing materials; similar to today's school backpack.

Roma (singular) or **Romani** (plural)—Self-described word for nomadic people who have their genetic and cultural origins in northern India and have migrated throughout most of Europe, the Middle East, and North Africa. Not to be confused with the Travelers of Ireland and the British Isles, who have a similar lifestyle but different origins. Both of these groups have historically been called Gypsies, which is misleading, inaccurate, and sometimes used offensively.

Reich—German term used by the Nazis for their political party and state. *Third Reich* roughly translates to "Third Realm" or "Third Empire." Literally, *Reich* means "rich," "wealthy," or "in abundance."

Reich Chancellery—The main administration building of the Nazi Party and government of the Third Reich, located in Berlin.

Reichsministers—German term for Hitler's cabinet of chief ministers within the government hierarchy of the Third Reich and the Nazi Party; also known as the Reichsführers.

Sauerbraten—A German roast beef dish marinated with white wine; literally means "sour roast meat."

Schadenfreude—German word, literally to mean "malicious joy," commonly used to mean "to take delight in another's misfortune or suffering."

scheusslich—German word meaning "awful."

schnell—German word for "hurry."

Schrebergarten—German word for a shared "community garden."

schrecklich—German word for "horrible."

Schwarz, Weiss, Rot—German phrase of reverence for the Nazi flag, literally meaning "Black, White, Red."

shiksa—Hebrew-derived Yiddish word with complex meaning depending on context. The word was originally used in ancient Hebrew and Eastern European Jewish culture to describe a woman who does not follow Jewish religious principles and is considered "impure" or not of the faith. The word eventually came to be used both lightheartedly for a non-Jewish woman marrying into a Jewish family and derogatively to denote a morally loose or unscrupulous woman and, sometimes, a prostitute.

Sei schnell.—German phrase for "Be quick."

Sieg heil!—Originally a German greeting or departure term, meaning "Good luck!" but used by the Nazis as an affirmation of power, and meaning, "Hail victory!" This greeting, which was accompanied by a straight hand salute among the Nazis, is now banned as a form of hate speech and considered a criminal offense throughout much of Europe.

Sonntag Abendbrot—German term for "Sunday supper," or dinner, often formal.

Spaetzle—A type of homemade German pasta noodle, sometimes taking the form of small dumplings.

Spam—American trademarked term for canned, processed ham, originally invented as a war ration but which later caught on as a popular civilian item in American grocery stores. Created and canned by Hormel, Spam stood for "shoulder of pork and ham" or, sometimes, "spiced ham," depending on which sources were cited. Spam is still available today.

Sprichst du Englisch?—German phrase for "Do you speak English?"

SS (not to be confused with the SS ship ID, as in SS *Marine Flasher*)—Common term for the Nazi Schutzstaffel, or Hitler's Protection Squadron. A paramilitary operation that came to the forefront under Heinrich Himmler, the SS was the foremost intelligence operation in Nazi Germany, seeking to eliminate any perceived threats to the Third Reich. This included the deportation and execution of Jews, Romani, Poles, and other minorities, as well as Germans perceived to be disloyal to the Nazi cause. The SS had the power to execute people on the spot if they so chose. They were actively tracked down after the war as war criminals and charged with crimes against humanity.

Star of David—A six-pointed star formed by two intersecting triangles, which became synonymous with the Jewish faith. Referred to in Hebrew as the *Magen David* (Shield of David), the symbol dates back to ancient Judaism. In the Old Testament, David was a pious shepherd musician who went on to slay the giant Goliath with just a simple slingshot.

A palm-sized, yellow cloth Star of David mandated by the Nazis to identify people of Jewish descent. Jews were required, under penalty of death, to sew the emblem onto their shirts and jackets in Germany and German-occupied regions. Even people of partial Jewish heritage were required to wear them.

Strassenbahn—German word for an electric streetcar, tram, or trolley.

swastika—The official emblem of the Nazi Party and Germany's Third Reich. Its distinguishing features are that of a cross with each arm continued as a right angle. An ancient image dating back to the Indus Valley and Mesopotamian civilizations, it originally symbolized divinity. In Hindu religion, the symbol also came to mean prosperity and good fortune. Hitler and the Nazis adopted the Swastika as the central symbol of its flag, where it was depicted as black against a white disc on an otherwise red flag.

synagogue—A word of Old English origin for "place of Jewish worship"; also sometimes referred to as "temple."

Tante—German for "aunt."

und alle Kinder—German phrase for "and all children."

Vielen Dank!—German phrase for "Many thanks!" or "Thank you very much!" and where *Dank* is employed as a noun.

Voilà!—French word adopted into English, meaning "There it is!" or "There you are!" Also used to introduce something with surprise.

Volksgasmasken—German word meaning "People's Gas Masks."

Volkssturm—German term for the People's Army, a desperate civilian draft of older German men and teenagers to shore up the failing German Army during the last years of the war. Literally, the "People's Storm," the Volkssturm was an official branch of the German military; it was punishable by death if one refused service.

Wehrmacht—German word for the consolidated branches of the German Army, commonly used interchangeably with the German Army in World War II.

Weihnachtsbäume—German word for "Christmas trees"; used by Germans as a dub for the magnesium flares utilized in bombing raids during World War II. The flares were dropped in advance of bombers to light up targets on the ground for bombers.

"Wiegenlied"—Traditional German lullaby, written by Johannes Brahms, first published in 1868.

Wie geht es dir?—German formal phrase for "How are you?" *Wie geht's* is informal for "How are you?" and similar to "How's it going?" or "What's up?" in English.

willkommen—German word for "welcome."

wir auch—German phrase for "we also" or "we too."

GLOSSARY OF HISTORICAL EVENTS

Authors' Commentary on the
Two World Wars and the Holocaust

The reasons behind the two world wars of the twentieth century are complex, intertwined, and certainly very difficult to collapse into brief summaries for the purposes of providing backdrop and perspective for *American Shoes*. Each of these catastrophic and epic wars involved most of the world's great military powers at the time and affected nearly all of the world's nations either directly or indirectly. When each war concluded, scores of millions had been left dead in military and civilian casualties across Europe, much of Asia, and parts of the Middle East and North Africa.

Both world wars involved heinous means of destruction and carnage fueled by rapid advancement in technology, the likes of which the world had never seen before. Such technological development allowed for progression from the centuries-old and often futile hand-to-hand combat to the use of armored vehicles, aircraft, and naval vessels, as well as the use of poisonous gas and chemical weapons. Rapid increases in communication technologies allowed information, both fact and bogus propaganda, to travel the globe in a matter of seconds, fueling international conflicts, escalating perceptions of potential threat, and stoking hatred between large groups of people. International conflict no longer seemed very far away as warfare was catapulted to doorsteps in the form of news reports, radio and telephone transmissions, and eventually television broadcasts.

By World War II, powerful weapons of mass destruction, enough to flatten large cities, came into use with the terrifying fire bombings in Europe and Japan and, in August of 1945, the detonation of two atomic bombs over the Japanese cities of Hiroshima and Nagasaki. These weapons could not only kill vast numbers of people in the blink of an eye but also cause cataclysmic economic and ecological disasters for years to come. Pervasive psychological fear and trauma caused by the use of such weapons and the potential use of such weaponry in the future continues to instill terror throughout the world to this day.

The dynamics of longstanding ethnocentrism, nationalism, and ethnic hatred are inextricably intertwined with human beings' longstanding history of war and international conflict and have often been a triggering factor in setting off hostilities within and between nations. For example, World War I, also known as the Great War, began with the assassination of an Austro-Hungarian leader and his wife, whose empire was seen as oppressors of Bosnian-Serbian national movements in the Balkans. This murder set off a cascading domino effect of complex international treaties ironically designed to maintain peace and a balance of power, and within weeks, the entire European continent was engulfed in war.

The stage for World War II was largely a predictable consequence of the punishing economic terms by the winning nations of World War I against the losing nations and empires. Economic hardship for common workers allowed for strong, charismatic but also vicious leaders to emerge amid cries of making their nation or ethnicity great again. Populations of entire nations were turned against themselves by leaders stoking legitimate economic frustrations into misguided patriotic fervor bent on attacking "outsiders" and "threats to our way of life," with minorities, immigrants, and various ethnic and religious groups providing convenient and tangible targets for nationalistic rage. In the case of World War II, millions of Jews, Romani, Muslims, and Poles were the target of German nationalistic hatred, which sought to remove and then exterminate them as threats to ethnic purity.

The history of events is very much a manifestation of those writing it, reflecting the biases of culture and society and those with the political or economic support to put forth and disseminate their historical accounts on a mass scale. We tend to believe that what we read or hear on the news is the gospel truth. This is not to say that all or even most references to historical events are lacking in truth, but what is brought to light and what is suppressed or overlooked have always been under the control of those who are in political, cultural, and economic power and dominance. Today, people from all walks of life lament that the telling of history has sadly become less of a science and more of a political tool to further political and nationalistic agendas. What is truth and what are lies no longer seem clear or reliable.

History has been largely taught—at least in the Western world—from the outside looking in, usually from the standpoint of the mainstream society. The perspectives of those exploited or oppressed by the dominant culture often go diminished, unrecognized, overlooked, or ignored. For this reason, *American Shoes* is important because it is told from the inside looking out and portrayed viscerally rather than through an emotionally detached, callous, and robotic set of facts and details. *American Shoes* shows us what war does to the innocents and indeed begs for an answer to the elusive, age-old question: are we are born to be easily threatened, confrontational, and violent, or instead taught to hate, judge, and fear?

In the end, that answer and its subsequent calls to action may rest with each of us as individuals and our collective push to restore the integrity and value of studying history. Readers are urged to review the wealth of information on each of these cataclysmic wars that is readily available online or in libraries and to draw their own conclusions. We have found that the online *Encyclopedia Britannica*, History.com, and Edtechteachers .net—to name just a few of the hundreds websites we consulted—provided excellent sources of information. For younger readers, Ducksters.com provides an excellent site for a better understanding of the world wars.

About the Holocaust

The Holocaust is a term that describes the mass murder and genocide of innocent people perceived as threats by the Nazis during World War II. Although many different ethnic, political, and religious groups suffered persecution, the term is often specifically reserved for the murder of Jewish people, who were explicitly targeted and killed by the millions, first across Germany and then all German-occupied lands.

Within months of being elected chancellor of Germany in 1933, Adolf Hitler, and his Nazi Party cohorts, passed a number of state-sponsored laws and policies that sought to identify, segregate, and ultimately remove Jews from integrated German society. Jews were soon forced to live in closed-off communities, called ghettos, throughout Germany and later, throughout all German-occupied countries. Some years on, as the German war machine overwhelmed Europe, Hitler proclaimed that isolation and segregation of Jewish people were not enough to stop "contamination" of German bloodlines and culture. By promoting what he and the Nazis called "The Final Solution," Hitler sought to wipe Jews from the face of the earth by building hundreds, possibly thousands, of concentration camps throughout German-occupied Europe. The largest of these camps became execution centers and included Auschwitz and adjacent Birkenau in German-occupied Poland; Belzec and Treblinka, also in German-occupied Poland; Jasenovac in German-occupied Yugoslavia; and Bergen–Belsen, Buchenwald, and Dachau in Germany. Packed inside train cars that were often no more than open livestock cars, innocent people were transported by the hundreds of thousands from far-reaching places across Europe and Asia. Auschwitz, for example, brought in Jews and other persecuted groups from places as distant as Greece, far western Europe, Russia, and Scandinavia. The number of deaths at Auschwitz-Birkenau alone numbered over one million.

There was a pecking order of sorts in many of the camps, drawn up and justified by bizarre Nazi ideology. Jews, Romani, and Muslims made up the lowest rung on the ladder and were subject to mass execution, while Slavic people, including Poles, Czechs, and Russians, were to be kept as slaves for the new German society, run by Hitler's "master race" of blond, blue-eyed *Aryan* people. Ironically and paradoxically, those physical attributes did not fit Hitler himself, or the majority of German people. Equally bizarre was the baby chosen in a 1935 Nazi-sponsored contest to find "the most beautiful *Aryan* baby": a Jewish girl named Hessy Levinsons.

Once inside the camps, prisoners were sorted by fitness and ability to work, age and gender, as well as selection for participation in gruesome "scientific" experiments. Prisoners were routinely killed if they resisted, questioned what was happening, or were deemed "unfit" to work. The elderly, babies, and very young children were nearly always murdered early in the sorting process. Virtually all prisoners were subjected to starvation, extreme heat and cold, poor sanitary conditions, deliberate medical neglect, and psychological torture. The lone exceptions were prisoners who were granted special privileges for keeping their barracks complacent and "in order." These individuals were sometimes Jewish themselves but usually chosen from other populations that were higher in the Nazi racial and ethnic hierarchy. For example, in Auschwitz-Birkenau, Slavic Poles were often designated to keep Jewish and other prisoners in line and compliant.

According to multiple estimates, upward of six million Jews were murdered by the Nazis during World War II. Entire families were separated and routinely killed. Many more died of disease, starvation, and medical neglect. Those who survived were few and were often spared only by chance, circumstance, and fleeting, often arbitrary decisions made by German officers. In Auschwitz, executions of those no longer deemed fit for work occurred regularly by their placement in chambers that piped in poison gases, often experimental in nature. The lifeless bodies were then placed into flaming ovens where a second hideous desecration occurred; their remains finally were dumped into mass graves and covered with lime to reduce the putrid smell and decomposition. An acrid, sickening odor of burning bodies hung in the air over the camps. Although the Nazis infamously tried to give enslaved workers false hope to keep them motivated and compliant ("arbeit macht frei" or "work will set you free"), the "work" they were forced to perform was often meaningless and perfunctory, used as a means to bide time and further torture victims before execution.

In the final year of the war, when Nazi leaders recognized that defeat was imminent, a mass campaign was conducted to kill as many Jews and other concentration camp prisoners as possible before Allied forces could liberate the camps. In Auschwitz, the killings were ramped up to frenetic proportions as the Russian Red Army approached, the bodies of those murdered hurriedly buried in mass graves in an attempt to hide the atrocities.

In the decades following the war, international tribunals were established among the Allied nations to systematically find and bring to trial all those who participated in the mass killings and related atrocities. Among those eventually captured and brought to justice for war crimes were many "upstanding" German leaders, businesspeople, scientists, and doctors once viewed to be pillars of German society. The hunt for surviving Nazi participants continues to this day.

On the Subject of Genocide

It is often thought that the Holocaust was a relatively unique and isolated event in human history, an aberration of sorts. It is not. Genocides have been common throughout both recorded and oral history, occurring on all continents and affecting the histories of many if not most nations and cultures of the world. The Crusades of the eleventh through thirteenth centuries saw the killing of many millions in Europe and the Middle East, as European Christians sought to "reclaim" Middle Eastern Holy Lands populated by Muslims. In the thirteenth and fourteenth centuries, expansion by the Central Asian Mongol Empire killed scores of millions in Western Eurasia and Eastern Europe, bringing with them Bubonic plague that further decimated European and Eurasian populations. The African slave trade of the sixteenth through nineteenth centuries killed millions of men, women, and children with many more millions subjected to brutal enslavement and forced labor in the Americas. Entire populations of Native Americans were killed or segregated when Europeans explored, colonized, and then populated the Americas and the Caribbean. Pogroms in Europe killed millions of Jews in the nineteenth and early twentieth centuries, well before Hitler and the Nazis came to power. Japanese forces murdered millions of Chinese and other mainland Asian people in the years leading up to World War II.

More recently, twentieth-century genocides have occurred in Cambodia, Bosnia, and in Rwanda-Burundi. China has sought to replace indigenous populations in Tibet and other regions under Chinese control with populations considered to be more "ethnically Chinese." In 2020 and 2021, Ethiopian forces slaughtered Tigray ethnic populations in northeastern Africa. The list goes on and on, nearly endlessly repeating across all regions of the globe, pointing to human beings' apparent intolerance and fear of people perceived to be different and assumed to be threats to precious resources or their way of life. The tragedies continue despite recent, groundbreaking DNA studies that have shown that all of the world's people have a core of fundamentally African genes and that more genetic differences tend to occur within an ethnic population than between ethnic populations. It can be argued that ethnic categories are an almost entirely manufactured human concept, designed to justify and enforce conquest, persecution, dominance, and control.

While information about the Holocaust and other genocides can readily be accessed online or in libraries from a myriad of sources, we have found that the U.S. Holocaust Museum, the Elie Wiesel Foundation for Humanity, and the Jewish Virtual Library all contain multitudes of information for further study and awareness. Readers are encouraged, if not implored, to invest in the honest study of world history, as the authors believe that the keys to peace lie squarely in the lessons of the past.

About the SS *Marine Flasher*

The SS *Marine Flasher* was commissioned by the United States Maritime Commission (MARCOM) and built by the Kaiser Shipyard in Vancouver, Washington.

With an initial capacity of nearly 3,500 passengers, the ship was originally commissioned and designed for use as a troop transport ship in World War II's Pacific Campaign. Finished in September 1945, the *Flasher* was readied just days before the war in the Pacific ended and never saw a day of wartime duty. Instead, its first voyage carried supplies and troops to postwar, American-occupied Okinawa, Japan, followed by a voyage to Allied-occupied Shanghai, China, and finally Inchon, Korea, in December 1945.

A Type C4-class ship, the SS *Marine Flasher* was 523 feet long, with a beam (width) of 72 feet, and a draft (submerged hull) of 29 feet. It was propelled by a single turbine steam engine system and could attain a maximum speed of 17 knots, or about 20 miles per hour. Able to carry freight cargo of up to 53,000 cubic feet, the SS *Marine Flasher* weighed in at well over 12,000 tons, with a range of nearly 12,000 miles.

On December 22, 1945, President Truman issued an edict for various American transport ships to aid in the rescue and immigration of thousands of Jews and "other displaced persons" who had survived the war and the Holocaust in Europe. The SS *Marine Flasher* would soon become one of those rescue ships. In the spring of 1946, the ship began runs between New York and Europe that would continue through September 1949. Typically, the ten-day cross-Atlantic journey started in Bremerhaven, Germany (the port for the city of Bremen), and made a stop in Le Havre, France, before passing through the English Channel into the open Atlantic. From there the ship headed for New York Harbor, some 3,400 miles to the west.

On my mother's voyage, which occurred between July 5 and July 15, 1946, there were just over one thousand passengers listed on the ship's log, with origins from all over Europe. Additionally aboard the *Flasher* were many U.S. citizens who, like my mother, had been trapped during the war. Scores of passengers were children. Passenger No. 155 was Rosemary (misspelled) Lengsfeld, a fifteen-year-old U.S. citizen, listed as traveling alone.

On my mother's trip, there were also over two hundred crewmembers, listed as "Seamen," from a number of different countries and American territories. A number of the seamen on this voyage were from Puerto Rico and Central America.

On or about July 11, the *Marine Flasher* encountered twenty-five- to thirty-five-foot waves in the North Atlantic shipping lanes far off the coast of Labrador, Canada. Days before, a rare, early-season tropical storm had formed off the coast of North Carolina, spiraling its way up the mid-Atlantic Eastern Seaboard as it grew in strength. The storm moved northeast into the open Atlantic, briefly becoming what would today be called a Category 1 hurricane with 80-mile-per-hour winds. Although the storm began to dissipate once over cold, Canadian waters, residual waves from this storm reached the *Marine Flasher* without warning. At their peak, the waves broke over the upper deck of the ship. Although certainly terrifying, there is no record of any of the passengers being seriously hurt.

In 1966, the SS *Marine Flasher* was rebuilt as a container freight ship and renamed the SS *Long Beach*. It made many runs as a freight ship but unfortunately ran aground in San Juan, Puerto Rico, in 1988. It was declared a "total constructive loss" following that accident and never sailed again.

ON THE WRITING OF *AMERICAN SHOES*

The evolution and writing of *American Shoes* took nearly eight years, a wild, enlightening, gut-wrenching, and unexpected journey into my family's past. It was a venture that began rather innocently, in 2012, when I took a German friend up on her offer to visit her in Munich.

I had met my dear friend, Ilona, in the States the year before. Having been divorced for a couple years, I was still reeling and wanted to do something "life changing." It was planned as a vacation, maybe an adventure, but instead it became a mission, if not a pilgrimage. After meeting me at the Munich International Airport, Ilona set me up in her apartment, and soon we were mapping out our course.

We traveled to five countries over the course of a month, visiting Germany, Poland, Austria, Italy, and the Czech Republic. For me, the most important site we visited was my mother's childhood home of Breslau, now Wroclaw, Poland. From there, we traveled on to the nearby Auschwitz-Birkenau Memorial, just outside of modern-day Krakow.

I cannot easily express how my trip through Eastern Europe affected me. Driving through the flowering, early summer landscape, I could feel the ghosts of my mother's past. Burned-out vestiges of the war were still strewn about the countryside. Machinery, vehicles, discarded weaponry, and abandoned buildings had been left as haunting reminders, frozen in time. In Auschwitz, the bizarre and sadistic inventions of murder and genocide that had left over one million dead were still covered with grime and soot. It was not that long ago.

For days, the air felt heavy. Included in my thoughts of those murdered was my daughters' great-grandfather's family. The evocative and unsettling imagery from my time in Europe left an indelible imprint within me. Those haunting images are forever embedded in my mind, never to be forgotten. How could they be?

In the winter of 2015–2016, after three years of grappling with the often-painful insights of my trip, I assigned my next mission: *Mom, I am going to take some of these demons from you; I will battle them alongside you.* My mother, silent about the war for her entire life, started talking, spurred on by the stories of my trip. Little by little, her memories began to unlock from the mental boxes that had held them in check, unable to be contained any longer.

The many intense feelings and recollections freed by my mother's interviews served as the catalyst for me to write *American Shoes*. At first, I had a handful of sketches from which to draw a story, hardly enough to fill the pages of even a modest book. Looking for a way to enhance the story, and thinking that her ten-day, cross-Atlantic voyage aboard the SS *Marine Flasher* might be an ideal setting from which to tell her story, I began putting my mother's harrowing experience to pen. Perhaps ironically, I decided to place my mother's recollections of true events as dreams that came back to her at night, which indeed is what happened during her voyage on the *Marine Flasher*. As I drew storylines around her sketchy memories of people aboard the *Flasher*, I could feel the ghostly presence of people my mother described as the walking dead—those silent, aloof, emotionally detached and physically depleted passengers beaten down by a cataclysmic, spirit-crushing war.

It is distressing to describe what my mother and I often endured writing this book. So many of my mother's demons appeared inside my own mind. I had frequent nightmares, sometimes waking up screaming. I went through months of depression. People around me noticed and asked what was going on with me. Was I having a crisis? But how could I dare to say anything about me? I was only experiencing her past indirectly, at most vicariously. For my mother, and for millions like her, these were not nightmares. These were real events she had endured and had lived through.

As the writing and story progressed, more and more of my mother's memories were freed. How they emerged over the next few years was almost always the same. "I like what you wrote, Garrett, but it wasn't like that—it was like this." As more and more memories came into the light, countless rewrites ensued, sometimes forcing entire chapters to be rewritten. Mom and I found ourselves trapped inside some sort of dark and nightmarish labyrinth, her war memories waiting for us at every fork and intersection, as we struggled to find our way out. Nearly lost at times, we found there was no way to turn back until we had finally passed the last of the dreadful memories and saw daylight ahead.

My mother's experiences are now preserved in these pages, a lesson for the wise, a warning that must remain relevant, across all time and the ages. I hope that *American Shoes* will serve as a harbinger of sorts, a haunting testament and reminder of a global tragedy we must never forget, lest it be repeated.

A skinny fifteen-year-old who looked more like an eleven- or twelve-year-old the day she arrived in New York Harbor, my mother fought the enduring grip of perhaps the world's most heinous war her entire life. Grappling with not only the suppressed horror of the war's atrocities, for eight decades she also struggled with feelings of abandonment, insecurity, self-doubt, and an inability to cry and grieve. She never gave up faith, however, telling me that she would one day overcome the darkness, find her way out of the maze of traumatic memories, and in that quest, step out into the light and into the realm of peace.

My mother finally has serenity now. She deserves it. If nothing more, she certainly has earned it. Those who know her remain awestruck that she was able to make it through the immense horrors and sadness of the war years and, in the end, find the way to create her own light.

Namaste, Mom, Namaste.

Garrett L. Turke

MAPS

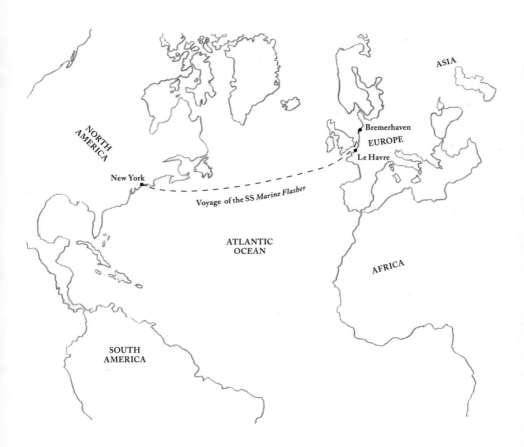

The North Atlantic and voyage of SS *Marine Flasher*

Europe

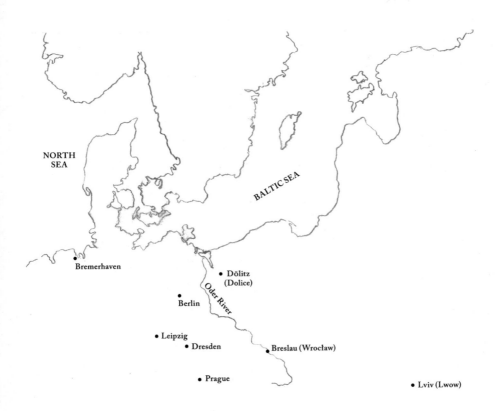

Silesia Region